CORPUS CHRISTI

Essays on

The Church and the Eucharist

by

E. L. MASCALL

Professor of Historical Theology in the University of London;
Emeritus Student of Christ Church, Oxford; Priest of the
Oratory of the Good Shepherd

. . . *ut tota ipsa redempta civitas, hoc est congregatio societasque sanctorum, universale sacrificium offeratur Deo per sacerdotem magnum, qui etiam se ipsum obtulit in passione pro nobis, ut tanti capitis corpus essemus, secundum formam servi.*

CORPUS CHRISTI

E.L. Mascall

First Edition 1953
Second Edition (Revised and Enlarged) 1965

Printed by Longmans, Green & Co: London

This Re-edition 2020
With a new preface by
Gerald McDermott

ACKNOWLEDGEMENT

The Publishing conglomerate Pearson, having purchased Longman, would have the first right to manage the copyright and re-issuing of this work, but they admitted to having insufficient records to establish their copyright management, and advised reaching out to the estate of E.L. Mascall directly. There is no publically recognizable manager of Mascall's estate, and so his writings have been determined to be de facto public domain. If this assessment is in error, please contact ben.p.jefferies@gmail.com

PREFACE TO THIS RE-EDITION

R EADING Anglican theologian Eric Lionel Mascall (1905-93) is like coming to the top of a hill on a foggy morning. After wandering slowly and uncertainly, you suddenly ascend to a place of light where the distance can be seen with refreshing clarity. After not being sure of where you are, now you know not only where you have come from but where you are going.

For example, this little book on the Eucharist helps readers see where Anglican Eucharistic theology has come from, having emerged from differences with Rome, Constantinople, Wittenberg, and Geneva. Mascall observes that Anglicans have followed the Fathers on sacramental grace perfecting nature rather than the Roman (Thomistic) view that transubstantiating grace destroys the nature of the elements (133-34). He explains that Anglicans have also rejected the (Eastern Orthodox) celebration of all of nature as sacramental because of its misplaced focus on the old creation and its fallen nature (40-41). Only the Anglican (and patristic) view recognizes that the sacrament brings the order of grace to make a new creation. Magisterial Protestants, on the other hand, either rejected the meaning of the Eucharist as sacrifice or reduced it to memorialism.

Mascall also shows us the road ahead. He charges that sixteenth-century Anglicans unwittingly perpetuated late medieval individualism and subjectivism, and need newer Anglican recognition of the sacrament as objective obedience of the whole Body to its Head's command to "do this *for his anamnesis*" (52). The Eucharist is not only for my own edification but also and more importantly for the unity and upbuilding of the whole Body of Christ.

Fresh vision on a foggy morning helps correct faulty notions of the terrain. So in this little book first published in 1953, Mascall tells us what the Eucharist is *not*. It is not, as some earlier Romans thought, a repetition of Calvary or a new sacrifice. Neither is it an imitation or recapitulation of the Lord's Supper, as many Protestants think. Rather, it simply *is* the once-for-all sacrifice of Christ in his life and death that is being continually — eternally — presented to the Father by our High Priest for the sake of Church and world.

But how is the once-for-all sacrifice also here and now? Mascall advises us not to think of *spiritual* as the fundamental mode of presence in the sacrament, as Calvin and some Calvinist Anglicans do, but of a *sacramental* mode. For "spiritual" suggests a Platonic disjunction between soul and matter, while "sacramental" retains the biblical and theological unity of matter and spirit, of Christ's humanity and divinity. The sacrament is the food *of* the whole Man *for* the whole man.

Another misleading view of the Eucharist that Mascall dispels is that in the sacrament Christ is dispersed on ten thousand altars throughout the world. This too misleads because it suggests division and scattering. In contrast, the Eucharist is the sacrament of unity by which a multitude of altars are drawn up into the one Messiah and his one sacrificial offering. It unites the faithful across the world to their Head and his saints and angels of all the ages.

That's why the Eucharist is not a mystical experience according to Mascall (70), that lifts me out of the world of matter and away from my neighbor and other believers. Instead it joins me, body and soul, to the messiah's Body of believers, those in the body now and those temporarily separated from their bodies until the final resurrection.

After clearing away all this *detritus*, Mascall gets to what the Eucharist *is*: the gospel in flesh. The good news is that "God the Son united human nature to himself in order to create a new human race" (38). (Note once again the corporate character of the gospel—not getting my soul to heaven but creating a new humanity.) The eucharist is the new creation at work with its own "new laws." It is the sacrifice by which the new creation is made—new because it is entirely different from the world of nature and even spirits. It is the one sacrifice in its totality present under a sign.

In this context Mascall makes a claim that is rare in modern theology, that the Incarnation effected a "real and decisive" change in the human race as a whole (11). One might wonder how this could be, for in many ways history since then has displayed greater and more manifold evils. Mascall does not here explain what he develops later in *The Christian Universe* (1966), where he suggests that just as baptism plants a real seed that its bearer can nourish or suppress, so too human nature in the last two millennia has manifested the glory of the divine image in unprecedented ways along with their demonic antitheses in unforeseen ways. He draws on Jesus' teaching that the Church is leaven in the lump of the world and a city shining on the hills of the world (*The Christian Universe*, 138). The Church can do one thing that the world cannot do for itself: "offer the world to be transfigured by his grace and to be taken into [Christ's] life" (140). She does this through her great high priest at the Eucharist and in the daily liturgy: "[Christ] continues his priestly work through the agency of the Church, which is ceaselessly engaged in praising the Lord and interceding for the salvation of the whole world. She does this, not only by celebrating the Eucharist, but also in other ways, especially by praying the Divine Office"

(142). In these ways the Church has changed the world for the last two thousand years.

Yet for Mascall the Eucharist is as much eschatological or proleptic as historical. It joins us to the "perpetual liturgy" (30) that is now going on in heaven, as we see in the book of Revelation (chaps. 4 & 5). There we behold a eucharistic liturgy, the messianic banquet.

Mascall takes us deeper into the mysteries of the Eucharist by digging down to its Jewish roots. First, he explains that "body and blood" is a Jewish idiom for full human personhood. In the Eucharist we have not just the divinity of the messiah but his humanity as well, as Chalcedonian Christology taught is always the case for Jesus Christ.

Second, Jewish blessing is a giving thanks for something that has been taken and set apart for God to fill with special grace. It is then *qadosh* or holy, literally "set apart." This is how Jews consecrate something, what the Jewish Jesus did with the bread and wine at the Last Supper, and what He promises to do when we obey His command to do the same. This is the Jewish background to eucharistic consecration.

But there is a third Jewish secret, which is that the heart of worship is sacrifice. For the Jewish Jesus and his Jewish disciples for whom the only Bible was the Old Testament, sacrifice does not always involve death but is always the *offering* to God of what is precious. That which is highly valuable is set apart and then (in some cases) killed. When this sacrifice is *offered* to God in thanksgiving, it is *transformed* by the grace of God. Here the meaning of sacrifice is revealed by its Latin roots: *facere* (to make) *sacer* (holy). Sacrifice offered (an oblation) with thanksgiving transforms not only what is given but also the giver (99).

The Eucharistic sacrifice offers what Calvary immolated. It "offers *after* the immolation the victim which the Last Supper offered *before*" the immolation (91).

Because Jesus said the Eucharist is an *anamnesis*, we know from this Jewish concept of the past coming into the liturgical present (as at Passover celebrations) that the Eucharist transcends time and place. It lifts the congregation into eternity or sacramental time where the sacrifice is being eternally offered to the Father by the One who was both victim and is High Priest, for the sake of Church and world.

What does the Eucharist do for the Church? Mascall says it is the function of the sacraments, and especially of this premier sacrament, "to extend, to vivify and to unify, the mystical Body of the whole Christ" (43). It does these two things not by reminding but by making and extending the Body of Christ so that the new human race "may be offered to God by the great High Priest" (45). As we saw, this is a service to society which society cannot perform for itself—not only the maintenance within society of the new human race in which all the mysteries of God are fulfilled, but also the offering of atonement for the sins of the whole world. At the Eucharist the one sacrifice of atonement is re-presented with new prayer that it be applied for the satisfaction of divine wrath against the sins of the world. It is during the Eucharistic prayer, when the veil between the visible and invisible worlds is thinnest, that the prayers of the people to call God's mercy down on a troubled world are particularly powerful.

But the effect of the Eucharist is not only to unify the Church, transform believers, and intercede for the world. It is also to offer "the redeemed material order to God the Father in the ascended Christ" (182). The Eucharist enables man to be the priest of the non-human creation, voicing the praises that irrational nature cannot articulate. Think of the psalmist who calls on the mountains and hills, fruit trees and cedars, wild animals and cattle and birds to praise the name of the Lord (Ps 148: 9,10, 13a). When the Eucharist offers bread and wine — wheat and grapes as fruits of the earth transformed by human hands — it offers to the Father not only redeemed human beings but a redeemed material order. It is therefore not just the Old Adam presenting the work of creation but the race of the New Adam anticipating the new heavens and new earth by presenting a renewed creation.

Mascall closes this beautiful little book by summarizing the "three aspects of the Eucharistic sacrifice" (185). First, it is a sacramental re-presentation of the one sacrifice of the Messiah that atones for sins, makes the Church, and calls God's mercy down on the world. Second, it is the means of making us acceptable to God by uniting us to the perfect life of his Son and thereby transforming us. Finally, it is the means of presenting to God his material creation, by the perfect Man in whom matter is united to the Godhead and therefore creation transformed by its acceptance by God.

It seems to me that Mascall's eucharistic theology is exceptionally helpful for twenty-first century Anglicanism. In an era when N.T. Wright and other scholars are showing that the biblical vision is profoundly Jewish and therefore the Kingdom of which Jesus spoke is more material and social than has been recognized, Mascall shows us that only a fulsome eucharistic theology such as his can consistently join the Kingdom gospel with sacramental reality.

Mascall's eucharistic theology also reinforces Anglican identity. On the one hand, his appeal to the Fathers shows that Anglicanism does not stand alone but rests on the catholic foundations of the undivided church of the first millennium. On the other hand, the beauty and profundity of this Anglican eucharistic theology reveal the weaknesses of other Anglican and Reformation eucharistic theologies that tend toward individualism, memorialism, or intellectualism. It also shows a better relation between nature and grace than that of Roman Catholic transubstantiation.

Mascall's last word on reservation of the sacrament might be helpful when attention to the objective character of the sacrament is causing adoration to be reconsidered. He observes that if Christ is present in the sacrament, we should worship him there. Hence such worship should be in a central and not peripheral place. But he notes that direct devotion to Jesus as an object of worship is not in the "official pattern" of the Church's prayer, which has always been *to* the Father *in* the Son *by* the Spirit. Furthermore, such devotion to Jesus did not begin until the twelfth century under the preaching of Bernard of Clairvaux.

Let's hear it, then, for more trips to the hilltop above the fog. Would that more Anglicans would read the works of E.L. Mascall, arguably the best Anglican theologian of the twentieth century. If they read *Corpus Christi*, they will discover that the Anglican tradition has a glorious sacramental vision that surpasses those of Rome and Constantinople. No need to swim the Tiber or the Bosporus to dispel the fog.

Gerald R. McDermott

Easter 2020

CONTENTS

Chapter   *Page*

FOREWORD TO THE SECOND EDITION   ix

FOREWORD TO THE FIRST EDITION   xi

I. THE ONE CHURCH   1
    i. The Church's Unity   1
    ii. Unity and the Apostolate   13
    iii. The Church Catholic and the
        Church Militant   20
    iv. Objections and Developments   26

II. THE CHURCH AND THE SACRAMENTS   36

III. THE EUCHARISTIC CANON   49
    i. The Primitive Eucharist   50
    ii. Doing and Describing   57
    iii. The Moment of Consecration   71
    iv. Liturgical Reform   77

IV. SONSHIP AND SACRIFICE   82
    i. Sacrifice in Human Religion   84
    ii. The Sacrifice of Christ   94

V. THE EUCHARISTIC SACRIFICE – I   105
    i. The Reformation Deadlock   106
    ii. A False Trail   119
    iii. De la Taille and Oblation   126
    iv. Vonier and Sacramental Significa-
        tion   131
    v. Masure and the Efficacious Sign   136

Chapter   *Page*

    vi. Journet and the Presence of the Sacrifice   146

   vii. Casel and the Cult-Mystery   150

VI. THE EUCHARISTIC SACRIFICE – II   155

     i. Recent Developments in Protestantism   155

    ii. The Eucharist and the Order of Creation   173

   iii. Who Offers What?   183

VII. THE EUCHARISTIC PRESENCE   199

VIII. THE EUCHARISTIC THEOLOGY OF ST. THOMAS   212

IX. THE EUCHARISTIC THEOLOGY OF CHARLES GORE   227

X. 'PRIVATE MASSES'   246

XI. 'ADORATION' AND 'BENEDICTION'   259

APPENDIX

Theology and Liturgy: some comments on the Liturgical Constitution of the Second Vatican Council   269

INDEX   283

FOREWORD TO THE SECOND EDITION

THE vitality of the subject with which this book is concerned is shown by the fact that, although barely a decade has elapsed since its publication, the central chapter, dealing with the sacrificial aspect of the Eucharist, has had to be split into three and entirely rewritten. At the moment of writing, the Roman Church is engaged in a drastic reform of its liturgy in accordance with the Constitution promulgated in December 1963 by the Second Vatican Council, with its revolutionary proposals for the wide recovery of the vernacular and for the fuller participation of the laity in the Eucharistic action and the Offices. In an Appendix I have commented on the admirable and very significant theological passages of the Constitution, which are in danger of being overlooked, owing to the avowedly practical and pastoral nature of the document, but which provide the foundation for the changes concerned. The rest of this book has required only small, but in some cases significant, modifications; the former appendix has been incorporated into the body of the work.

I may perhaps be allowed to mention that further discussion of a number of points of ecclesiology and Eucharistic theology may be found in two other of my books, *Christ, the Christian and the Church* and *The Recovery of Unity.*

E. L. M.

King's College,
London

FOREWORD TO THE FIRST EDITION

S OME, though not all, of the essays which comprise this book have appeared during the last few years as articles in various theological journals. In revising them for publication in more permanent form I have not attempted to impose upon them more unity of theme than they naturally possess or to remove all traces of repetition. Nevertheless, it will, I think, be found that, while in no way constituting a systematic treatise on Eucharistic theology, they are in fact dominated by one over-arching conception, the conception of the church as a reality of the sacramental order, the mystical Body of Christ, preserved and nourished by the Sacrament of the Lord's Body and Blood. This is a theme which I have indeed previously discussed at some length in an earlier book entitled *Christ, the Christian and the Church*, and, apart from a few minor points which will be sufficiently obvious to readers of the present volume, I do not think that there is much in that book which I should wish to recant. There is, however, a good deal in it which needs development and expansion, and I am more conscious than I was when I wrote that book of the extent to which the traditional Anglican formulations of Eucharistic doctrine need examination for undiscarded relics of late mediaevalism. I do not, of course, wish to suggest that everything which can be shown to be mediaeval is thereby shown also to be bad, and I am impressed by the extent to which developments in

liturgy and spirituality which owe their origin to the
influence of unbalanced theological emphases frequently (though not of course always) prove to be of
permanent value and to be worthy of retention when a
more inclusive outlook has been recovered. This is,
after all, only what one will expect if one believes that,
in spite of the imperfections of her members, the
Church is under the guidance of the Spirit of God; we
ought at all costs to avoid that theological and liturgical
purism which assumes that to our own age and to it
alone God has granted a fully integrated and perfectly
balanced comprehension of the revelation given to the
Church in Christ. Nevertheless, it may well be the case,
as the report entitled *Catholicity* suggested in 1947, that
we are now in a better position than Christendom has
been in at any time in the last four hundred (or perhaps
in the last sixteen hundred) years to recover something
of that wholeness of outlook which, however imper-
fectly, characterised primitive Christianity. And if we,
as Western Christians, are to make this attempt we
must be more ready than we have commonly been to
call in question the attitudes and formulations that
have become habitual among both Catholics and
Protestants as a result of the disputes of the sixteenth
century.

I do not think that an Anglican need feel that he is
being in any way disloyal to his own Church in adopting such a questioning attitude. He is, I would maintain, bound to adhere to that appeal to primitive wholeness which so notably distinguishes the great post-
Reformation Anglican divines, with their emphasis
upon Scripture and the Fathers. But I cannot see that
he is bound to hold that either the Anglican liturgy or

the Anglican divines were at all points successful in
making that appeal; the last thing that the Anglican
divines would have claimed for themselves is infalli-
bility, whatever may be true of some of the Continental reformers. It has, I think, become clear in
recent years that the great tragedy of the Reformation
lay in the fact that, while the great majority of the
Reformers were desperately anxious to return, for both
their ecclesiastical order and their liturgical forms, to
the practices of primitive Christianity, neither they nor
anyone else at the time had any adequate knowledge
of what primitive Christianity was. A good many
features were rejected as mediaeval accretions which
were in fact primitive, and a good many features were
retained as primitive which were in fact merely
mediaeval. Furthermore – and this is of even greater
significance – there were a number of highly questionable assumptions which had become so deeply in-
grained in the minds of mediaeval Christians that they
never rose to the level of consciousness at all and in
consequence became the implicit premisses of the arguments of Catholics and Protestants alike. When, in
addition to this, religious persecutions and wars had
hardened prejudices into inhibitions, the climate was
ideal for that condition of deadlock and mutual incom-
prehension which has continued in the West down to
our own time. Perhaps the most hopeful feature of the
theological situation today is the appearance in more
than one quarter of a readiness to get behind the
sixteenth-century alignments and confrontations, to
unearth first, and then to examine ruthlessly, our unconscious mediaeval inheritance, in the determination
to escape from the stuffy and thundery atmosphere of

post-Reformation theology into a fresher and serener clime. For this task of theological psychotherapy the Anglican Church would seem to be peculiarly fortunately placed, for it is fettered neither by the late-mediaeval theological rigidity of the Council of Trent nor by the personal domination of the tremendous figures of the Continental reformers. Appealing as it does to Scripture and the Fathers, it is peculiarly fitted to grasp the opportunities of a situation in which the most vigorous movements in theology are in the realms of Biblical exegesis and patristic study. Free, as the dogmatic Protestant is not, to see the Bible steadily and see it whole, and free, as the modern Roman Catholic is not, to see the Fathers as they are and not as recast in the mould of the Council of Trent, the Anglican theologian today is uniquely favoured for the task of recovering the lost unity of an integrally Catholic theology. It is this conviction that has inspired the writing of the essays which are collected in the present work. They make no pretence to completeness and their deficiencies will be obvious. But they do at least attempt to reopen some issues that have been closed for too long, and that is my justification for offering them to the attention of those who are willing to read them.

E. L. M.

Christ Church,
  Oxford

Chapter One

THE ONE CHURCH

I. THE CHURCH'S UNITY

'I BELIEVE ... in one ... Church.' This is a provocative statement and, on the lips of an Anglican, it would not appear at first sight to be a particularly sensible one. When uttered by a Roman Catholic this clause of the Creed is easily intelligible to anyone who hears it; the Church to which it refers clearly means the totality of Christians who are in peace and communion with the see of Rome, and, in view of the tightly knit organisation which it manifests, this totality can obviously be described as 'one' in a quite straightforward sense. Nor does the clause raise any special difficulty for those Protestants who hold that the Church is entirely invisible; the Church consists of those whose identity is known to God alone, who are united to Christ by justifying faith, and their unity is in no way impaired by the fact that there are a number of separated and sometimes mutually hostile groups of people who call themselves Christians, for those groups, as visible organisations, have simply nothing to do with the Church of which the Creed speaks. For Anglicans, however, and indeed for Eastern Orthodox and many Protestants, the assertion that the Church is one has, at any rate *prima facie*, a highly paradoxical ring. (In passing, it should be noted that although, from the

I

strictly canonical point of view, the Eastern Orthodox Church holds that it and it alone is the Catholic Church of Christ, very few of its theologians are today prepared to defend this position without qualification.) No one would, I imagine, be prepared to maintain that the Catholic Church was simply identical with the Anglican Communion. Nevertheless, Anglicans continue to affirm their belief in one Church, while the great majority of them would certainly deny that the Church is purely invisible. It might be thought that the explanation of this was simply that Anglicans are thoroughly unreflective and illogical. No doubt many of them are, but many of them are not. And I think that if we inquire how it is possible to maintain that the Church is one when we believe that it is neither purely invisible nor, on the other hand, a mere unity of organisation, we may be led to a more profound understanding of the unity of the Church than we should otherwise have had.

It will help to clear the ground if we begin by recognising that the word 'one' is highly ambiguous. As St. Thomas Aquinas reminds us,[1] we must distinguish between 'one, which is the principle of number' and 'one, which is convertible with being', that is, between numerical and ontological unity. As a matter of grammar and syntax, 'I believe in one Church' might mean no more than 'I believe that there is one Church, and not two churches, or six, or three hundred and sixty-five'. And of course it does mean that; we do believe that the Church, holy, catholic, and apostolic, the Church of which the creeds speak, is numerically one. But if that was all that was meant by unity, we should,

---

[1] *S. Theol.* I, xi, 1.

I think, as Anglicans hardly profess our belief in the unity of the Church at all. Unless we believed that the Church was one in some deeper sense we should in all probability say, when we looked at Christendom as it is, with all its divisions, that there was not one Church, but a very large number of churches; we should use the word 'church' as it is used, for example, in the title 'World Council of Churches', and that would be all. We might perhaps profess our belief in one Ecumenical Movement, but hardly in one Catholic Church; and that is, in effect, what a good many liberal Protestants seem to do.

When, however, Catholic Christians profess their belief in one Church, they mean much more than that the Church is one numerically. They mean by the unity of the Church that the Church is one organically, an organism, a coherent whole and not a mere aggregate of items. They believe, furthermore, that what holds it together and makes it one is not merely the psychological forces of moral and emotional attraction between its members, their sense of loyalty to one another and the inspiration which they derive from their mutual fellowship; this kind of organic unity can be found in many societies that are not specifically Christian, or even religious at all, such as the Antediluvian Order of Buffaloes or the Surrey County Cricket Club. Nor, for Catholics, is the Church's unity constituted by the psychological forces of moral and emotional attraction between its individual members and Christ, their sense of loyalty to him and their feelings of gratitude for all that he has done for them. Such a unity would be a purely human one, in the sense that it would be constituted simply by the acts of men, even though those acts were made by them in response to the redemptive work of Christ. For Catholics the Church is made one by a unifying principle which, while it works in men and binds them both to one another and to Christ their Lord, has supervened and still supervenes upon them from outside themselves and unites them in a way beyond anything that their own activity could achieve. What, then, is this super-natural principle which makes the unity of the Church? That is the first question to which I shall address myself. There are several lines by which we might approach it, but I shall take as my starting point the seventeenth chapter of the Gospel of St. John.

On the night before his Passion, in his high-priestly prayer, the Incarnate Lord prayed to the Father for his disciples that they might be one. And this *Ut omnes unum sint* has become the watchword of all movements for Christian unity. It is, however, remarkable how often these words are interpreted without reference to their context. They occur twice in the prayer. In the first place they refer to those who are already one with Christ in the Father and for whom Christ prays that their unity may continue: 'I pray not for the world, but for them which thou hast given me, for they are thine. And all mine are thine, and thine are mine, and I am glorified in them ... Holy Father, keep through thine own name those whom thou hast given me, that they may be one ...'[2] In the second place he prays for those who are not yet his disciples but will be brought to him through the ministrations of his Church: 'Neither pray I for these alone but for them also which shall believe on me through their word;

[2] John xvii, 9–11.

that they all may be one ...'³ But what is this unity
into which they are to be brought? It is nothing less
than the unity with which the Father and the Son are
already united. In the first case, the prayer is 'that
they may be one, *as we are*';⁴ in the second, 'that they
all may be one, *as thou, Father, art in me and I in thee,
that they also may be one in us*'.⁵ The unity which binds
together Christians in Christ is nothing other than the
unity which binds Christ to the Father. And this unity
is not simply the moral unity which Christ enjoys with
the Father through his perfect obedience and self-
dedication. He goes on to say: 'The glory which thou
gavest me I have given them, that they may be one,
even as we are one, that they may be made perfect in
one.'⁶ They are to be one, then, with the glory which
the Father gave to the Son and which the Son has given
to them. And what is this glory? The beginning of the
prayer tells us: it is 'the glory which I had with thee
before the world was',⁷ the glory which the Son enjoys
with the Father from all eternity in the unity of the
Blessed Trinity. Let us note, then, the movement of
thought. (1) The divine Word is one with the Father
in unity of substance of the Trinity: 'the Father is God,
the Son is God, and the Holy Ghost is God; and yet
there are not three Gods but one God'. He is 'God
from God, Light from Light, very God from very God,
begotten of his Father before all worlds, consubstantial
with the Father'. (2) By the Incarnation this unity is
communicated to the human nature which the Son has
united to his divine Person in the womb of Mary, so
that with his human lips he can say, 'Thou hast sent

³ John xvii, 20, 21.   ⁴ John xvii, 11.   ⁵ John xvii, 21.
⁶ John xvii, 22, 23.   ⁷ John xvii, 5.

me into the world ... Thou, Father, art in me and I in thee.'[8] (3) And, finally, this unity is communicated to all those who are adopted and incorporated into Christ: 'that they may be one, *even as we are one*'.[9] In other words, the unity with which the Church is one is nothing other than the unity with which the Persons of the Holy Trinity are one, and this unity is communicated to men, as it were, by a bridge with two arches. The first is the arch of the Incarnation, by which the divine Person of the eternal Son unites human nature to himself in Jesus Christ – the hypostatic union; the second is the arch of our adoption into Christ, by which we are incorporated into his human nature.

The principle of the Church's unity, the dynamic act which makes the Church an organism, is, then, the selfsame act which makes the Holy Trinity a consubstantial unity of love; 'that the love *wherewith thou lovedst me* may be in them, and I in them'[10] are the concluding words of the high-priestly prayer. This realistic view seems to me to be inevitable, but I am fully conscious of the problems to which it gives rise. It may well be that it is here that we touch on the real issue that divides Catholics from Protestants. It would, I think, be unfair to say that Protestants believe in a purely fictitious or imputed union of man with God, but it is, I think, true to say that they tend in general to look upon this union as consisting in an influence exerted upon man by God and in a consequent stimulation of man's moral powers towards God, rather than in a real communication of God to man; they are, I think, reluctant to take *au pied de la lettre* the words of

---

[8] John xvii, 18, 21.   [9] John xvii, 11.   [10] John xvii, 26.

II Peter: 'that ye may become partakers of the divine nature'.[11] The reason for this hesitation is obvious and it is one with which one cannot but sympathise. It is the fear of obliterating the distinction between God and the creature, of holding that a man can be entitatively transformed into God. The very word 'deification', which has traditionally been used by Catholics both in East and West to describe the effect of grace upon the soul, fills Protestants with dismay. It is, however, not true that Catholic theology teaches any such entitative transformation, any conversion of the creature into the Creator. I will give two examples of this, one from the West and the other from the East. St. John of the Cross has been quite unfairly condemned by some, and applauded by others, as being really only a Hindu mystic who had the misfortune to live in sixteenth-century Spain. They point to such statements as that in which, describing the highest form of mystical experience, he writes that the soul is 'united in [God] and absorbed by him, and is thus God by participation in God'.[12] Nevertheless, in the very sentence in which these words occur he writes: 'The substance of this soul … is not the substance of God, for into this it cannot be substantially changed.' And Eastern Orthodox theologians, following St. Gregory Palamas, commonly draw a distinction between the divine essence and the divine energies deliberately in order to maintain a deification of man which does not destroy his creaturely status; God, they say, really communicates himself in his energies, though his essence is incommunicable and

[11] II Pet. i, 4.
[12] *Living Flame*, 2nd redaction, II, 34 (ed. Peers, III, p. 159).

unknowable.[13] We are admittedly contronted here with one of the most difficult notions with which Christian theology has to contend. Just as in the cognate question of grace, and indeed in that of the Incarnation itself, what is involved in the existence of the Church is nothing less than the fact of the Infinite Being really imparting himself to the finite being without destroying the finite being's finitude. *Infinitus fit finitus* – that is the Incarnation. But in that very fact, *finitum fit infinitum* – this is that assumption of manhood into God which is the foundation of both grace and the Church. Yet neither can God be converted into a creature, nor a creature converted into God. There is ample room here for argument between the Thomist and the Palamite, and also between the Thomist and the Augustinian, as to the way in which this amazing example of divine mercy is best expressed in human words, but on the fundamental fact Catholic West and Orthodox East will, I think, agree: that the life of the Church, the organic act which constitutes its unity, is the life of the Holy Trinity imparted to men in Christ. This is indeed a great mystery, but I speak of Christ and the Church.

I will put forward at this point one consideration which may, perhaps, make this realistic doctrine of the Church's unity less difficult to accept. It will, I suppose, be universally agreed that the Church is the Spirit-bearing body of Christ, that the Holy Ghost really dwells in the Church and maintains its life. This is a view upon which Protestants, no less than Catholics,

[13] See, for example, the account in V. Lossky, *The Mystical Theology of the Eastern Church*, and my discussion in *Existence and Analogy*, pp. 148f.

have been ready to lay great stress; indeed they have sometimes gone so far as to accuse Catholics of substituting the Pope or the Blessed Virgin Mary for the Holy Ghost as the indwelling principle of the Church's unity. Now to say that the Holy Ghost is the life or the soul of the Church is, if one is doing anything more than employing a picturesque metaphor, to say that God is really communicating himself to men, that the Church consists of deified humanity. For the Holy Ghost is God himself. Furthermore, there is a persistent tradition in Christian theology that, in the interior life of the Holy Trinity, the Spirit, as consubstantial love, is the bond of unity between the Father and the Son, the hypostatic principle of the unity of the tri-personal Godhead. If this view is correct (and it seems to go back at least as far as Athenagoras[14]), to say that the Church is the Spirit-bearing body is only another way of saying that the principle of the unity of the Holy Trinity and the principle of the Church's unity are identical, for the principle of unity of both is the Holy Ghost.[15]

How, then, do men enter into this unity, which is the unity of God? Not merely by a moral act, however necessary faith and repentance may be in the man who comes to enter into it. The unity between God and his creation is never set up by a merely moral approach from the side of the creature; so far as the Incarnation is concerned, the Church made this quite clear in the condemnation of Nestorianism. Like everything else in the Church's life, our incorporation into the divine unity is a sacramental act; that is to say it is (1) an act

[14] Cf. F. J. Hall, *Dogmatic Theology*, IV, p. 273n.
[15] Cf. my further remarks on this point, p. 99 *infra*.

not of men but of God, but nevertheless (2) an act performed by God through human agents and by means
of material instruments. This raises important questions of detail to which it is not easy to give a confident
answer. Is the sacramental rite of initiation baptism
alone, or baptism and confirmation combined, as they
were in the early Church and still are in Eastern Orthodoxy today? Can we hold that in the West, where
baptism and confirmation have become two distinct
rites, usually separated by an interval of anything from
seven to fifteen years, some of the effects of confirmation
have been transferred to baptism? What is the relation
to the Church of those who have been baptised but not
confirmed? Or of those who, while sincerely devoted
to Christ, have been kept from baptism by invincible
ignorance or prejudice? Or of those who, seeking for
God according to their light, have never received baptism because they have never come into contact with
the Church and never heard of Christ? There are a
host of problems of this kind, which have been much
discussed by theologians in recent years, but the central
fact is plain. A man is brought into the life of the Holy
Trinity by baptism into Christ as a member of his body
the Church, and so becomes a member of the new, the
re-created and renovated, human race. And if we
accept the view that the bond of unity in the Holy
Trinity is God the Holy Ghost we can understand why
it is that in the Church's initiatory rites so much stress
has always been placed on the action of the Spirit.

There is one important question to which reference
must be made at this point. It is difficult to deny that
there is a very real sense in which the human race was
re-created and brought into the life of the Trinity

simply by the Incarnation, death and Resurrection of Christ, for what Christ united to himself was neither, on the one hand, the human nature of one individual man, as Nestorianism held, nor, on the other hand, a merely abstract universal manhood, a purely logical category; it was manhood in the concrete, the manhood of which we are part. A strong patristic tradition can be quoted along these lines. *Universitatis nostrae caro est factus*, writes St. Hilary. 'He incorporated himself in our humanity,' writes Fr. de Lubac, summarizing this doctrine, 'and incorporated it in himself.'[16] Now there is an ultra-realist metaphysical doctrine about universals which, if it were true, would involve that the assumption of human nature by Christ *ipso facto* regenerated every member of the human race and so transformed the whole human race into the Church of God by one instantaneous act. But neither Christian tradition nor the facts of experience support so extreme a view. Whatever may be the correct metaphysical doctrine about universals and particulars as regards the lower creation, where man is concerned neither such an extreme realism nor the opposite extreme of nominalism, according to which the Incarnation would have had no effect upon anyone except Jesus himself, meets the case. Something real and decisive happened to the human race when the divine Word became flesh, but it was not something that removed it from the historical process or brought history to an end. Presumably one of the reasons for this is that many of the human beings whom Christ came to redeem had not even come into existence at the moment of the Incarnation; the concrete universal of humanity was not then, and is not

[16] *Catholicism*, p. 9.

yet, complete. If a metaphysical doctrine of universals and particulars can be constructed which will do justice to the Christian facts, so much the better, but we must not construct a metaphysical doctrine *a priori* and then demand that the Christian facts should conform to it.[17] So we must, I think, say that, although the Word became flesh for the salvation of all men and in a sense renewed the human race by that very fact, yet in another sense it was only his own individual human nature, the human nature of Jesus of Nazareth made personal by its union with the Word, that was constituted in its primal perfection at that moment. Like the old Adam, the new Adam is in one sense the whole human race, but in another sense he is simply himself, not identical with, but the Father of, the human community. Christ's human nature is both universal and particular. The fact remains that the human race is not the Christian Church, even although the Church is meant for all men and claims them all, and although there is no man who is altogether excluded from the Church's redemptive life, which, like a river in flood, overflows its formal boundaries and irrigates the surrounding land. There is a sense in which Christ's redemptive work has communicated the divine life to all mankind. There is even a sense in which the act of creation itself has communicated the divine life to the whole created order: 'that which was made was *life in him*', according to a very probable reading of the prologue to St. John. But, as a fully operative reality in the historical order, it is the Catholic Church that is the supernatural organism in which men, by sacra-

[17] I may perhaps refer to the discussion in my book *Existence and Analogy*, pp. 58f.

mental incorporation into Christ, are elevated into the life of the Holy Trinity and, by the Sacrament of the Eucharist, are maintained therein.

II. UNITY AND THE APOSTOLATE

So much, then, for the Church's unity in its inner constitutive reality. We must now come down to another plane. For the Church is not only a mystical organism, the Body and Bride of Christ, *ecclesia de Trinitate et de Christo*. It is also a community of men and women living within the historical order, the City and the Army of the living God, *sponsa Christi quae per orbem militat ecclesia*, marked out indeed from other human societies by its supernatural endowments and its concern for man's eternal end, but none the less visible, tangible and entangled with all the relativities of history. It would therefore be surprising if there were no visible organ by which the Church's unity is expressed and maintained, although that unity is not a merely moral, political or organisational unity but an inner and sacramental one. Such an organ is, I would suggest, to be found in the Apostolate, instituted by Christ in the Twelve and expanded through the centuries into the universal Episcopate. It is, I think, noteworthy that the patristic tradition lays primary stress upon the Episcopate as the link between the local and the universal Church and upon the function of the bishop as the supreme minister of the Church's sacraments and the supreme guardian of the Church's faith and tradition.

I would remark at this point that this last-mentioned function of the bishop, namely to guard the Church's faith and tradition, seems to correspond precisely to the New Testament insistence upon the Apostle as the eye-witness of the Lord's ministry and Resurrection;[18] it is precisely what the function of witnessing becomes when the events to which witness is borne have moved into the chronological past. And this seems to me to be the answer to those who allege that the Apostolate could only be a temporary institution, on the ground that the first generation, which included the eye-witnesses, was bound to die out in the course of time.

Some such view of the Apostolate as this would seem to be necessary if we are to account for its existence at all. It is perhaps significant that those Christian bodies which look upon the Church either as entirely invisible or else as a merely human contrivance can find no place for the Apostolate as an enduring element in the Church. Nor do they find it easy to make sense of the Apostolate even as a New Testament institution, though, in view of the plain evidence of the Gospel, they cannot deny its existence. But what is surprising is the fact that those very bodies which are most concerned to set forward the Church of the New Testament as the primitive pattern to which the Church in all ages is bound to conform should be anxious to maintain that the institution of the Apostolate, which is one of the New Testament Church's most prominent features, was meant to be purely temporary and transient. It is no doubt difficult, in view of the sheer lack of evidence, to trace the exact steps which connect the New Testament Apostolate with the Episcopate of the second century, but when we consider the place which the Apostolate holds in the Church of the New Testament we ought not, I think, to be surprised to find later on

[18] Cf. Acts i, 21, 22.

that there are persons in the Church who claim, and are recognised as having, the apostolic character; and the simplest explanation is that they are in fact what they profess to be. For the obvious significance of the institution of the twelve apostles is that they are the patriarchs of the new Israel as the sons of Jacob were the patriarchs of the old. However, the new Israel being open to the whole human race and being the substance of which the old Israel was but the shadow, the new Patriarchate – the Apostolate – is not limited in its number nor restricted to one generation; it expands and grows as the Church expands and grows. It is an *apostolic* patriarchate, charged with the mission to preach the Gospel to all nations. It is the function of the Episcopate, as the perpetual Apostolate, to manifest and preserve the unity of the Church throughout space and time, a unity which is not merely schematic, static or (in the modern sense of the word) formal, but organic, dynamic and expansive, because it is the unity of a living body and because its vital principle is nothing less than the life of the Holy Trinity communicated to men.

I have, of course, been stating a theory – or, I would prefer to say, a doctrine – about episcopacy, but this seems to me to be a very important thing to do. Some words of the late Archbishop of Armagh are, I think, highly relevant in this connection. Commenting on what he described as 'an over-accommodating readiness to treat historic disputes on the subject of Church Order with some indifference', Dr. Gregg wrote as follows:

> I am not sure if a good deal of this laxity of conviction is not to be traced to the very dangerous suggestion which

has been current for some twenty years past, to the effect that, while the acceptance of episcopacy as a practice is indispensable for those who would enter into communion with the Anglican Church, no particular theory of epis-copacy need be insisted on. I regard this view as both unsound and unprincipled. It seems to me nothing less than the rankest ritualism. To urge the acceptance of an institution without insisting on any reasoned meaning of it reduces it, in my opinion, to something like mumbo-jumbo. To have no philosophy of the institution which episcopacy is, is to undermine the Ordinal, which insists on episcopal ordination, and to leave it to be supposed that this insistence rests only on antiquarian pedantry or sectarian prejudice. Whereas if episcopacy is invested with no apostolic association, and is treated merely as a desirable, because an early, practice, we rob it of any final and ultimate authority. If it represents merely the result of an evolution upwards out of the presbyterate, and if it represents anything less than a devolution down-wards from the apostolate, it is hard to see any vital reason why it should not rank with any other experi-ment in administration which happened to justify itself on utilitarian grounds.[19]

I would add to this admirably lucid statement that to accept the historic Episcopate without insisting on any theory about it can, in practice, only mean accep-ting the Episcopate in the form which, in the course of history, it has come to take. And that is to destroy all hope of correcting the abuses with which it has become infected. For you can only reform any institution by applying to it in its actual condition some theory about

[19] *Reunion*, p. 8. Pax House, Westminster, for the Council for the Defence of Church Principles. Cf. K. E. Kirk, *Beauty and Bands* (1955), p. 244.

its essential nature and so bringing it into closer conformity to that pattern. It is, in this connection, perhaps relevant to point out that in the mission field it is the low-church Anglican societies which have tended to reproduce overseas the customary features of twentieth-century English ecclesiastical organisation – to treat Anglicanism as a matter of all-or-nothing – while the Catholic-minded societies have shown themselves ready to abandon any customary Anglican features other than those which, on the basis of theological doctrine, they have believed to be essential to the Church's life. This is a question of real importance, for there can be few more unattractive ideals of Christian reunion than that which would bind upon the Church of the future the distinctive features of modern Anglican episcopacy, accepted moreover not on grounds of theological principle but merely as a concession to the obstinacy of Anglicans.

To return to our previous point, the Church, as a visible and tangible society, living in the historic process, needs a visible and tangible organ of its unity, though that union is, as I have emphasised, an interior and mystical unity and not a moral or political one. The Church is a visible and tangible society, but it is a sacramental one, and the organ of its unity will be a sacramental organ. This is why, as I see it, the apostolic Episcopate precisely fulfils the requirements for such an organ, for the episcopal character is conferred by a sacramental act. And this is why it seems to me impossible to locate the organ of the Church's unity in the Papacy, for the papal character is not conferred by a sacramental act at all, but by the purely administrative and organisational process of election. Whether the Papacy has, by divine providence, a unique status in the Church and, if so, what are the functions which rightly attach to it are, of course, important questions, but by its very constitution the Papacy does not, so far as I can see, possess the nature which is required in the organ of the Church's unity. It might be an adequate organ if the Church's unity was the unity of an organisation; it does not seem to be adequate to the unity of a sacramental organism. (Neither would the Episcopate be an adequate organ if it were in its essence what many people believe it to be, a merely governmental and organisational contrivance; but it is adequate if it is, as Catholic theology maintains, a reality of the sacramental order.) It is perhaps an unconscious realisation of this fact that has led the Pope to appropriate more and more exclusively to himself the episcopal character, to the detriment of his episcopal brethren. There were, I believe, some theologians who held that all the episcopal character primarily inheres in the Pope as universal bishop and that other bishops possess it only by delegation from him; it is certainly commonly maintained by Roman Catholic theologians that the Pope has a direct and immediate episcopal relation to every one of the faithful. I do not deny that the Pope is the successor of Peter, but the common post-Tridentine Roman attitude seems to me to make Peter not merely the Prince of the Apostles but, in effect, the only apostle. I think the Roman Church is right in insisting that the Church is a visible and not an invisible body, but I think it has gone wrong in treating the Church's visibility as an organisational rather than as a sacramental one, and so in locating that unity in the organisational organ of the

Papacy rather than in the sacramental organ of the Episcopate; and the consequence has been, as I have suggested, that the Papacy has infringed upon the Episcopate and, in the Papal Communion, has all but absorbed it. However I do not think that the remedy is for the Episcopate to claim that it is collectively what the Pope claims to be individually; that would only perpetuate the error in another form.[20]

I would maintain, then, that as a visible reality in the historic order, the Church's unity is established in our Lord's institution of the Apostolate, which is continued in the universal Episcopate; the bishop is the link between the local and the universal Church. This fact is reflected in the ancient requirement that for the consecration of a new bishop at least three bishops are normally required as consecrators; that is to say, although the diocese gathered round its bishop is the self-coherent local manifestation of the Body of Christ, its perpetuation requires, at least in principle and ideally, a repeated recourse to the universal Apostolate. This requirement, which had largely become obsolete in the West, was restored by the Church of England in the sixteenth century; it has, I gather, never been abandoned in the Eastern Church. With the devolution of so many of the bishop's sacramental functions upon the second order of the ministry – the presbyterate – the status of the diocese, gathered round its bishop, as

[20] Some important thought has recently taken place in the Roman Church on the relation between Papacy and Episcopate, cf. K. Rahner and J. Ratzinger, *Primacy and Episcopate* (1962). Cf. also my *Recovery of Unity* (1958), chh. ix and x. If the progressive element makes its weight felt fully, the way may be open for a reconsideration of the whole question of the Papacy in ecumenical circles.

3

the organic local manifestation of the Catholic Church has, of course, become very much obscured. It is the parish priest, rather than the bishop, round whom the faithful are normally assembled for the great liturgical action by which the Church's life is maintained, though I am told that in the small dioceses of such countries as Greece the bishop has retained more of his primitive liturgical position. Nevertheless, the sacramental functions of the presbyterate are limited and partial, and nowhere in Catholic Christendom has the bishop abandoned his status as the sole minister who can sacramentally delegate, even partially, the apostolic character to others. Every presbyter has received his partial apostolate from the hands of the bishop in the sacramental rite of ordination; while the bishop himself has received his full apostolate from those other bishops who together represent the Apostolate of the universal Church. The diocese, gathered round its bishop, is thus not merely a *part* of the Church of God, but is its full manifestation in a particular place. Like the cell in a living organism, it is a coherent organic entity, yet it lives only because it coheres in the whole body. Like the sacramental Body of Christ in the Eucharist, the mystical Body of Christ which is the Church is not divided into portions by its extension in space and time; it is *tota in toto, et tota in aliqua parte.*

III. THE CHURCH CATHOLIC AND THE CHURCH MILITANT

It is necessary at this point to introduce a new consideration, which is of the utmost importance and the neglect of which has done more than anything else to confuse the discussion of the theology of the Church in recent years. The part of the Church which is militant here on earth is only the fringe or the outpost of the whole Catholic Church of Christ. To put this same point in another way, the Catholic Church, of which the local church is the manifestation, is not just the Church militant but the whole Church on earth and beyond the grave, militant, expectant and triumphant. I must emphasise this point, for it is, as I see it, quite central to the question of the Church's unity. Only too often the Church has been thought of as a purely earthly society, which we enter by baptism and leave by death, a continuing terrestrial organism with a constantly changing membership, comparable in this respect to the Royal College of Surgeons, or the Worshipful Company of Fishmongers. On such a view the Episcopate also is a group with a constantly changing membership, like the governing bodies of the two societies just mentioned, and if the bishops are conceived as having any relation to the apostles at all it is merely the relation of being the apostles' successors. Now I do not deny that the phrase 'apostolic succession' can be given a legitimate meaning; one bishop succeeds another bishop in his see, and each bishop is consecrated at the hands of other bishops. But the natural suggestions of the phrase seem to me to be highly misleading; it suggests that the episcopal office is like a relay-race in which each runner drops out when he has handed on his baton, and it gives some colour to the Protestant accusation that the Catholic view of the ministry is magical and materialistic. The truth, however, is that, although the Church has an earthly part which we call the Church militant, it is not just an earthly reality,

and the Church militant at any particular epoch is
only a minute fraction of the Church catholic. The
Church's membership does indeed change as time goes
on, but it changes simply by increasing. Men enter
the Church by baptism; they do not leave it by death.
And what is true of the Church is true of the apostolic
Episcopate; a man enters the Episcopate by consecration, but he does not leave it by death. The Church
grows with the passage of time, and the Episcopate
grows within it. Thus a newly consecrated bishop is
not in the strict sense a *successor* of the apostles; he is
simply a new apostle.[21] The Church militant is, of
course, the only part of the Church through which a
man can enter into either the Church itself or its Apostolate; there are not, I imagine, baptisms and ordinations
in either purgatory or heaven. This does not, however,
affect the fact that the Church into which a man is
baptised is not the Church militant, but the whole
Church of God, and that the ministry into which a
man is ordained is not just the ministry of the Church
militant, but the universal Apostolate. There are many
problems, historical and theological, bearing upon the
Church's unity and its ministry which I cannot discuss
here, but they cannot even be seen in their proper setting if we identify the Church for all practical purposes
with the Church on earth. And it hardly needs pointing out how much this identification has been made in
recent years. It is a commonplace in the Ecumenical
Movement and in contemporary reunion schemes. It
has been almost invariable in Papal and other Roman
Catholic pronouncements; even the famous encyclical

[21] I have expounded this conception more fully in my book
Christ, the Christian and the Church, pp. 122f.

of 1943, *Mystici Corporis Christi*, is strongly coloured with it. And it is painfully evident in the encyclical letter and the resolutions of the Lambeth Conference of 1948, which in consequence show a remarkable hesitancy and incoherence.[22]

This unhappy identification of the Church catholic with the Church militant seems to underlie a suggestion made by the late Dr. O. C. Quick which has introduced great confusion into interconfessional discussions about the ministry. I mean the suggestion, which was made in his book *The Christian Sacraments*, that 'in a divided Church the validity of orders becomes inevitably a matter of degree'.[23] If the Church in which a man was consecrated or ordained were merely the Church militant, this might perhaps be so, at least if the further assumption were made that consecration and ordination simply consisted in the conferment by the totality of the Church upon one of its members of a commission to perform certain functions in its name. (Even so, the concept of partial validity gives rise to some very perplexing questions. Can a priest whose ordination is only partially valid only celebrate partially valid sacraments?) If, however, the Church in which the consecration or ordination takes place is the whole Church of God and if the ordinand is being incorporated into the Apostolate, the conclusion simply does not follow. It must, I think, be admitted that we are in fact confronted with two radically different doctrines of the ministry between which it is extremely difficult to see any possibility of reconciliation. There

[22] Cf. *Lambeth* 1948 *Reviewed*: A Report of the Theological Committee of the Church Union, pp. 3–7.
[23] P. 145.

is, on the one hand, the doctrine that ordination is an act (whether divinely instituted or humanly invented) by which one of the constituent parts of the Church militant, to the extent to which it is competent to do so, authorises one of its members to perform on its behalf certain functions which any Christian is in principle already capable of performing. And there is, on the other hand, the doctrine that ordination is an act by which the universal Apostolate, most of whose members are not on earth at all, acting through its earthly part incorporates a new member into itself.[24] This view, it must be stressed, does not mean that the Apostolate is a kind of inner ring which operates in isolation from the Church as a whole. It is an organ within the Church; ordination therefore takes place in the setting of the Church's liturgy, in the presence of all the faithful. Whatever episcopal activities may take place in secret session, ordination is not one of them. Nevertheless the minister of ordination is the bishop, the local apostle, not the congregation as a whole. For what is happening, in essence, is the creation of a new apostle.[25]

It will, I think, be clear that the conception of the Church and its ministry which I have been expounding is fundamentally eschatological. Dom Gregory Dix has very clearly shown[26] that for the first three centuries the Church was looked upon by its members as a

[24] There is also the doctrine held, I am told, by some Protestant bodies, that ordination does not *make* a man a minister at all but is nothing more than the recognition by the earthly Church that a man has already been made a minister by the call of God.

[25] See, for example, the prayer for consecrating a bishop in the *Apostolic Tradition* of Hippolytus (trans. G. Dix, pp. 4, 5).

[26] *The Shape of the Liturgy*, ch. xi, 'The Sanctification of Time'.

divine and supra-temporal reality into which a man or woman was admitted by baptism and confirmation, and that it was only after the official recognition of Christianity by the Roman Empire that this view was gradually overshadowed by the conception of the Church as a society operating within the temporal process and primarily concerned with the refashioning of the secular order. These two views are, of course, not formally contradictory; moreover it would, I think, be quite untheological to suggest that the Church ought to have refused to be recognised and quite unrealistic to suggest that it could in fact have done so. It is, however, important to remember – and it was in forgetting this that the great defect of mediaeval Christendom lay – that the Church's temporal mission is only the external manifestation of her supra-temporal and interior reality and can only be understood in terms of it. In calling this concept 'eschatological', it is perhaps necessary to explain precisely how one understands the term. I do not mean, as many of its exponents apparently do, simply that the New Testament, following a contemporary Jewish idiom, frequently describes things that have already happened or are now going on as if they had not yet occurred, in a way which has consistently misled the Church throughout the centuries. I mean rather that, in his membership of Christ and of the Church, the Christian experiences here and now realities whose manifestation in the natural chronological process of history will not take place until the end of time, and that he is able so to experience them because in the unseen realm they already exist and inhere in the ascended Christ. They are future in history, but they are present in the Church, because they are present in Christ. Thus the Church militant, while it is neither an illusion nor a perversion, can only be properly understood if it is seen as the manifestation on earth, and the communication to men, of the human nature which the eternal Word united to himself in the womb of Mary. Our membership of the Church therefore endures as we pass from the Church militant into the Church expectant and triumphant. If we identify the Church of God simply with the Church militant, we shall look upon it as a society with a membership that is constantly *changing* as new members enter it by baptism and old ones leave it by death, after the pattern of any other earthly society. If, however, we remember that the Church militant is only the lower fringe of the whole Church, we shall see the Church as an organism, a body which is constantly *growing*, which is being built up into the measure of the stature of the fullness of Christ. And what is true of the Church as a whole is, I have maintained, true of the apostolic ministry, for that is the organ of the body's unity.

IV. OBJECTIONS AND DEVELOPMENTS

There are one or two objections to the view of the ministry which I have put forward which ought to be taken note of. I have heard it complained that, if one holds that a bishop or priest remains a bishop or priest after his bodily death, the necessary implication is that through all eternity some Christians will be in a position of superiority in relation to others. I must confess that this seems to me to be a most extraordinary objection, but the fact that it has been raised is perhaps illuminating. For I suspect that a very similar objection underlies the common Protestant refusal to give any serious recognition to the saints; there appears to be a lurking feeling that there is something undemocratic in the suggestion that in heaven one star differs from another in glory. I can only reply that this objection seems to be based upon a totally false notion of the kind of superiority that a bishop has to a priest, or a priest to a layman. I was on one occasion astounded to find that a distinguished Free Church theologian genuinely thought that the Catholic doctrine of the ministry implied that a priest is *pro tanto* morally holier than a layman is. Any respect in which there is in fact superiority is surely totally unobjectionable; it is like the superiority which St. Paul ascribes to the eye over the ear and to the hand over the foot, a superiority which is entirely compatible with mutual need and mutual love. And presumably when we are made perfect in heaven, neither will the clergy pride themselves on their 'superiority', nor will the laity envy them for it; so what harm will it do? The blessed are able, in Dr. C. S. Lewis's phrase, 'to play great parts without pride and little ones without dejection'.[27] In the words of Peter Damian's great hymn,

> *Caritas hoc facit suum quod amat in altero;*
> *Proprium sic singulorum fit commune omnium.*

But the very fact that the objection can be made is perhaps a tragic indication of the abuses to which the apostolic office has become subject in the course of the ages and to the kind of superiority over the laity which it has seemed to imply. We can hardly wonder at the

[27] *Arthurian Torso*, p. 145.

misgivings of Protestants about episcopacy if it has
appeared to them as typically embodied in Wolsey,
Richelieu and Manners-Sutton. And this all goes to
show the importance of having a theory about the
historic Episcopate and not simply accepting it as a
fact.

Perhaps a more serious objection is that which finds
it difficult to suppose that the ministerial character
persists beyond the grave since it is hard to see what
there can be there for the Christian minister to do.
There are presumably no sacraments to celebrate, no
sermons to preach, no parishioners to visit, no Sunday
schools to run. And whatever spiritual ministrations
are needed by Christians beyond the grave, the layfolk
might seem perfectly capable of giving them to one
another, without any need for clergymen. Furthermore, if the general Catholic teaching about the nature
of purgatory and heaven is reliable, the Catholic priesthood, no less than the Gospel ministry of Protestants,
would seem to have singularly little opportunity of
exercise in the other world. I believe that this objection
rests partly upon a misconception of the real nature of
the ministry and partly upon a confusion between the
essence of the ministry and its earthly exercise. To take
the first point, I have noticed that in discussions between Free Churchmen and Anglicans about the
ministry there has been a strong tendency upon the
part of the Free Churchmen to look upon the ministry
entirely in terms of pastoral activity, while the Anglicans (or at any rate many of them) have laid the
primary stress on its sacramental and liturgical functions. In consequence, the Anglican clergy have seemed
to the Free Churchmen to be almost entirely pre-

occupied with devising and conducting church services and to be lacking in concern for people's souls. Now it is, of course, unfortunately true that some of the Anglican clergy are 'spikes'. But it needs to be emphasised that, when we say that the primary function of the Christian minister is sacramental and liturgical, we are thinking of him neither as a machine for saying masses and pronouncing absolutions, nor as a professional organiser of inspiring ecclesiastical functions. It is indeed true that his priesthood is most fully and publicly exercised when he is standing at the altar as the celebrant of the liturgy. But what is the liturgy itself? It is the perpetuation in the Church's midst of the redemptive act of Christ, the means whereby the people of God are made one and the sins and needs of the world are brought before the throne of the Father. And this, so far from excluding the pastoral character from the priesthood, necessitates it. For the pastoral activity of the Christian minister is concerned with saving men into the Church as members of Christ, so that they may be offered in Christ to the Father in the totality of their functions and activities, that their life and their liturgy may become one. The Eucharist is therefore both the source and the focus of the priest's pastoral action. And the Christian priest is a priest only by participation in the priesthood of the Good Shepherd, who gave his life for the sheep in order to bring them into the Father's fold and who identified himself with them to the point at which he himself became the Lamb of God that takes away the sin of the world.

So much for the first point. I said also that I believed that the objection with which we are dealing rested upon a confusion between the essence of the ministry and its earthly exercise. I meant by this that the ministry *is* something in itself apart from what it *does*. This is, of course, connected with the fact that in ordination a man receives what is technically described as an indelible *character*, that he becomes, not intellectually, morally or physically, but sacramentally and really, *different* from what he was before.[28] It is, of necessity, extremely difficult to say precisely in what this 'character' consists, because, as in the case of other realities of the Christian religion, there is nothing else exactly like it; 'every thing is what it is and not another thing'. Any description of it must be highly analogical. But it does give its recipient a share (a full share if he is a bishop, a partial share if he is a presbyter) in the Apostolate with which Christ has endowed his Church as the organ of its unity; and, while that apostolicity will be most clearly manifested in the priest's sacramental ministrations and supremely when he stands at the altar as the celebrant of the Eucharist, it attaches in one way or another to everything that he *does*, for it arises out of something that he *is*. And so he will take it with him beyond the grave. It should be added that though, according to the common teaching, sacraments will cease in heaven, there is a sense in which the liturgy will not cease. For the worship of

[28] It should be remembered that the Anglican archbishops explicitly stressed the doctrine of sacerdotal character in their reply to the papal condemnation of Anglican orders in 1897. It should be added that it does not seem correct to say, as is sometimes said, that the Orthodox Church denies the indelibility of character. It does seem to hold that in certain circumstances the Church can suspend or, as it were, 'paralyse' the ministry of a degraded priest. But if he is subsequently readmitted to the exercise of his ministry, I do not think he is ever reordained.

heaven is an organic, symphonic, differentiated and corporate worship; and it is significant that in the Apocalypse it is described under the figure of the Eucharist. So, after the Second Coming of Christ at the Last Day, in the General Resurrection (which is the Resurrection of Christ's Body the Church), there will be transfiguration but not destruction. The apostles will have received their thrones as the judges and patriarchs of the New Israel. They will be seated with their Master, who is himself the Apostle of the Father, at the Messianic Banquet, which, because it is the banquet of his crucified and ascended Body and Blood, is at the same time the perpetual Liturgy wherein the Father is glorified by the Eucharistic offering of him who is the Son by nature and who includes within himself all those who, because they are his members, are the sons of the Father by grace and adoption, and who in their organic unity are his mystical Body and Bride the Catholic Church, one flesh with him. And in this perpetual Liturgy, wherein the Church will for ever contemplate and adore the Father, gazing at him as it were through the eyes of Christ who is her head, everything will be transformed but nothing will be destroyed. However different its expression may be, the Church's apostolate and priesthood will remain, as 'the whole and holy society of the redeemed and sanctified city is offered unto God by that great Priest who gave up his life in so mean a form for us to make us members of so great a head'.[29]

There is a further point on which I must touch. I think a good many Protestants would agree that Christ has communicated his apostolic character to the

[29] Augustine, *De Civ.*, X, 6.

Church, but they would say that it is the Church as such that is apostolic and not merely some one of its organs. Similarly they would say that the whole Church is priestly, and not merely the ordained presbyter; I have heard a high-church Methodist argue that every Christian by his baptism becomes a priest in precisely the sense in which Catholic theology alleges that a man becomes a priest by ordination. Now I do not deny that the whole Church is in a real sense both priestly and apostolic. But if nothing more is to be said than this it seems to be quite impossible to make sense of the plain New-Testament fact that Christ chose from those whom he called unto him twelve whom he named apostles,[30] and that after his Resurrection he breathed into them his Spirit, gave them the authority to bind and loose,[31] and commissioned them to teach and baptise all nations.[32] However, this will perhaps not seem strange if we return to the point from which we began and remember that the unity of the Church is the unity of the Holy Trinity. For the unity of the Holy Trinity is a differentiated unity, in which the Son is eternally begotten by the Father as apostle and priest. It is, I think, generally recognised today that both the apostolic and the priestly function of our Lord do not begin with the Incarnation but are the manifestation in human flesh of eternal realities; *missiones sequuntur processiones.* As the Epistle to the Hebrews insists, Christ's priesthood is a priesthood 'after the order of Melchizedek',[33] grounded in the eternal realm. And his apostolicity and his priesthood are nothing more than the two aspects of his eternal generation. As

[30] Luke vi, 13.
[32] Matt. xxviii, 19.
[31] John xx, 21–23.
[33] Heb. v, 6; vii, 17.

begotten from the Father he is the *apostolos*, the one who is *sent*, who *comes forth*; as the loving and obedient Son, who delivers himself back to the Father in joyful and filial self-oblation, he is the eternal *priest* who offers himself as the archetypal sacrifice.[34] By his Incarnation this dual character of his sonship is communicated to his human nature; and by the baptismal incorporation of men and women into him it is communicated to the Body the Church. In so far then as the Church is his Body, *ecclesia de Christo*, she is apostolic and priestly, and so is every Christian, though not as an individual but as a member of the Church. This is entirely true and must not be minimised. There is, however, another truth that must be borne in mind. The Church is not only *ecclesia de Christo*; she is also *ecclesia de Trinitate*. Her life and unity are the life and unity of the Holy Trinity. The pattern of her life is the pattern of the life of God, into which she is taken up. And the life of God is not an undifferentiated but a trinitarian life, in which Father, Son and Spirit, though united, are distinct, and in which sonship, with its two aspects of apostleship and priesthood, is not common to all three Persons but is proper to the Son alone. So I would suggest, with all the deference that should accompany speculation in such high matters, if we remember that the Church is *ecclesia de Trinitate*, mirroring the pattern of the triune God, as well as *ecclesia de Christo*, mirroring

---

[34] There is, of course, no suggestion that this eternal sacrifice is a sacrifice for *sin*; it is not a propitiation but a homage. Nor does it involve destruction; it is self-giving, not destruction, that is the essence of sacrifice, though when sacrifice is made in a world of sin the element of destruction is bound to be present, though even there it is subordinate to the element of transformation. Cf. Masure, *The Christian Sacrifice*, *passim* and ch. iv *infra*.

the pattern of the Incarnate Lord, we can see how congruous it is that, in addition to the apostolic and priestly character of the whole Church as *corpus Christi*, there should be an apostolic and priestly character that adheres in the ordained ministry alone. Furthermore, if the Spirit is the principle of love, binding the Son to the Father in the inner life of deity and, so to say, making the procession of the Son from the Father something that does not split the Godhead but, by the act of filial response, contributes to its unity, then it seems wholly appropriate that ordination should be recognised as the peculiar work of God the Spirit, who confers the apostolic and priestly character upon the new minister as something which is not to set him up as separate from or antagonistic to the Church, but to make him an agent and instrument of the Church's unity. I must make it plain that I do not put forward the above reflections as proofs that there must be in the Church an apostolic and priestly ministry which is not just co-extensive with the Church itself; the existence of the ministry rests not upon theological speculation, but upon Scripture and tradition, as the Preface to the Anglican Ordinal asserts. But such speculation may be of value as providing *rationes convenientiae*, to illuminate and show the mutual coherence of truths that have been already accepted. And this is, after all, the main positive task that the human reason can perform in the sphere of divine revelation.

Having just made use of the appeal to Scripture and tradition, I will conclude by pointing out what, in the light of the view of the Church that I have been expounding, the nature of this appeal is. Only too often it appears, I am afraid, as purely reactionary and anti-

quarian, and therefore tends to exasperate many of
those who are most conscious of the urgency of the
Church's present-day task. If, however, we are conscious of our solidarity with the Church beyond the
grave we shall see that the appeal to tradition is not an
appeal to our remote predecessors but to our contemporaries. It is the guarantee that the whole Church
believes the same faith. No more than the ministry is
the Church's tradition to be looked on simply in terms
of succession, but in terms of organic development and
identity. The appeal to tradition has been defined, in
a fine phrase, as 'the democracy of the dead', and this
is true. But, since God is the God not of the dead but
of the living, and since those who die in Christ are alive
in him, the appeal to Christian tradition is the appeal
from the part to the whole. For we are 'come unto
mount Zion and unto the city of the living God, the
heavenly Jerusalem, and to innumerable hosts of angels,
to the general assembly and church of the firstborn who
are enrolled in heaven, and to God the judge of all,
and to the spirits of just men made perfect, and to Jesus
the mediator of a new covenant, and to the blood of
sprinkling that speaketh better than that of Abel'.[35]

[35] Heb. xii, 22–24.

* The Constitution *De Ecclesia* of the Second Vatican Council
has appeared too late for consideration to be given to it in this book.
Its bearing upon some of the questions raised in this chapter will be
obvious.

Chapter Two

THE CHURCH AND THE SACRAMENTS

I T is impossible to consider either the sacraments in general or the Sacrament of the Eucharist in particular with any approximation to adequacy unless we see them as organically related to the Catholic Church. It is one of the great tragedies of Christian history that the great efflorescence of sacramental theology, which began in the Middle Ages and continued right through the controversies of the Reformation and after, took place in the almost entire absence of any comparable development in the thought of theologians about the Church itself, and indeed at a time when the primitive Catholic conception of the Church had fallen almost entirely out of view. It must of course be admitted that in the minds of the greatest of the mediaeval thinkers some grasp of the Church's true nature and of the organic connection between the Church and the sacraments was not altogether lacking. Does not St. Thomas Aquinas tell us that the ultimate effect, the *res*, of the Eucharist is the unity of the mystical Body?[1] But where, even in St. Thomas, shall we find an adequate discussion of the mystical Body itself? Only in the last thirty years or so have theologians recovered and put in the forefront of their thought the understanding of the Church's true nature which was the common instinctive possession of Christians down to the time of

[1] *S. Theol.*, III, lxxxiii, 3.

36

Augustine, though Anglicans may be proud to find traces, and more than traces, of it reappearing in the works of Hooker at the beginning of the seventeenth century, and to find Robert Wilberforce nearly a hundred years ago anticipating the main features of the writings of Mersch, Congar and de Lubac in our own time. In the Middle Ages, however, and more and more as time went on, the Church appeared to the eyes of men primarily in the guise of a great supra-political corporation, having much the same structure and organisation as the kingdoms of this world, differing indeed from them in being concerned with a supra-temporal end, but grossly over-preoccupied with temporal affairs and with the construction of a vast system of legal administration. The sacraments, on the other hand, came to be considered predominantly as means of individual salvation and stimulants of individual devotion; and except for the ominous fact that the Church controlled the sacraments and could bestow them upon the individual or withhold them from him at will, the relation between the Church and the sacraments was hard to discern. The Reformation, whatever its effects for good and bad in other spheres, in this respect certainly made things worse rather than better. Since the break up of mediaeval Christendom, Catholics and Protestants have indeed differed widely about Church order and also in their views about many points of sacramental theology, but on one point they have quite unconsciously and most lamentably agreed almost down to the present day. They have alike been bemused by their common inheritance of the individualism and subjectivism of mediaeval sacramental devotion, by the assumption that the ultimate concern of the sacra-

ments is with the spiritual edification of the individual
recipient and that their ultimate effect is to be seen in
the change which they bring about in his behaviour
and in his feelings. And, paradoxically enough, the
fact that both parties to the dispute have agreed unre-
flectively in this common assumption is the main reason
why their conscious differences on other points of sacramental theology have been at once so violent and so
irreconcilable. For each party has been able to see the
distortions which the common assumption has produced in the other party's outlook, while failing to
recognise that their source is one which has been influential in moulding its own. It is, in fact, very largely
true that the antagonism between post-Reformation
Catholics and Protestants has been due not so much to
their obvious and conscious differences as to their
latent and uncriticised agreement. Both sides have so
often been right in their denials, and wrong, if not in
their assertions, at least in their assumptions.[2] Only in
quite recent years have we begun to realise that the
resolution of the Reformation and post-Reformation
conflicts demands the recovery not merely of a pre-
Reformation but of a pre-mediaeval understanding of
the nature of the Church. And it is in the setting of this
primitive and catholic doctrine of the Church that we
must place our consideration of the sacraments.

We can sum up the essence of the Christian gospel in
the assertion that God the Son united human nature to
himself in order to create a new human race. But he
did not simply call a new world into existence to re-
dress the balance of the old. He did not abandon fallen
humanity to its own devices and put an entirely novel

[2] Cf. p. 106, *infra.*

and independent creation in its place. He made a new human race out of the very substance of the old, so that the old might itself be renewed. God sent not his Son into the world to condemn the world, but that the world through him might be saved. The eternal Word did not bring his human nature with him from heaven; he took it from a human mother. He did not create a new human race out of nothing; he re-created the human race which he had created at the beginning and which had fallen away from him into sin and misery. He is, as St. Paul insists, the second Adam, the Father of the new human race, but he became the second Adam by becoming the lineal descendant of the first Adam. When the fullness of the time was come, God sent forth his Son, born of a woman, born under the law, that he might redeem them that were under the law.[3] He renewed man's nature by entering himself into man's fallen condition and by taking upon himself the supreme penalty of man's sin. He fought his battle not *against* man but *within* man, in order that by his victory man might not be destroyed or enslaved but restored and redeemed. He used the very material of the old creation as the substance of the new. He took a perfect and complete human nature from his Virgin Mother in order that men and women might be able to become part of the new creation by being incorporated into him. By our physical birth we are descendants of the first Adam, part of the old creation, members of the fallen human race; by our new birth in Christ, who is the second Adam, we become part of the new creation, members of the restored human race which is the Catholic Church.

[3] Gal. iv, 4.

In the light of this fundamental truth about the nature of the Church and our status as Christians, we can, I think, readily see how inadequate is any discussion of the sacraments which is content to base itself merely upon a so-called 'sacramental theory of the universe'. The phrase which I have just quoted does indeed stand for a very important and fundamental truth, though it describes it in a highly misleading and confusing way. It is, of course, true that the world, just because it is the creation of God, manifests his glory to those who have eyes to see it. 'The heavens declare the glory of God and the firmament sheweth his handiwork.'[4] 'The invisible things of him since the creation of the world are clearly seen, being perceived through the things that are made, even his everlasting power and divinity.'[5]

> *Earth's crammed with heaven,*
> *And every common bush afire with God.*[6]

It is to be hoped that we shall never exalt the devil to such an equality of power with God as to suppose that, even in a fallen world, the devil can blot out the mark of God's workmanship from his creation or that he can obliterate the image of God from the human soul. All this is very wonderful and very true and we must never allow ourselves to forget it. But it has little or nothing to do with the doctrine of the sacraments, which belong to an order of God's activity which is more wonderful still. There is, of course, an organic relation between the order of nature and the order of grace. Grace necessarily presupposes nature as the material in which it works, perfecting nature but not destroying it. But

[4] Ps. xix, 1.   [5] Rom. i, 20.   [6] E. B. Browning, *Aurora Leigh*, vii.

the two orders are distinct, and the sacraments belong to the order of grace, not to that of nature. They derive their existence and their efficacy not from the act by which God omnipotent perpetually preserves the world in existence, lovely and beautiful even in its fallen condition, but from the act by which God incarnate, entering into his world and, as it were, making himself part of it, died and rose again that it might be created afresh and be made more lovely and beautiful still. 'The sacraments be effectual', says Article XXVI, 'because of Christ's institution and promise.' They belong to the new order, the new world, the new creation, the world of grace and of the Church, of the Church which is the new Eve, the mother of all living, the bride of the new Adam, born from his side as he slept in death on the cross. This is incidentally why no amount of worshipping God 'under the blue dome of heaven', however good in itself it may be, can ever be an adequate substitute for coming to Mass; it is the worship of the old creation, not of the new.

'By grace', wrote that great Anglican divine Richard Hooker, 'we are every one of us in Christ and in his Church, as by nature we are in those our first parents. God made Eve of the rib of Adam. And his Church he frameth out of the very flesh, the very wounded and bleeding side of the Son of man. His body crucified and his blood shed for the life of the world, are the true elements of that heavenly being, which maketh us such as himself is of whom we come. For which cause the words of Adam may be fitly the words of Christ concerning his Church, "flesh of my flesh, and bone of my bones", a true native extract out of mine own body. So that in him even according to his manhood we according to our heavenly being are as branches in that root out of which they grow.'[7]

To return to our subject, where mediaeval and post-mediaeval thought about the sacraments has so frequently been defective is not in emphasising the part which they play in the personal sanctification of the Christian, but in looking upon that sanctification as brought about primarily by the stimulation of devout feelings in the recipient and in forgetting the organic relation in which both the individual Christian and the sacraments stand to Christ's mystical Body the Catholic Church. That is to say, our view of sacramental efficacy has been both psychological and atomistic. Now if it were true, as so many people have assumed, that what actually enables us to receive Christ into our souls is the fervour of our feelings of devotion towards him, it would follow that the sacraments are valuable only in so far as they produce those feelings and that anything else which produces them will be equally valuable. And so we shall look upon the Mass as good for those to whom it appeals, and Evensong or *The House of the Octopus* as precise and legitimate substitutes for the Mass for people whose devout feelings are stimulated by them. And is not this in fact the attitude of most English Christians? However, the fact remains that 'the sacraments be effectual because of Christ's institution and promise', and the most fervent admirer of Archbishop Cranmer or of Mr. Charles Williams – and in the latter of these two classes at least I am proud to claim membership – could hardly make this assertion for the evening office or the *Octopus*. It must be repeated that the sacraments do not operate by their effect upon

[7] *Eccl. Polity*, V. lvi, 7.

our feelings, nor is their primary purpose our individual edification. They operate because they are the acts of Christ in his mystical Body the Church, and their purpose is the building up of the Body of Christ by the ever closer and fuller incorporation of his members into him. It is the function of the sacraments to establish, to maintain and to extend, to vivify and to unify, the mystical Body of the whole Christ, made up of Head and members in one organic and coherent pattern of life, to the glory of God the Father. 'All the whole and holy society of the redeemed and sanctified city', writes St. Augustine, 'is offered unto God by that great Priest who gave up his life in so mean a form for us to make us members of so great a head.'[8] And here it is, I think, necessary to say something about the sacraments in their social aspect.

We have heard a great deal in recent years about the social implications of the sacraments, and I for one would not wish to deny what has been said. But just as the phrase 'the sacramental view of the universe' can easily mislead us, so too can the phrase 'the social implications of the sacraments'. For it can and it sometimes does suggest – though it need not and ought not to do so – that the sacraments are chiefly to be valued for their implications in the sphere of economics and politics and that this is the main justification of their existence. We must put the matter in its true proportions.

It is perfectly true that the sacraments have these implications, and Christians have been only too reluctant to admit them. One of the glories of the Catholic movement in the Church of England has been the

[8] *De Civ.*, X, 6.

courage and persistence with which such great men as Scott Holland, Marson and Gore insisted on them. The fact that in the sacraments man finds his deepest needs and aspirations satisfied in the context of a social gathering does, indeed, remind us that the true pattern of human living is neither that unrestricted struggle of individual man against individual men which has been the curse of capitalist industrialism, nor yet that submergence of the individual in the collective which has been so glaringly destructive of human freedom in the totalitarian states. It sets before us a picture of society in which both the personal and the social aspects of human nature are united in an ordered harmony of authority and freedom. The fact that the sacraments are concerned with the redemption of sinful men warns us, on the one hand, against that superficial optimism which, as Peter Drucker has pointed out, led the humanitarians of the nineteenth century to identify universal education with the power to know the true, and universal suffrage with the power to will the good, and forbids us, on the other hand, to fall into that cynical pessimism which believes that men and women can only be safe to themselves and their fellows as long as they are kept in chains. The fact that in the sacraments man's eternal destiny is advanced by the divinely ordained use of material things reminds us that man is neither a pure spirit temporarily imprisoned in an alien fleshly body nor yet merely the most advanced product of the process of biological evolution, but is a mysterious unity of flesh and spirit, in which flesh and spirit alike are included in God's eternal purpose for him. The fact that the greatest of all the sacraments can only be performed at all when certain products of human labour – bread and wine – have been manufactured and transported by a process of unimaginable intricacy which has involved, directly or indirectly, the co-operation of countless human beings, many of whom are altogether indifferent or hostile to God, reminds us that the Church is necessarily implicated in the life of mankind as a whole and that she cannot, without being false to her very nature, ignore the interests and the problems, the joys and the sorrows, of the outside world and enclose herself simply in the sanctuary and the sacristy. These social implications of the sacraments are of the utmost importance, and we are constantly forgetting them.

And yet in the last resort the sacraments do not exist to remind us of anything, but to make and preserve and extend the Body of Christ, the holy people of God. They exist as the means by which Christ draws men and women into his own self in order that his Body the Church, the new human race, the 'whole and holy society of the redeemed and sanctified city', may be offered to God by the great High Priest. The sacraments have social implications, the Church has social implications, only because the Church itself is a divine and supernatural society. 'Ye as living stones are built up a spiritual house, to be a holy priesthood, to offer up spiritual sacrifices acceptable to God through Jesus Christ.... Ye are an elect race, a royal priesthood, a holy nation, a people for God's own possession, that ye may show forth the excellencies of him who called you out of darkness into his marvellous light.'[9]

The Church has many functions *in* society, but it can never become a mere function *of* society, for it *is* a

[9] I Pet. ii, 5, 9.

society – the Society of God, the life of the Holy Trinity communicated to men. Before the Church teaches, it lives; and before it teaches about society it lives as a society, as the supernatural and sacramental society that it is. The sacraments are not concerned in the first place with having implications for society at large; to suppose so would be to fall into another of those confusions of the order of nature and the order of grace to which human minds are so prone. The sacraments have implications for society at large which are startling and far-reaching, but they have these implications only because in the first place they are concerned with something else, namely the maintenance of the Church's life as the worshipping Body of Christ, the new creation, the family of God in which a man can live as a son in the house of his father, the restored human race. And it is in fact in simply being itself and living its own supernatural life that the Church performs its greatest service to the world. Many of the services that the Church can perform for society are services that, at least in principle, society, once the way has been pointed out, can perform as well or better for itself. We have seen the state take over from the Church more and more of those functions which the Church originally performed when the state never thought of performing them – the teaching of the young, the care of the sick and the poor, and such like – and opinions will no doubt differ as to how far this transition is to be applauded. Be that as it may, the supreme service which the Church performs for society is one that society *cannot* perform for itself – the maintenance in the midst of society of the new human race in which all the mysteries of God are fulfilled. The world may misunderstand this or ignore it or resent it or even welcome it, but it cannot itself perform it.

Because Christ died for the whole world and commissioned his Church to preach the gospel to all the nations, the Church's sacramental life is the means by which not only the affairs of Christians but of all men are brought under the mercy and the grace of God. The sacrifice which the Mass perpetuates was offered for the sins of the whole world as their full, perfect and sufficient sacrifice, oblation and satisfaction. The grace which God pours into the Church through the sacraments overflows the Church's visible boundaries and floods the whole of creation with its regenerative power. It brings under the eyes of God all human misery and suffering, it claims for God every act of human love, it pleads God's mercy for every act of human selfishness and hate, it claims all God's creation as his possession. To outward view the Church may appear to be merely a rather queer gathering of very miscellaneous men and women, inexplicably preoccupied with old-fashioned ceremonies, strangely excited about apparently irrelevant issues, and patently failing to live in accordance with the ideals of human life in which they profess to believe. But in its inner reality the Church is the re-created human race, the holy people of God, the divine community in which the Son of God patiently and tenderly draws men and women into his own perfect human nature and offers them to the Father as his members made one with him and clothed with his glory. Such is the Church of God, black with the sins of its members but comely with the beauty and holiness of its Head, and of this Church the sacraments are the very life.

There is one further point on which I must briefly touch. One day sacraments will cease. The life of the Church and the sacraments, by which, even while we are in this mortal flesh, God gives us his very self and draws us into his being, is a gift of surpassing wonder exceeding anything that we could conceive or desire. And yet God has something more wonderful in store. If by his mercy we attain the end for which he has made us, we shall see him and enjoy him no longer under the veil of material appearances but in his own glory and splendour. 'Now we see in a glass darkly but then face to face.'[10] 'Now are we the children of God, but it doth not yet appear what we shall be. But we know that when he shall be manifested we shall be like unto him, for we shall see him as he is.'[11] No one, I suppose, has ever sung the wonder and the glory of the greatest of the sacraments with such fervour as St. Thomas Aquinas, and yet four out of his five great sacramental hymns end with the prayer that God will bring us at last to our home in heaven, where there are no longer any sacraments but in their place the beatific vision of the Holy Trinity.

> *All praise and thanks to thee ascend*
> *For evermore, blest One in three;*
> *O grant us life that shall not end*
> *In our true native land with thee.*

'Thine eyes shall see the King in his beauty; they shall behold the land that is very far off.'[12]

[10] I Cor. xiii, 12.   [11] I John iii, 2, 3.   [12] Isa. xxxiii, 17.

Chapter Three

THE EUCHARISTIC CANON

I INTEND in this chapter to offer some reflections, from the point of view of a dogmatic theologian, upon the development of the Eucharistic canon. It is important to recognise at the start that the whole question of the origins and history of the Christian Eucharist is a highly complicated and difficult one in which at the present time a large number of historical and textual scholars are engaged. There are many points of the highest importance upon which there does not seem to be anything like substantial agreement among those who are best qualified to judge, and the conclusions to which they have severally come are not very readily available to the non-expert.[1] However much trouble he may take to inform himself adequately, he is inevitably exposing himself to some danger in expressing himself upon the subject at all. In spite of this, there seem to be certain broad results emerging which are of considerable interest to the dogmatic theologian as such, and of not less concern to the working parish priest and the people to whom he ministers. This must be my excuse for venturing upon a discussion which inevitably involves matters in which I can claim no special competence, but which, so far as I have been

[1] For this reason among others I am glad to express my gratitude to the Rev. A. H. Couratin for the great help which I have received from him while writing this chapter.

able to understand the points at issue, have certainly provided me with much food for thought.

I. THE PRIMITIVE EUCHARIST

There are certain theories about the origins of the Eucharist which can, I think, now be set aside without very much argument. Few scholars today would hold that the Eucharist is simply a foreign and more or less magical intrusion from gentile mystery-religions into a fundamentally non-sacramental Jewish ethical movement. Few again would hold that our Lord celebrated the Last Supper under an entire misapprehension of the whole future course of events. There is, however, wide and unresolved conflict of opinion as to the character, from the point of view of Jewish religion, of the meal at which the Eucharist was instituted. Was it the Passover meal or some other sort of meal held on the previous day? And if the latter, what sort of meal was it – a *kiddûsh*, a *chabûrah*-meal, or something else? Nothing like agreement is yet to be found on these questions.[2] It is therefore fortunate that for the purposes of the present discussion it is not necessary to give an answer to them. I shall need only to make the following assumptions, which will, I think, be readily granted by anyone who is prepared to accept the Eucharistic narratives of the New Testament as substantially accurate and who finds it inconceivable that the central rite of the Church's worship, by which the followers of Christ have lived throughout the centuries,

[2] See, for example, Srawley, *The Early History of the Liturgy*, 2nd ed., pp. 1f; Higgins, *The Lord's Supper in the New Testament*, pp. 13f; Dix, *The Shape of the Liturgy*, ch. iv.

should rest upon a complete misunderstanding, on the part either of Christ himself or of the first generation of Christians, of the significance of the acts which he performed and the words which he spoke in the upper room at Jerusalem the night before his Passion.

The first assumption is that he blessed the Eucharistic bread at the beginning of the meal.

The second assumption is that he blessed the Eucharistic cup with the prayer of thanksgiving at the end of the meal.

The third assumption is that the significance of the Eucharist is not to be found in the mere fact of the blessing of the bread and of the cup, which were in fact part of the normal ceremonies of a formal Jewish meal, but in certain mysterious words which he said as he distributed them for consumption and which, by their similarity of form as well as by their unexpected character, link together these two widely separated blessings and single them out from all the other blessings of food during the meal. These words, as recorded by St. Paul in I Corinthians are as follows:

(*a*) At the distribution of the bread: 'This is my body, which is for you. This do for my *anamnesis*.'

(*b*) At the distribution of the cup: 'This cup is the new covenant in my blood. This do, as oft as ye drink it, for my *anamnesis*.'

There are three points which ought to be emphasised before we pass on. First, the words just quoted accompanied the distribution, not the blessing; in modern terminology, they were a formula of communion, not of consecration. Secondly, as Dom Gregory Dix has so forcibly shown,[3] the command of Christ is not simply

---

[3] *The Shape of the Liturgy*, pp. 57f.

to *do this*, for what had been done was part of the
normal ceremonial of a formal Jewish meal and would
therefore be done in any case, but to do this *for his
anamnesis*, whatever the precise significance of the word
anamnesis may be. Thirdly, the Jewish manner of
blessing an object was not by an indicative formula –
'I bless this thing' – nor even primarily by a precative
formula – 'May God bless this thing' or 'O God, bless
this thing' – but by blessing God and thanking God
over the object and for it. Thus the Hebrew language
has only the one word *berakah* to denote what we
describe by the two words 'blessing' and 'thanksgiving' – in Greek, *eulogia* and *eucharistia* – for, in
Jewish usage, it was by giving thanks to God for an
object over it that the object was set apart and made
holy.

In passing, it may be well to observe that the com-
mand of Christ was 'Do this for my *anamnesis*' and not
'Do something else for an *anamnesis* of this'. The
difference is profound, whatever precise significance
we give to the much debated word *anamnesis*. The
Eucharist of the Church is not either a commemoration
or a dramatic imitation of what was done at the Last
Supper;[4] it is *the same thing*. 'Do *this*.' Both the Last
Supper and the Eucharist bring about the *anamnesis* of
Christ; neither of them is the *anamnesis* of the other. It

---

[4] In denying that the Church's Eucharist is a dramatic imitation
of the Last Supper, I do not intend to deny that the Church is
bound to repeat the essential acts which Christ performed at the
Supper (though we shall see in the sequel how free the Church felt
to modify whatever was not essential). What I do deny is that the
Eucharist is related to the Supper simply in the way in which, for
example, a scene in a pageant is related to the historical event
which it depicts.

therefore seems to me to be an unfortunate lapse when Dom Gregory Dix says that the Last Supper is not the Eucharist but rather the sowing of its seed.[5] There is, of course, a difference, as well as an identity, between the Last Supper and the post-Resurrection Eucharists, and I do not think I disagree with anything that Dom Dix was trying to say. But it seems to me that it is something that is much better expressed by Père de la Taille's distinction between the *oblatio hostiae immolandae* and the *oblatio hostiae immolatae,* than by Dom Dix's distinction between the sowing of the seed of the Eucharist and its reaping. This, however, is a digression, and we must return to our main theme.

The upshot is that the absolutely primitive Eucharist, by which I mean the rite as celebrated by our Lord at the Last Supper and presumably as celebrated by the Church in the years immediately succeeding the Resurrection, had what Dix describes as the 'seven-action' shape; it consisted of four acts performed with the bread at the beginning of the meal and three acts performed with the cup at the end. Diagrammatically, we may represent it as follows:

A. *At the beginning of the meal*		B. *At the end of the meal*	
1. He took		1. He took	
2. He blessed	the	2. He blessed	the
3. He broke	bread	[3. lacking]	cup
4. He gave		4. He gave	

There were thus what might almost be described as two separate services, one concerned with the bread and the other with the cup, the two being separated by

[5] *The Shape of the Liturgy*, p. 76.

the normal length of time that a meal would occupy. What linked the two and distinguished them from the rest of the meal was simply the words which Christ had said as he distributed the bread and the wine, and which gave these two articles a new and mysterious significance, namely the declaration that the bread was his body and that the cup was the new covenant in his blood, and the command that this was in future to be done for his *anamnesis*. It was, no doubt, in the gentile churches that everything in between was removed to become the separate rite of the *agape*-meal and then got abandoned altogether; for there was no particular reason why gentile Christians should follow the ceremonial directions of the Jewish religion when they met together for a meal. The state of affairs that is indicated by I Cor. 11 shows that it was by no means easy to reproduce and maintain the specifically *religious* character of a Jewish meal among a miscellaneous body of gentile Christians, and it may quite well have been as a result of such disorders as those at Corinth that the separation of the *agape* took place. But the two features to which the Lord had given such a new and solemn significance – the taking, blessing, breaking and giving of the bread at the beginning of the meal, and the taking, blessing and giving of the cup at the end – these could not be abandoned, and the removal of the intervening meal brought these two features into immediate juxtaposition. The final step was presumably taken on grounds of convenience; it consisted in dovetailing together the two services of the bread and the cup. The seven acts which Christ performed at the Last Supper still survive, but their order is changed and they are combined into four. We thus get the 'four-action' shape which is found in the earliest liturgies which have come down to us, and which may very well go back to the days of the Apostles themselves. It may be represented diagrammatically as follows:

1. He took the bread and the cup.
2. He blessed the bread and the cup.
3. He broke the bread.
4. He gave the bread and the cup.

And these four actions are respectively enacted in the four great acts of the Church's liturgies as follows:

1. The offertory.
2. The *sursum corda* leading into the canon.
3. The fraction.
4. The communion.

This is the pattern which we can see, for example, in the early third-century liturgy of the Apostolic Tradition of Hippolytus.[6] It survives in all the great liturgies of East and West, though it has become complicated by later additions and modifications, and in particular by the prefacing of the Eucharist proper with the originally separate service of the *synaxis*, consisting of lessons, chant, sermon and prayers. It appears clearly in the Western Latin rite from the offertory onwards, if we remember that in origin the preface and the canon are one continuous prayer of thanksgiving on the

[6] It cannot be taken as certain that the fifth-century Verona palimpsest, upon which Dom Dix based his edition of the *Apostolic Tradition*, precisely reproduces the third-century Greek original (cf. E. C. Ratcliff, 'The Sanctus and the Pattern of the Early Anaphora', in *Journal of Eccl. Hist.*, I, i and ii, 1950). This will not, however, affect the general argument in the text. Cf. also G. A. Michell, *Landmarks in Liturgy* (1961), pp. 83f.

Jewish model and that the singing of the *Sanctus* and *Benedictus* by the choir, however natural and edifying it may be, is really an interruption of the primitive pattern. We may notice in particular that the offertory is followed immediately by the opening of the Eucharistic prayer with the *sursum corda*, and that these are not separated by anything like the prayer for the Church militant and the 'communion devotions' of the Anglican rite. There is also nothing like the interposition of 'communion devotions' between the fraction and the communion of the people which is found in the modern Roman rite. The insertion into the Eucharistic action of prayers by which the individual communicant expresses penitence for his sins and is given a general absolution is in fact a typical piece of late mediaeval individualism which is altogether foreign to the objective and corporate character of the classical Eucharistic rite; the Anglican Church has inserted it between the offertory and the Eucharistic prayer (indeed, it has wedged the 'prayer of humble access' into the Eucharistic prayer itself), while the Roman Church has inserted it between the fraction and the communion. It is in any case most unfortunate that, when in 1661 the offertory was explicitly restored to the Anglican rite, it was placed before the prayer for the Church and not after the communion devotions.

Nothing that I have said so far is in any way original. It has been pointed out many times before, and in particular by Dom Gregory Dix in *The Shape of the Liturgy*. It is, however, needed as a prelude to what will follow, and there is some convenience in having summarised in a few pages the essential and less disputable points of a long and intricate discussion.

II. DOING AND DESCRIBING

The blessing of the bread at the beginning of a Jewish meal, as preserved in the tractate *Berakoth* of the Mishnah, and as used by pious Jews at the present day, is quite brief and, *mutatis mutandis*, serves for other kinds of food as well. 'Blessed be thou O Lord our God, eternal King, who bringest forth bread from the earth.' The formal prayer of thanksgiving, said at the conclusion of the meal, is, as would be expected, much longer and ceremonious. According to the Mishnah, on formal occasions it was recited over a cup of wine, and it seems clear that this must have been the practice in our Lord's day. Only so can we account for the fact that the early Eucharistic canons all have the form of a more or less protracted prayer of thanksgiving. Clearly what happened is that when, with the vanishing of the rest of the meal from the Eucharistic rite, the two services of the bread and the cup got dovetailed together into the four-action shape, the short formula for blessing the bread was absorbed into the longer formula for blessing the cup, so that henceforth both bread and cup were blessed with the long thanksgiving prayer. What then was the structure of this prayer? After a preliminary interchange of versicles and responses, which correspond fairly closely to the *Gratias agamus* of the Christian liturgies (one of them, given in the Mishnah for use when there are a hundred people present, has the actual form 'Let us give thanks unto our Lord God') the host or other person presiding recited the prayer, which fell into three main parts. In the first of these, God was blessed for bringing food from the earth and giving it to men; that is, broadly speaking, for the work of creation. In the second, he was blessed for bringing his people out of Egypt and giving them the Law and the Covenant; that is, for the work of redemption. In the third part (though the form of it which survives is clearly later than the Fall of Jerusalem) petitions appear to have been offered for God's continued favour towards his people. Presumably in our Lord's time the wording of the prayer had not become absolutely fixed, and in any case we can hardly doubt that he would have modified it so as to express the fact that the supreme act of God's redemptive power in which all preceding acts were fulfilled and transcended, was that in which he himself was the central figure. At any rate, it is clear, from the novel and tremendous words with which he distributed the bread and the cup, that, as now enacted by the Messianic King who was none other than God incarnate, the significance of the rite had been transformed beyond human imagination. *Antiquum documentum novo cedat ritui. Vetustatem novitas, umbram fugat veritas, noctem lux eliminat.* The precise form which the blessing took at the Last Supper is a matter about which we can only speculate, but there is one thing about which we can be certain – that the Church knew herself to have received from her Master the command to do this for his *anamnesis.*

The point which is of primary importance for our present purpose is this – that what Christ had commanded was that they should do this for his *anamnesis,* not that they should *say* that they were doing it.[7] If

---

[7] 'On ne récite pas une rubrique, on l'exécute' (P. Benoit, *Rev. Bibl.* XLVIII (1939), p. 386, cit. J. Jeremias, *Eucharistic Words of Jesus,* p. 159.

they carried out his commands with complete literality, they would do precisely what he did at the Last Supper. They would not give any verbal description of anything that he did then – they would simply do it. They would thank God for his work in creation and redemption in the very words in which their Master had thanked God for it the night before he died, but this would not involve – it would indeed exclude – any announcement that this was what they were doing. A simple illustration will make this point clear. Let us suppose that an actor is engaged to play the part of Hamlet in Shakespeare's play of that name. This will involve his reciting all the lines of his part with whatever accompaniments of voice and gesture he considers will be most effective in expressing their significance. But what it will not involve – and will indeed positively exclude – is any announcement by him in the course of the play that he is acting the part of Hamlet in Shakespeare's drama. If on his first entrance he were to say to the audience, 'This is *Hamlet* by William Shakespeare, and I am Mr. X in the title-role', he would not be fulfilling the instructions of the author and the producer at all. It will, of course, be obvious to the audience that they are watching Mr. X in the play of *Hamlet*, and the fact will be advertised on the posters and in the programmes. But no reference to this will occur in the play itself. Mr. X is engaged to play the part of Hamlet, not to talk about playing it. And if he does talk about playing it while he is playing it, he will, to that extent, not be playing it at all. Now the parallel with the Eucharist is not, of course, exact, because the Church, in its Eucharistic celebration, is not bound to conform to the example of Christ with

that literal accuracy with which an actor is bound to
conform to the book of the play. In fact, the Church
has felt at liberty to depart rather strikingly from the
rite of the Last Supper, as we have seen, for example,
in the dovetailing of the original seven-action liturgy
into the four-action shape.[8] The words 'Do this ...'
are to be interpreted in substance and not in detail.
Nevertheless, the illustration which has been given
may serve to make this point clear, that what is necessary, *absolutely speaking* (I italicise these words, for what
is not necessary absolutely speaking may conceivably
become necessary for other reasons, e.g. by ecclesiastical ordinance) – what is necessary, absolutely speaking,
for the Eucharistic rite, is that the Church, by duly
qualified ministers, shall be doing, in obedience to
Christ's command and for his *anamnesis*, what he did at
the Last Supper, namely taking, blessing, breaking and
giving the bread, and taking, blessing and giving the
cup. And since, at the Last Supper, Christ did what he
did but did not say that he was doing it, so, in following
Christ's example, the Church must do what he did but
need not say, in the course of this, that she is doing it.
This is surely the explanation of the fact, which has
puzzled many and scandalised not a few, that the East-
Syrian liturgy of SS. Addai and Mari (as indeed a
number of other liturgies) appears never to have contained a full narrative of the institution of the Eucharist
at all. It takes the bread and the cup and blesses them
by thanking God over them for his mighty acts, and it
identifies these mighty acts with the redemptive work

---

[8] We may notice also that even as early a rite as that of Hippolytus feels at liberty to substitute its own words of distribution for
those used by Christ.

of Christ. It apparently even goes so far as to address the prayer itself to the Second Person of the Trinity, rather than the First. But, while doing in all essentials what Christ did at the Last Supper, it no more gives a *description* of what Christ did there than he gave while he was doing it. It is, of course, necessary that it shall be perfectly clear that what is being made is the *anamnesis* of Christ, and not, for example, merely the rite of an ordinary *chabûrah*-meal. So far as I can see, this could be done perfectly well by a preliminary announcement, or even by the setting in which the rite takes place. In fact, Addai and Mari does it by bringing into the canon a specific reference to the redemptive work of Christ and by affirming that 'we ... are gathered together in his name ... and have received by tradition the example which is from him'. But it does not find it necessary to incorporate into the prayer a detailed description of the circumstances under which the prayer was recited by Christ, and so it makes no mention of what we now call 'the words of institution'.

It is not difficult to see how the words of institution found their way into almost every extant Eucharistic canon, and, given the legitimacy of any liturgical development at all, their introduction need not be deprecated. In thanking God over the bread and the cup for his mighty acts of redemption, the Church could hardly restrict herself to the mighty acts of the Old Dispensation and make no reference to the supreme redemptive act of the New Covenant, in which the acts of the Old Covenant received their fulfilment and of which they were only the foretaste and the shadow. We can hardly doubt that, in his thanksgiving-prayer at the Last Supper, Christ himself would

have offered praise to the Father for the sacrifice of
himself in which all previous sacrifices were now fulfilled; the more so as it appears to have been normal
for a *berakah* to contain some verbal reference to the
divine word by which the particular observance which
was being celebrated was authorised. And in fact, in
almost every surviving liturgy the New Covenant has
altogether swallowed up the Old, in verbal expression
no less than in theological reality. And once the New
Covenant has found its place in the canon, what can be
more appropriate than that an explicit account should
be given of the solemn act in which, on the night before his Passion, King Messiah consecrated himself to
be the victim of the new covenant-sacrifice, especially
as, in the very rite in which it is now engaged, the
Church is re-enacting that solemn act in obedience to
his command? Nothing could be more fitting or more
natural, but the consequence is a striking one which
has had remarkable repercussions. It is that, within
the performance of the Eucharist, which the Church is
making in obedience to the command of Christ, there
is henceforth found in miniature a description of the
rite as originally celebrated by Christ himself. Thus,
while the primordial and essential structure of the
Eucharist in its four-action shape is the following:

1. Offertory[9] – 'Taking'.
2. *Sursum*, preface and canon – 'Blessing'.
3. Fraction – 'Breaking'.
4. Communion – 'Giving'.

[9] 'Offertory' here means the taking of the elements by the
celebrant, not the bringing of them up by the people. Cf. pp. 179f.
infra.

the scheme which has become practically universal in Catholic Christendom is this:

1. Offertory – 'Taking'.
2. *Sursum,* preface and canon – 'Blessing'.

    Narrative within the canon:

A		B	
(i) 'Christ took ...	⎫	(i) 'Christ took ...	⎫
(ii) 'Christ blessed ...	⎬ the bread'	(ii) 'Christ blessed ...	⎬ ...the cup'
(iii) 'Christ broke ...	⎪	—	⎪
(iv) 'Christ gave ...	⎭	(iv) 'Christ gave ...	⎭

3. Fraction – 'Breaking'.
4. Communion – 'Giving'.

It is, in fact, as if the 'four-action' Eucharist is now wearing on its breast a small picture of itself in its original 'seven-action' form.[10]

Once this has happened, the almost inevitable tendency is to look upon the narrative which has been incapsulated in the canon as being the real performance of the Eucharist in obedience to Christ's command. After all, we find ourselves saying, we do not profess to be doing anything other than Christ himself did; indeed, the Eucharist is nothing else than Christ's own action in his Body the Church. Surely, then, the priest should take the elements when he says that Christ took them, should bless them when he says that Christ blessed them, and so on. Nothing could seem more fitting. And yet the consequence is that the whole action of the Eucharist tends to be compressed into

[10] It is not necessary for our purposes to enter into a discussion of the various 'strata' of the Eucharistic prayer. See Dix, *The Shape of the Liturgy,* ch. viii.

what is really a part of it. I am sure that almost any educated Anglican or Roman Catholic at the present day, if he were asked at what point of the Eucharist the priest follows the example of Christ in taking the bread, would reply without hesitation, 'When he takes the host into his hands just before the consecration'; very few would reply, 'At the offertory.' And yet, from the point of view of history, the latter is the right answer.[11]

An even more striking example of my point is provided by an extraordinary rubric at the consecration of the host in the Sarum Missal. The whole passage is as follows:

Here let the priest ... lift up the host, saying, Who on the day before he suffered took bread into his holy and adorable hands, and lifting up his eyes to heaven, *Here let him raise his eyes,* unto thee, his Father, God Almighty, *Here let him incline and afterwards raise himself a little,* gave thanks to thee, bles ✠ sed, brake, *Here let him touch the host, but not so as to break it, as some do; for although the order of the words seems to imply that Christ brake before consecrating, tradition teaches the contrary,* and gave it to his disciples, saying, Take and eat ye all of this,
FOR THIS IS MY BODY....

It is quite obvious what has happened. The original Latin liturgy follows quite straightforwardly the example of Christ, except of course for the telescoping of the bread and the cup into the four-action shape; he took, he blessed, he broke, he gave. Not even the incapsulation of the institution-narrative in the canon has been able to remove the communion of the people from its proper place after the end of the canon; to make that transference was to be the work of Cranmer

[11] Cf. T. S. Garrett, *The Liturgy of the Church of South India*, p. 65.

in 1552. And, in the Sarum rite, the fraction as well retains its ancient place between the canon and the communion. But the writer of the rubric is a true mediaeval. For him, the blessing of the bread means the recital of the 'words of institution', words which, in the Biblical narratives, accompany not the blessing of the bread, but its distribution. He has never thought of the canon as the great consecratory prayer, which blesses by giving thanks. Thus, for him, the fact that, *in the narrative*, the *mention of the fraction* precedes the *mention of the words of institution* is in effect a statement that *at the Last Supper* the *fraction itself* preceded the *consecration*. The only way in which the rubrician can get out of his difficulty is by appealing to tradition against the words of Scripture, by saying that, 'although the order of the words seems to imply that Christ brake before consecrating, tradition teaches the contrary'. It never occurred to him that the order of the words implies nothing of the sort.[12] By the end of the Middle Ages the view that the recital of the narrative of the institution was really the whole Eucharistic action, to which all the rest of the service was simply an edifying but inessential setting, had spread so widely that, in the fourteenth and fifteenth centuries, not only Western Catholics but (of all people) Egyptian Copts had begun to make a fraction during the narrative, though this did not, either in Europe or in Egypt, succeed in abolishing the fraction at the traditional place.[13] The Sarum rubrician forbids this innovation,

[12] Cf. the passage from Pope Innocent III (*De sacro altaris mysterio*, Migne, *P.L.*, ccxvii, c. 888) quoted by George Every, *The Baptismal Sacrifice* (1959), p. 77.
[13] Dix, *The Shape of the Liturgy*, p. 49n.

but prescribes the curious custom of touching the host instead; among the Copts, the fraction during the narrative persists at the present day.[14] In the Anglican rite, no direction as to the place of the fraction occurs in 1549, nor any mention of it at all from 1552 onwards; when it was restored in 1661, it was inserted in the narrative and remains there still.[15] In the reformed Roman missal of Pius V, there is no direction for either touching the host or breaking it during the narrative; nevertheless, the priest is told to take the host into his hands at the words *accepit panem* and to make the sign of the cross over it at *benedixit*, and similarly for the chalice. In all these instances we see different manifestations of the assumption that in order to do anything at the liturgy you must be simultaneously describing it, an assumption which comes to its climax in the intolerable verbosity of most of the reformed liturgies of the sixteenth century. The action which it is most difficult to synchronise with the narrative is clearly the distribution of the elements in communion, on account of the marked interruption which it would introduce into the prayer; nevertheless, the reformers attempted it, and also tried to return from the four-action to the seven-action shape. Thus, in Luther's 'German Mass', we are told: 'I think that it would be in accordance with the Last Supper if the sacrament were distributed immediately after the consecration of the bread before

[14] *The Coptic Liturgy*, trans. by John, Marquis of Bute, p. 99; Attwater, *Catholic Eastern Churches*, p. 144.

[15] It is interesting to note that the Scottish liturgy of 1929, which prescribes the fraction in the traditional place, has not suppressed the fraction which the seventeenth-century rite placed in the narrative of the institution; so that here the fraction takes place not once but twice!

the blessing of the cup.'[16] Zwingli explicitly made this provision.[17] Cranmer adopted an ingenious compromise; he did not attempt to restore the seven-action shape, but in 1552 he removed the communion from the mediaeval place after the canon and the Lord's prayer, which it still occupied in 1549, and inserted it, with the Lord's prayer, immediately after the narrative, so that it was followed by what was substantially the latter part of the 1549 canon or by the 'prayer of thanksgiving' which was provided as an alternative. It is clear that, in all these reconstructions the various reformers were doing their best to be scriptural and primitive. But it is equally clear that they were all dominated by the mediaeval conviction that the narrative of the institution is the essence of the Eucharist; and all that they did was to go a little farther than the mediaevals in packing as much as possible of the Eucharistic action into the narrative. The Calvinist rites form an exception to this generalisation; structurally they are refreshingly primitive, but they are appallingly dominated by preoccupation with human corruption and by the desire not to miss the opportunity of turning the Eucharistic prayers into statements of godly reformed doctrine. 'If Lutheran worshippers are "laeti triumphantes",' writes Dr. Horton Davies, 'Calvinists are "miseri et abjecti".'[18] But, he also tells us, 'the real difference between the Lutheran and Calvinist reforms in worship may be summed up as follows: Luther will have what is not specifically condemned by the Scriptures; whilst Calvin will have only

[16] Kidd, *Documents of the Continental Reformation*, p. 200.
[17] Ibid., p. 447.
[18] *The Worship of the English Puritans*, p. 24.

6

what is ordained by God in the Scriptures'.[19] The real
tragedy of the liturgical reforms of the sixteenth century is that nobody at that time really understood what
a scriptural liturgy would be like. Dr. G. A. Michell
has pointedly remarked that 'as a comparison between
the evidence from Christian antiquity, the Canon and
Cranmer's prayer of 1549 makes abundantly plain,
Cranmer's prayer follows the Canon, where the Canon
deviates from the primitive pattern, but deviates from
that part of the Canon, which faithfully adheres to
primitive usage'.[20]

The incapsulation within the Eucharistic canon of a
miniature of the Eucharistic rite has of course been a
gradual process, though it clearly began very early. In
the early third-century Roman rite of Hippolytus
(which ought, however, not to be taken as embodying
a rigid and invariable form) the miniature refers explicitly only to the taking and blessing of the bread and
the cup, not to the breaking and giving, and there are
no directions for any manual acts to be made by the
celebrant at this point. In the Egyptian rite of Sarapion,
of the middle of the fourth century, three of the four
acts – the taking, the breaking, and the giving – are
mentioned in connection with the bread, though there
is strangely no mention of the blessing either of the
bread or of the cup: 'The Lord Jesus Christ in the
night in which he was betrayed took bread and brake
and gave to his disciples, saying ... The Lord Jesus
Christ taking a cup after supper said to his own
disciples, Take ye, drink ...', and the narrative is less

[19] *The Worship of the English Puritans*, p. 16.
[20] *Landmarks in Liturgy*, p. 131. The 'Canon' is that of the Latin
mass.

closely integrated into the thanksgiving prayer. In the East-Syrian liturgy of Addai and Mari, as we have seen, there is no account of the institution at all, but only the extremely general reference to 'the example which is from thee'. In nearly every other extant liturgy the narrative of the institution is explicit, even when, as in the Eastern Orthodox Church at the present day, it is not considered as marking the moment of the Eucharistic consecration.

I shall conclude this section of the discussion by pointing out that, while the incapsulation within the liturgical canon of a narrative of the institution has undoubtedly obscured the fact that the primordial essence of the consecration consisted not of narration but of thanksgiving, it has had one result of the highest importance for which we cannot be sufficiently grateful. It has anchored the Church's Eucharist to its foundation in history;[21] it has made it quite inescapably clear that in her liturgy the Church is doing, in obedience to Christ's command, what he did at the Last Supper. I have pointed out already how necessary it was for the Church to make it evident that any Eucharist which she was celebrating was the *anamnesis* of Christ, and not merely a solemn Jewish meal within the framework of the Old Dispensation. I have also pointed out that this does not necessarily require that the canon should incapsulate within itself a narrative of, or even a reference to, the institution itself. Nevertheless, there could hardly be a more effective way of doing what was needed than to incapsulate such a narrative within the canon; and, in view of the fact that it was apparently normal for a Jewish blessing to contain some mention

[21] Cf. G. Dix, *Jew and Greek*, pp. 107–8.

of the divine ordinance which authorised its performance, it is, as we have seen, highly likely that at
least some reference to the institution would have been
made in the apostolic liturgy. Judaism was, however,
not the only danger to which the early Church was
exposed. There were the various gnostic systems, and
there were the various mystery-religions. And, however much these may have differed from one another,
they were at one in their profoundly unhistorical
character. They were myths rather than history, they
offered salvation by an intellectual or an emotional
technique rather than by a personal union with a concrete historical individual. The historical status of such
figures as Mithras or Osiris is, to say the least, highly
ambiguous, nor was it of the least importance to the
religion of their devotees. In contrast, the central fact
of the Christian faith was the crucifixion of Jesus of
Nazareth under Pontius Pilate, and the Church staked
its very existence upon the assertion that this particular
Jew had risen from the dead. Hence the fundamental
fact about the liturgy was, in the words of Ignatius of
Antioch, that 'the Eucharist is the flesh of our Saviour
Jesus Christ, which flesh suffered for our sins and which
God the Father raised up'.[22] It is, of course, possible to
find here and there in Christian liturgical forms traces
of thought and language which may be derived from
mystery-religions. There is nothing that need disquiet
us in this. Christianity is the fulfilment of the mystery-
religions, as it is of all human aspirations and intuitions,
however imperfect and distorted these may be. What
was, however, essential was that the Church and its
liturgy should remain firmly rooted in the flesh and

[22] *Smyrn.*, vi. 2.

blood of Jesus the Messiah. However difficult it may be to unravel the various strands of the Church's early liturgical tradition, the practically universal incorporation of an account of the institution of the Eucharist into the canon witnesses to the Church's determination to maintain these roots. What the Church is doing when it celebrates the liturgy is not offering a mystical experience to the initiates of an ecstatic cult, but fulfilling the command of the incarnate Lord to do as his *anamnesis* what he did at the Last Supper, for the gathering into unity of the people of God.

III. THE MOMENT OF CONSECRATION

I shall now say something about the vexed question of the 'moment of consecration'. Those who wish to rebut what they conceive to be materialistic views of the Eucharistic presence are accustomed to assert that the whole Eucharistic prayer is consecratory, and not any particular section of it; and they may possibly feel that the preceding argument supports their view. Up to a point, no doubt, it does, for I have stressed the fact that the Jewish method of blessing food or drink was to thank God for his mercies over it, and that at the Last Supper Christ instituted the Eucharist in just this way. If all that the Eucharistic consecration consisted in was the setting aside of the elements for the solemn use of a sacred meal, this would be a sufficient description of it. We have, however, not only to take account of the features that our Lord took from the Jewish rites but also of those that he added to them. As we have seen, when he distributed the elements which he had previously blessed, he did so with the words 'This is

my body which is for you. This do for my *anamnesis*'
and 'This cup is the new covenant in my blood. This
do, as oft as ye drink it, for my *anamnesis*.' This identification of the elements with his body and his blood was
something altogether novel, and it makes the Christian
Eucharist something altogether different from the mere
ceremony of grace at meals on which it was founded. It
did in fact establish the Eucharist as a sacrifice, and
the implications of this are discussed in the following
chapter of this book. We are not, however, directly
concerned with this at the moment, but with the
Eucharistic presence, and it is perhaps well to remember how extremely realistic and unmetaphorical the
doctrine of the early fathers on the Eucharistic presence
is. 'The Eucharist', writes Ignatius in words already
quoted, 'is the flesh of our Saviour Jesus Christ, which
flesh suffered for our sins and which God the Father
raised up.'[23] 'The food which has been eucharistised',
writes Justin, 'is the flesh and blood of that Jesus who
was made flesh.'[24] 'How', asks Irenaeus, 'can [the
gnostics] claim that the bread which has been eucharistised is the body of their Lord and the cup is his
blood if they confess him not to be the Son of the
Creator of this world?'[25] appealing to a belief in the
Eucharistic presence common to Catholics and gnostics
alike. In the face of expressions like these it is obviously
impossible to interpret such words as *antitypon*, *figura*,
symbolon, and the like, when used of the elements, as
indicating belief in a merely metaphorical presence, or
to understand the transition from symbolist to conversionist language in the fourth century as marking
the beginning of belief in a presence that is real and

[23] *Smyrn.*, vi. 2.   [24] *Apol.*, I, 66.   [25] *Adv. haer.*, iv, 18, 4.

unmetaphorical. The difference between symbolist and conversionist language is not the difference between belief in a metaphorical presence and belief in a real one; it is simply the difference between two ways of looking at the real presence. In the earlier period, the question which is in effect being asked is 'How can bread and wine be the body and blood of Christ?' and the answer is 'By the fact that they are the *figures* or *symbols* of the body and blood'; where 'figures' and 'symbols' mean outward signs of invisibly present realities. (That this approach to the matter is not altogether outmoded may be seen by reference to the discussion of sacramental signification on pp. 131f. below.) In the later period, the question which is in effect being asked is 'How can what was formerly only bread and wine be now the body and blood of Christ?', and the answer is 'By the fact that the bread and wine have been changed into the body and blood'. This does indeed show a great change of attitude and of interest; it manifests in the Eucharistic realm that transition from an eschatological to a historical outlook which came over Christian thought and activity in all their aspects when, with the gradual acceptance of Christianity by the Roman world, the Church found herself faced with the task of christianising the temporal order. But there is no change from a metaphorical to a literal view of the Eucharistic presence; and the quotations which have just been made from patristic writers in the earlier period are quite sufficient to show this.

To return to our main point, it is the words with which our Lord accompanied the distribution of the elements that indicate the change that they have undergone. At the moment of reception they are no longer ordinary bread and wine, but have become the Body and Blood of Christ. For several centuries the Church gave little or no thought to the question of the precise moment at which the change had taken place; all its attention seems to have been concentrated upon the Eucharistic action, upon the liturgy as the work of Christ in his body the Church. But as soon as the mind is turned to the consideration of the elements themselves, as distinct from the action in which they are the focal objects, the question of the moment of the change is bound to arise, and it seems quite wrong to suggest that the posing of it shows a materialistic or superstitious attitude. In whatever terms the Eucharistic presence is conceived, the fact remains that the elements were formerly ordinary bread and wine and that they are now the Body and Blood of Christ. Since they are objects in space and time, there must be some instant at which they ceased to be ordinary bread and wine and became the body and blood. To deny the validity of this statement is not a sign that one holds a pure, unsuperstitious and spiritual doctrine of the Eucharistic presence; it is merely a sign that one is suffering from confusion of mind. If anything is likely to lead to a materialistic doctrine of the presence, it is surely the view that the Eucharistic change is a gradual and imperceptible process to which no exact moment can be assigned; for the only changes in material objects which can take place in this way are changes in their material properties, such as, for example, the liquefaction of wax on the application of heat or the change of colour in a piece of cloth that is being bleached. It is simply inconceivable that the bread becomes the outward sign of Christ's body by a gradual process, so that at one moment it is more the outward sign of the body than it was shortly before. It might, of course, be argued that we have no means of *knowing* at what moment the change takes place; but this is not to say that there is no such moment. We should then not be denying that there is a 'moment of consecration', but simply saying that we do not know when it is. And there is a good deal to be said for such reticence.

If we consider what happened at the Last Supper itself, we can surely say that the change in each element had taken place by the time that Christ delivered it in communion, for he gave the bread with the declaration that it was his body, and the cup with the declaration that it was the New Covenant in his blood. It seems likely that the change in fact took place in each of the elements while he was reciting over it the formula of blessing. But it might, I suppose, be held that each of them underwent a twofold consecration: that, as at any other Jewish meal, it was solemnly dedicated to God as his gift to man by the recitation of the formula of blessing, but that it only became the body or blood of Christ when he uttered the mysterious words at the distribution. In this latter case, the words 'This is my body ...' and 'This cup is the new covenant in my blood ...' would be, to use a phrase of the modern logicians, not descriptive but performatory.[26] I cannot see any way of settling this point. But it seems to be clear that, in the West at least, the Church was so conscious of the fact that it was these words and these

[26] Thus, for example, Tertullian says explicitly that at the Last Supper, Christ made the bread his body *Hoc est corpus meum dicendo* (*Adv. Marc.*, iv, 40).

words alone that differentiated the Last Supper from any other solemn Jewish meal, that, when, in the way which we have already seen, the narrative of the Last Supper became incapsulated in the Eucharistic canon, they were taken as not only describing but effecting the change in the elements. This represents, no doubt, a departure from the primordial rite, though, as we have seen, the Church seems from the beginning to have felt at liberty to act with considerable freedom in liturgical matters, as for example in the dovetailing of the original seven-action pattern into the four-action form. It is perhaps not altogether impious to suggest that the ascended Lord may have been ready to endorse such action taken by the Church which is his Bride and his Body, an action which at least shows her recognition of the fact that the whole significance of the Eucharist for her life and for the lives of her members lies in the things which her Master said and did on the night before his crucifixion as he sat at supper with his apostles. It seems at any rate easier to associate the change in the elements with the words by which Christ himself declared their true significance than, as has come to be the practice in the Eastern Church, with words of purely ecclesiastical origin. I do not think we can be very confident in our conclusions, but this discussion has at least shown two things. The first is the Church's clear recognition of her absolute obligation to do for the Lord's *anamnesis* what he himself did at the Last Supper and commanded her to repeat. The second is the quite extraordinary freedom which she has felt entitled to exercise in the way in which she has carried out this obligation.

IV. LITURGICAL REFORM

I am not without hope that the following out of this line of thought may have to some degree deepened my readers' understanding of the Christian liturgy; at least I am sure that it has very considerably deepened my own. I should like to conclude by making it quite plain that I have no intention of pleading for a radical reconstruction of our existing liturgical formularies in the name of primitivistic purism. I am convinced that liturgical development can lead, and has led, to the apprehension of truths about the liturgy which were formerly unrecognised, as well as to the obscuration of truths that were formerly explicitly held. And the only way in which forgotten truths can be restored to their rightful place is by thinking about them and talking about them and finally, with every possible consideration of the effect upon the ordinary worshipping layman – the brother for whom Christ died – by giving them liturgical expression. At all costs we must avoid the tempting short cut which assumes that you can revive the apprehension of a forgotten truth simply by prohibiting or abandoning something else. In the sixteenth century the Church of England had the wholly laudable desire to restore to the layfolk their rightful place as participants in the liturgy and not merely spectators of it. Instead, however, of adopting the positive and arduous course of instructing the laity in the real nature of the liturgical action and of their membership of Christ's mystical Body, the Church's controllers adopted the draconic and wholly negative line of prohibiting the celebration of the liturgy unless a minimum number of persons had previously registered themselves as intending communicants. The consequence is notorious: instead of lay communion becoming universal, the celebration of the Eucharist became almost extinct. In some high-church Anglican circles today it appears to be believed that the best way to get the laity to take their full part in the Eucharistic action is by stopping the clergy from celebrating what are inaccurately described as 'private masses'; it is perhaps sufficient to point out that there is no warrant for supposing that you can persuade one person to do something by stopping another person from doing something else. Again, it is not uncommon to find liturgically minded Roman Catholics who are so dismayed by the way in which, in many of their churches, the Mass has become overshadowed by the rite of Benediction of the Blessed Sacrament, that they would like to abolish Benediction altogether. More surprisingly still, there are Anglicans who urge the same reason as a ground for prohibiting the adoption of extra-liturgical devotions to the Blessed Sacrament in the Anglican Church, where no such overshadowing has taken place. It is surely clear that, if the Mass has in some places become overshadowed by Benediction, this is not because the laity have come to overvalue Benediction but because they have come to undervalue the Mass. It is, of course, true that people learn not merely by *listening* but by *doing*. It is, however, also true that to introduce them to unfamiliar liturgical activities without instructing them first may result in a diminished, rather than an enhanced, understanding of the liturgy. There are, I fear, some 'liturgical' circles in which emphasis upon the 'parish communion' and upon the importance of the offertory has led to a serious misunderstanding of the corporate character of the liturgy. It has produced the impression that what makes the liturgy corporate is simply the fact that a large number of people are together at the same time in the same place, rather than the fact that, whether the communicants be few or many, the liturgy is essentially corporate because it is the act of Christ in the *Corpus mysticum*. It is perfectly possible for the parish communion to result in a far more morcellated and fragmented conception of the Church and of the liturgy than can be produced by any number of 'private masses'. For once people get into the way of assuming that the corporateness of the liturgy is produced by a merely geographical togetherness of the worshippers, they will almost inevitably take the further step of assuming that every liturgy at which a good crowd of people are present is complete in itself, and the fact that the very nature of the liturgy is that it transcends space and time and makes one Body out of all the children of God, wherever they may be, will have entirely fallen out of view. On the other hand, when the fact is fairly faced that a number of priests saying Mass at different altars are not in fact doing different things but are all doing (not merely generically, but numerically) the *same* thing, the real nature of the unity of the Mass and of the Church becomes impressively clear. I am not, of course, arguing for the abolition of all that is represented by the idea of the parish communion. Nor am I denying that 'private masses' can be understood in a thoroughly individualistic and even superstitious way.[27] But I am arguing that no change in liturgical practice will produce a

[27] Cf. ch. x *infra*.

good effect unless it is both based upon and accompanied by a sound liturgical theology.

Again, I would urge that, however certain he may be of the correctness of his own views about the nature of the liturgical action, no priest ought to introduce changes in the accepted manner of conducting the liturgy without exercising the greatest circumspection. For, after all, he may very well be wrong, and he may even come to see this.[28] It is possible to point to parishes whose priest is an enthusiastic amateur liturgiologist, where the layfolk have to adapt themselves at regular intervals to fresh modifications in the rite and ceremonies of the Mass in agreement with the stage now reached by their pastor in his researches. Liturgism of this kind is simply individualism run riot. No method of celebrating the liturgy can claim absolute universality, however universal the liturgy may be in itself. It is of the essence of the liturgy that, under the forms which are given to it by the Church of each time and in each place, it makes present there and then the redemptive act of Christ. We are no doubt right in being acutely conscious of the deficiencies of the mediaeval and post-mediaeval expressions of the liturgical act. But we must also be prepared to admit

[28] It is relevant in this connection to refer to the question of the position of the celebrant at the Eucharist. The notion that the only primitive and genuinely 'liturgical' arrangement is for the priest to face the people across the altar has received some severe shocks from experts in liturgical history. See, e.g. J. A. Jungmann, *The Early Liturgy*, pp. 137f.; L. Bouyer, *Rite and Man*, pp. 175f.; C. E. Pocknee, *The Christian Altar, passim.* 'Facing the east', seems at times to have mattered more than anything else and to have led to the situation in which, if the altar was in a western apse, priest and people alike had their backs to the altar and the priest prayed over their heads from behind!

that, in permitting the liturgy to be expressed in those forms, the ascended Lord was allowing Christians of those times to worship him in the only ways that they could understand. And, however much we may pride ourselves upon our revived insight into the true nature of the liturgy, we have no warrant for holding that the whole truth about the liturgy has been revealed to us in the twentieth century. When we wonder at the blindness which prevented our forefathers in the Faith from seeing the truths about the nature of the liturgical action which are so obvious to us, it is salutary to remember that they were men of not less piety and intelligence than ourselves and to reflect that the theologians of the twenty-third century may well wonder at the blindness which prevented us from seeing the truths which are so obvious to them. This is not, of course, an argument against liturgical experiments and development. In the history of the Church there have been periods of liturgical efflorescence, as well as periods of liturgical stagnation, and, however much it may shock the legalists, it looks as if, after the regimentation of the last four hundred years, a new period of development has begun, though it may well be a period whose keynote will be simplification rather than elaboration. Such a period will call for a combination of qualities which we are unlikely perfectly to achieve, though this does not exempt us from trying to achieve them. It needs diligence and intrepidity, restraint and humility. And above all it calls for great charity towards the flock of Christ.

Chapter Four

SONSHIP AND SACRIFICE

O NE of the most remarkable celestial phenomena
in the theological firmament today is undoubtedly the multiple conjunction that has taken
place between a large number of Catholic and Protestant luminaries on the subject of the Eucharistic
Sacrifice, a conjunction that is all the more striking
because it does not seem in all cases to have been either
intentional or even recognised. Such names as those of
Masure[1] and Journet,[2] developing the earlier con-
tributions of de la Taille[3] and Vonier[4] on the Catholic
side, and of Benoit,[5] D. M. Baillie,[6] Cullmann and
Leenhardt,[7] Geddes MacGregor,[8] Thurian,[9] Aulén[10]

[1] E. Masure, *The Christian Sacrifice* (1944); *The Sacrifice of the Mystical Body* (1954). The French originals were published in 1932 and 1950 respectively.

[2] C. Journet, *La Messe, présence du sacrifice de la croix* (1957).

[3] Two volumes of an English translation of M. de la Taille, S.J., *Mysterium Fidei* (1915), have been published under the title of *The Mystery of Faith* (1940, 1950).

[4] A. Vonier, O.S.B., *A Key to the Doctrine of the Eucharist* (1925).

[5] J. D. Benoit, *Liturgical Renewal* (1958).

[6] D. M. Baillie, *The Theology of the Sacraments* (1957).

[7] O. Cullmann and J. Leenhardt, *Essays on the Lord's Supper* (1958). The French originals were published in 1936 and 1955 respectively.

[8] G. MacGregor, *Corpus Christi* (1959).

[9] M. Thurian, *The Eucharistic Memorial*, 2 vols. (1960–61).

[10] G. Aulén, *Eucharist and Sacrifice* (1958).

and Prenter[11] on the Protestant, will be sufficient indication of this; and if among Anglicans there has been little in recent years to set by the side of F. C. N. Hicks's ponderous but influential work, *The Fullness of Sacrifice*,[12] this may be attributed at least partly to the deeply rooted tendency of Anglican theologians to direct their energies into other channels than that of dogmatic theology.[13] It is important not to exaggerate the extent to which agreement has been achieved, either between the two camps or within them severally. Nor should we forget that on the equally burning question of the Eucharistic Presence little agreement has up to now been either attempted or attained; and, while I would hold that the Sacrifice is primary to the Presence and not *vice versa*, I cannot agree with those who hold that without a satisfactory doctrine of the Presence an adequate understanding of the Sacrifice is either possible or sufficient. Perhaps on this point Lutheran theology may have some help to offer. Nevertheless the *rapprochement* on the question of the Sacrifice is highly significant, and it is in the hope of advancing it a little further than I propose in this chapter to discuss first the nature of sacrifice in general and then that of the Sacrifice of Christ as a background for our later consideration of the Sacrifice of the Eucharist.

[11] I am indebted to the Rev. A. M. Allchin for information about Professor Regin Prenter's Danish work on creation and redemption, *Skabelse og genløsning*, which has not been translated into English. (There is a German translation, *Schöpfung und Erlösung*, 2 vols. (1958–60).)

[12] F. C. N. Hicks, *The Fullness of Sacrifice* (1930).

[13] As exceptions to this generalisation I might mention F. Hastings Smyth's *Sacrifice: A Doctrinal Homily* (1953) and two small works, C. F. D. Moule's *The Sacrifice of Christ* (1956) and George Every's *The Baptismal Sacrifice* (1959).

I. SACRIFICE IN HUMAN RELIGION

First, then, let us consider sacrifice in general. I must leave it to the anthropologists to classify the extreme variety of sacrificial rites that have characterised human religion throughout the ages and the differing interpretations that men have placed upon them. I would, however, stress the virtual universality of sacrifice as a central feature, if not indeed *the* central feature, of human religious activity. The secularism that has more and more become the dominant mental presupposition of men and women in the sophisticated technological civilisation of the post-Renaissance Western world, and has more recently begun to swamp the ancient cultures of the East and of primitive societies, must be reckoned as a highly exceptional phenomenon in human history, whether we interpret it as marking the long-awaited emancipation of the human race from the fetters of superstition and degradation or the atrophy and inhibition of a normal human faculty. Not less questionable is the assumption that it is a healthy and noble thing for human religious practice to be purely mental and spiritual and that the institution of sacrifice itself, and not merely perverted and horrible forms of it, is a deviation, an excrescence, or an outworn survival. If I may use a rather crude illustration, throughout almost the whole of human history and in almost every human social group, man's natural and spontaneous reaction, when he is perplexed about existence in general, anxious about his own future, desirous to recognise the claims of a supernatural order of reality, tormented by the problem of evil or burdened by the consciousness of sin, is not to chant the appropriate lyric from Robert Bridges's anthology *The Spirit of Man*, or even *Hymns Ancient and Modern*, but to take the healthiest and plumpest chicken from his farmyard round to the local shrine and there cut its throat. Indeed, one of the main difficulties in deciding what is the essential meaning of sacrifice on anthropological grounds arises from the fact that men find themselves offering sacrifices simply because it seems to them the obvious thing to do long before they ask themselves why they are doing it. In consequence, doctrines about sacrifice tend to have the character of *a posteriori* rationalisations of an existing practice rather than of *a priori* reasons for instituting it.

It is in any case notorious that one of the greatest obstacles that confronts the Church today in its evangelistic and teaching functions arises from the twin facts that the religion of the Bible, in both Testaments, is expressed predominantly in sacrificial terms and that the institution of sacrifice has become totally unfamiliar to modern industrialized man. I believe Sir Edwyn Hoskyns used to say that he wished that a heifer could be regularly sacrificed on the Backs at Cambridge, in order that every theological student at some time in his career might understand what the religion of the Jewish Temple was like. Where the word 'sacrifice' has survived in modern speech it has completely lost its traditional theological connotation, so that we get such instances as that of the advertisement in the *Church Times* for an exchange of benefices that ends with the words, 'Cannot sacrifice' – a phrase that properly could only signify that the cleric in question was unable or unwilling to celebrate the Holy

Eucharist – and the notice in the window of a tailoring establishment, 'These trousers will be offered at a great sacrifice.' Nevertheless, in spite of the exceptional character of our own time and setting, sacrifice is a central and universal feature of human religion as such, and both anthropologists and theologians have recognised this.

I have referred to the fact that the institution of sacrifice precedes all attempts to explain it; and indeed when the explanations appear they are bewilderingly numerous and often mutually incompatible. There has, however, been a tendency, which has had the most unfortunate consequences, to assume that the essence of sacrifice consists in the destruction of some valuable object, preferably a living one, in order to honour or to propitiate a deity, a destruction which, in the case of an animal victim, will involve its slaying and, in other cases, will involve some ritual act of equivalent significance. Nor is it only in the lower and more primitive forms of religion that this simple identification of sacrifice with mactation has been made; it has obtained a firm foothold even in the Christian Church and has provided the guiding concept for many doctrines of the Atonement. As Masure,[14] Galy[15] and Mersch[16] have shown, the great leaders of the French

---

[14] Masure, *The Christian Sacrifice*, p. 31.

[15] Galy, *Le Sacrifice dans l'école française de spiritualité* (1951), pp. 145f., 302f., 350, etc.

[16] Mersch, *The Whole Christ* (1938), Part III, ch. 10. He writes *à propos* of Condren's teaching about Christ's offering of his nothingness to the Father,

This is indeed a wonderful vision, and yet ... there is something frightening about it, like an immense desert landscape. The constant repetition of our nothingness, but most of all the

School of spirituality, Bérulle, Condren and Olier, found it very difficult, as appears from their liking for such terms as *anéantissement*, to shake off the idea that God is glorified by the destruction of his creatures in homage to him and in recognition of his sovereignty.

It is therefore a matter for deep satisfaction that in recent years there has come to the fore a wider and more positive notion of sacrifice which, while finding a real place for the insights of what we might call the established view, altogether avoids its weaknesses. This movement, which is at least as much a recovery as an innovation, has resulted from a convergence of biblical, anthropological and strictly dogmatic considerations. The chief honour for it must be given to the French theologian, Canon Eugène Masure, whose remarkable book, *Le Sacrifice du Chef*, has been translated into English by Dom Illtyd Trethowan under the title of *The Christian Sacrifice*. His argument has received confirmation from a quite independent work by an American Episcopalian scholar, Dr. R. K. Yerkes, *Sacrifice in Greek and Roman Religions and Early Judaism*.[17] While fully recognising the grim and even horrible character that sacrificial rites have sometimes assumed,

---

peculiar glory that God is said to take in the fact that his Son is offered to him dead, are depressing details.

And of Olier he writes,

He is quite as exacting as Condren, except that he speaks rather of effacement than of immolation: one is reminded more of a candle burning itself out than of a victim being slaughtered. Apart from this, his doctrine presents exactly the same rigour as that of Condren and we explain the two as one doctrine (op. cit., pp. 547–8).

[17] R. K. Yerkes, *Sacrifice in Greek and Roman Religions and Early Judaism* (1952).

Yerkes warns us not to be misled by the fact that most sacrifices involve the slaying of an animal into concluding that the notion of sacrifice is essentially tragic or gloomy; the Greek *Thusia*, he points out, for example, was joyous and thankful.[18] I shall not attempt here to summarise his argument or to pass judgment upon its details. That would be beyond both the scope of this chapter and the competence of its author; but I think it may be said that, even if some of the detailed interpretations were questioned, Yerkes's main point would stand firm, that sacrifice in its essence is not a gloomy or destructive activity but a joyous and affirmative one. We might perhaps emphasise his basic caveat by remarking that the fact that the central figure of a Christmas dinner is customarily the carcass of a slaughtered bird does not imply that the participants are engaged in a grim and terrible commemoration of its demise. Even of the primitive blood-rites Yerkes is able to write:

> We are apt to think of these as eerie, barbarous rites devoid of all spiritual content. If so we forget that those who performed them were striving, in the best way they knew, for that solid union in which alone is strength.

And he adds that 'blood, to all ancient men, was symbolic, never of death, always of life. Blood and life were synonymous',[19] making the same point with regard to primitive religion that was central to Hicks's account of the religion of Judaism.

To turn now to Masure. While he opens his discussion by giving some quite horrifying descriptions of

[18] *Sacrifice in Greek and Roman Religions and Early Judaism*, pp. 102f.
[19] Ibid., p. 44.

sacrificial rites, he insists that the basic meaning of sacrifice is not the destruction of the creature but its offering to God for his acceptance in joyful homage. So, he remarks in a luminous phrase, 'what was really immolated was, in men's minds, not the victim but the offerer'.[20] I shall develop the subsequent argument in my own way, but before doing so I should like to emphasise my indebtedness to Masure, who seems to me to be one of the most brilliant and original of present-day theologians.

I shall therefore define sacrifice as the offering of a creature to God in recognition of him as its Creator, in order that it shall be accepted by him and transformed by his acceptance. We shall, I think, see that this definition will take us very far indeed.

First, we must observe that in being offered to God in sacrifice a creature is simply fulfilling the law of its being as a creature. God is both its efficient and its final cause, its alpha and omega, its beginning and its end. It is made by him and for him; its *esse* is both *esse a Deo* and *esse ad Deum*. The sacrificing of a creature to God is the ritual expression of its ontological status. The part that is normally played in this process by slaying or some equivalent action will be considered in a moment.

When the victim is a lifeless or an irrational object the sacrifice can hardly be more than symbolic or external, for neither the understanding nor the will of the victim has any part in it. As Masure points out, what is morally and effectively offered is not the victim but its owner, who offers it as a token of his own homage. And, as the Old Testament emphasises, it is the intention of

[20] Masure, *The Christian Sacrifice*, p. 37.

the offerer and not what happens to the victim that is in fact pleasing to God. 'The sacrifices of God are a broken spirit. A broken and a contrite heart thou will not despise' (Ps. li, 17). It is only when sacrifice is offered in righteousness in the rebuilt Jerusalem that God will again take pleasure in burnt offerings.

The true sacrifice, the sacrifice that God can accept and transform and that when transformed is then of value in itself, is the offering by a rational creature of himself. And in order to see the full implications of this truth we must, I suggest, give full weight to the biblical truth that man is made in the image of God and indeed trace back the essence of sacrifice to its prototype in the Holy Trinity.

We are accustomed to remember that, according to orthodox trinitarian doctrine, the Father eternally begets the Son by an act of complete self-communication, a self-communication so complete in fact that the Son who results from it is in no way inferior to the Father but coequal with him. We do not, I think, so often reflect on the correlative truth that the Son eternally responds to the Father in an act of filial self-giving, a self-giving that is no less complete because he who makes it is not an inferior but an equal. I have argued elsewhere[21] that the truth for which St. Athanasius contended against the Arians can be summed up in the phrase 'derived equality', to describe the status that is enjoyed by the Son in conquence of the Father's eternal act of generation; I shall now use the phrase 'filial response' to describe the correlative act by which the Son, eternally recognising the Father as the source of his personal distinc-

[21] E. L. Mascall, *Via Media* (1956), ch. ii.

tion, offers himself back to the Father as the Father's loving Son. It is this that St. John expresses when he tells us that in the depths of eternal Being, 'in the beginning', the divine Word was not only *theos* but *pros ton theon*, leaning, as it were, towards the Father.[22] We might make the point by saying that it was the achievement of Nicene orthodoxy to see clearly that both derivation and response are strictly compatible with equality. In Masure's fine phrase, the Father's Almighty Word has sung his glory eternally in an invisible silence.[23] It would not, I think, be correct to describe this eternal response by the term 'homage', for that would seem to imply that the Son was inferior to the Father; still less could we describe it as 'worship' or 'sacrifice'. But it is, I suggest, the uncreated prototype of the homage, worship and sacrifice that a rational creature is bound to offer, for the Son is the Father's Image and man is created in God's image to be not only his creature but also his beloved and loving son. Adam, St. Luke tells us, was the son of God (Luke iii, 38).

Man, then, created by God and for God, was meant to achieve his fulfilment and beatitude by offering himself to the Father in a life of joyful and loving filial obedience which would be an analogous reflection on the created level of the eternal act of filial response made by the Son on the uncreated level in the life of the Trinity. And if this offering had been made and maintained God's acceptance of it would, we cannot doubt, have transformed beyond our powers of imagination the nature of man and of the material world of

[22] Cf. E. Masure, *The Christian Sacrifice*, p. 130.
[23] Ibid., p. 70.

which he was part. Here, then, there would have been
established a relation between man and God that
would have strictly conformed to the definition of
sacrifice from which we began, the offering of a
creature to God in recognition of him as its Creator, in
order that it shall be accepted by God and transformed
by his acceptance. The capacity of the creature to be
thus transformed by God's acceptance is, of course,
what theology calls the potentiality of nature for grace.
In this there would have been neither pain nor death
but the joyful return of the creature to its Creator, of
the son to his Father, to enjoy all the riches of the
Father's house. And in this sacrifice man would have
been both victim and priest, for he would have been
offering himself. 'The substance of sacrifice ...,' writes
Masure, 'is ... the return of the creature to him who
has made it for himself so that it may find its end and
therefore its happiness in him and for his glory....
Sacrifice is the movement or action by which we try to
bring ourselves to God, our end, to find our true
beatitude in our union with him. *To sacrifice a thing is to
lead it to its end.*'[24] And Masure quotes the famous
sentence of St. Augustine: *Verum sacrificium est omne opus
quod agitur, ut sancta societate inhaereamus Deo, relatum
scilicet ad illum finem boni, quo veraciter beati esse possumus.*[25]
'It is because of sin', writes Masure, 'that death now
precedes and conditions life, and that *without shedding of
blood there is no remission. But, in the beginning it was not
so.*'[26]

Sin, however, has entered in and man is, in the

[24] Masure, *The Christian Sacrifice*, p. 41.
[25] *De Civ.*, X, 6.
[26] Masure, *The Christian Sacrifice*, p. 38.

biblical phrase, at enmity with God (Rom. viii, 7). He cannot make this free and joyful offering of himself; indeed his very will is perverted and internally divided. (I need only refer in passing to the classical description of this state given by St. Paul in Romans vii.) The consequence is that sacrifice now becomes something extraordinarily deviant and ambiguous. Man knows in the depths of his being that he can no longer offer himself to God, with the lower creation incorporated into his offering, so he finds himself offering other creatures to God instead of himself. The truth that he cannot apprehend but that will one day be revealed is that what is needed is not that he should offer other creatures instead of himself, but that someone other than himself should offer *him*. The offering is, he believes, indeed accepted and transformed and may be returned, in whole or in part, to him as a sacred food, by partaking of which he may himself be accepted and transformed. But now at the centre of his sacrifice there lies the death or destruction of the victim.

For man can no longer offer himself and his gifts to God spontaneously and effortlessly, in an act in which, because his will is set wholly upon God in loving and obedient sonship, what God wills and what man wills are the same. He can in his fallen and divided condition only put his gift into God's possession by removing it totally from his own. Therefore he slays or burns his offering so that it may wholly pass into the presence of God. But let us note that even here there is no suggestion that God is glorified by the destruction of his creature, for if it could be literally destroyed there would be nothing left for him to accept and transform.

It is not being destroyed but transferred to him in such a way that it is no longer under the control of selfish and sinful man. But when it has been accepted and transformed it may be given to man as the vehicle of God's own life in a meal eaten at God's own table, where man sits down in his Father's house as the reconciled and once again accepted son.[27]

Now all these things were done in an allegory, for the blood of bulls and goats cannot take away sin. All that even the sacrifices of the Old Law, still less those of heathen religions, could in fact do was to keep alive the memory of what needed to be done. And even this memory was clouded and curiously inverted; for as we have already seen, when man had become incapable of offering himself to God, what was needed was not that man should offer something else but that someone else should offer man. And here we enter on the second part of our discussion, that of the Sacrifice of Christ.

II. THE SACRIFICE OF CHRIST

Nowhere, I think, has the simple identification of sacrifice with slaying done more harm than in the

---

[27] Cf. Fr Roland de Vaux, O.P., on sacrifice in Judaism: 'The purpose of this destruction is not merely to destroy. In opposition to the theory that sacrifice consists in annihilation, and in opposition to a certain modern school of spirituality, we must maintain that God, who is Lord of life and of all being, cannot be honoured by the destruction either of being or of life ... Two reasons may be given for the destruction of the victim's carcase or of the vegetable offerings upon the altar, and they are complementary to each other. The first is that such destruction makes the offering useless, and makes it, therefore, an irrevocable gift ... The second reason is that destruction is the only way to give the offering to God by transferring it into the realm of the invisible' (*Ancient Israel: Its Life and Institutions*, p. 452).

thought of theologians about the redemptive work of Christ. At its worst it has led to crude and horrible substitutionary theories of the Atonement, as exemplified by the preacher whose sermon reached its climax in the words, 'And when Jesus cried, "My God, my God, why hast thou forsaken me?" God struck him dead – instead of you!' Now I have no intention of minimising the central and ineradicable significance of the death of Christ in the economy of redemption; I shall try later on to show what that significance is. And I think it would be unrealistic to attempt to eradicate from Christian speech such phrases as 'The sacrifice of Calvary' and 'The altar of the Cross'.[28] Nevertheless, if we are to interpret sacrifice by the threefold definition of offering, acceptance, and transformation, we shall see that the Sacrifice of Christ includes in its sweep not only the death but the whole incarnate life of the eternal Son.

For when the divine Word took flesh in the womb of his Virgin Mother, it was surely in order that in manhood there might be made that perfect offering of filial homage to the Father that man throughout his history had so signally failed to make. (I may remark in passing that in the case of the Virgin Mother there are certain special considerations, arising out of her unique role in the Incarnation and out of the fact that she is, so to speak, *within* the redemptive act from the start, which I shall not develop here.) In virtue of the hypostatic union the manhood of Jesus is taken up by its union with the divine Person of the Eternal Son into that act of filial response that the Son ever makes

[28] *Cujus corpus sanctissimum*
In ara crucis torridum ... (Office hymn for Eastertide).

to the Father in the life of the Trinity. In Masure's words, 'His nature [viz., his human nature] like his Person is *pros ton theon*, because the Son keeps in his humanity his eternal attitude, his single unvarying direction; the activity which was his and from the beginning ... he now performs in his finite and created nature, as St. Paul says, *sōmatikōs*.'[29]

Elsewhere Masure rather puzzlingly writes: 'We have therefore a sacrifice initiated on Calvary and crowned in heaven, and because it is there consummated, it is there eternally prolonged'; but I think the word 'initiated' marks an unintentional lapse, as Masure almost immediately says:

> The immolation of Christ is a continuation in the sequence of acts and gestures accomplished by the Incarnate Word for the purpose of establishing him for all eternity as our intermediary between his Father and us, *semper vivens ad interpellandum pro nobis*.[30]

Dr. S. H. Hooke writes:

> At the heart of all beginnings, the beginning of the new creation, we have what may well be taken as the interpretation on the highest level of the baptismal scene, the Word *pros ton theon*, the Son, as it were, confronting the Father in an attitude of filial trust and obedience receiving from the Father the word by which he was to live.[31]

Thus, in Christ, human nature has once again become fully filial and more wonderfully than in man's first creation. God indeed wonderfully made the dignity of

---

[29] *The Christian Sacrifice*, p. 144.
[30] Masure, *The Sacrifice of the Mystical Body*, p. 59.
[31] S. H. Hooke, *Alpha and Omega* (1961), p. 129.

man's substance, but has yet more wonderfully restored it. Unfallen man in the original creation – the first Adam – would merely have reflected and analogically reproduced in his own life, in that union with God that we call grace, the filial response to the Father that the divine Son makes eternally in the life of the Triune Godhead; in the second Adam, the man Christ Jesus, human nature is literally taken up into that eternal filial response, for this human nature is lived in, and this human life is led by, none other than the Person of the divine Son himself. The Apollinarians were right in their recognition that the Person of the divine Son was eminently fitted to be the subject of a perfect human life, though they were wrong in supposing that he had to displace a constituent of human nature in order to do this.

Thus from the moment when the divine Word took flesh in Mary's womb, throughout his earthly life and beyond his Ascension to his present glorified condition in heaven, the human life of the divine Son and the human nature in which he lives it are one continuous offering to the Father, continuously accepted and continuously transformed. Because, up to the Ascension, this life is lived under the conditions of human history, a succession of events and a development are inherent to it, and we can discern in it various stages, the Baptism, the Transfiguration, the Passion, the Resurrection, the Ascension, but it is all one thing, the perfect offering of a human life that is the human life of the divine Son, a human nature that is filial because it has received filiality from the person of the Son who is eternally filial. (In passing we may remark that the status of the man Jesus as the human Son of God derives immediately from the hypostatic union and not from the overshadowing of Mary by the Spirit. The Spirit does not take the place of a human father, to the destruction of Mary's virginity, but makes her a virgin mother, which is quite a different thing.) This whole complex of offering, acceptance, and transformation is not a static object but a developing process worked out in the detailed and contingent events of a human life, lived in one particular place at one particular time among a particular group of people, but it reaches its culmination as complete, and therefore no more subject to vicissitudes, in the Ascension and the heavenly session, in which all the previous stages and events that have contributed to its fulfilment are included as causes in their effect.[32]

I must now say something about the part played in this by the Spirit. The scriptural indications are that, among its other functions, the gift of the Spirit indicates and implements the Father's acceptance of the object that is offered to him; by promitting the Spirit upon it the Father seals it as his own. Thus in the baptism of our Lord, Christ's offering of himself as the obedient Son who has come to fulfil all righteousness is ratified by the Father's declaration from heaven, 'Thou art my beloved Son, in whom I am well pleased', and by the descent of the Spirit, in virtue of which the baptism that Jesus himself will institute will

---

[32] It is, I think, the rigid restriction of Christ's sacrifice to his death on the Cross that gives such an extremely unprogressive and unco-operative character to the learned and in many ways illuminating papers read at the Oxford Conference of Evangelical Churchmen in 1961 (published under the title *Eucharistic Sacrifice* in 1962) and contrasts them so sharply with much contemporary writing by Protestant theologians outside England.

be no longer merely a symbolic baptism of water but a transformed and transforming baptism of water, Spirit and fire. We may see this same pattern exemplified at the Annunciation, when Mary's offering of herself in the words, 'Behold the handmaid of the Lord, be it unto me according to thy word', is accepted and replied to in the descent of the Spirit who transforms her into the Mother of God; at Pentecost, when the Spirit comes upon the potential or latent Body of Christ, waiting and offering itself in silent obedience to the Lord's command, and transforms it into the fully and actively energised Spirit-bearing Body; and, if we can accept the common Eastern Orthodox Eucharistic doctrine as expressing at least a part of the truth, in the descent of the Spirit upon the Church's offering of the Eucharistic elements to signify the Father's acceptance of them and to transform them into the true Body and Blood of Christ.[33] As Nicholas Cabasilas writes, 'God makes these holy offerings so much his own that he transforms them into the Body and Blood of his only-begotten Son. Surely it is not possible to conceive of anything to equal such an appropriation, nor to set a measure to the way in which these gifts are accepted.'[34] There is strong patristic support for the view that the Spirit is properly to be thought of as the Gift of the Father both to the Incarnate Son, to his Church and to his individual members. We find this, for example,

[33] In fact the doctrine that the Spirit as well as the Word is concerned in the Eucharistic consecration does not seem to be specially 'Eastern'. Professor E. C. Ratcliff traces it in the West from Paschasius Radbertus by way of Gratian (*Theology*, LX (1957), p. 232).

[34] *A Commentary on the Divine Liturgy*, tr. J. M. Hussey and P. A. McNulty (1960), p. 105.

in St. Augustine,[35] and St. Thomas asserts that 'Gift'
is the Holy Spirit's proper name.[36] Now I have argued
that this whole pattern of offering, acceptance, and
transformation, which in the created order is the
essence of Sacrifice, is an analogical participation or
reflection of the loving intercourse of the Son and the
Father in the life of the uncreated Trinity. We might
therefore expect to find in the Trinity the prototype of
the gift of the Spirit in the created analogue. So we
should expect to find in trinitarian doctrine the notion
of the Father bestowing his Spirit on the Son to seal the
Son's filial response to the Father's love in begetting
him. I gather that neither the fathers nor the scholas-
tics appear to have taken this step. It would, however,
seem to be thoroughly in accord with the accepted
principle, *Missiones sequuntur processiones*, that the opera-
tions of the Divine Persons in the created realm are, as
it were, copies and prolongations of their mutual self-
expressions in the Trinity itself, and we might suspect
that attention to this notion could have done something to soften the acuteness of the *Filioque* dispute. I
would add that, as regards the element of transformation, the uncreated prototype cannot in this case, any
more than in the case of the elements of response and
acceptance, involve any *change* in the Son. What it does
involve is his eternal embracement by the Father in an
utterly complete and loving interchange of self.

To return, now, to our main theme, we should, I
have suggested, see the sacrifice of Christ as extending
from the moment of the Incarnation, through all the
episodes of Christ's earthly life, into his present glorified

[35] *De Trin.*, V. xv; XV, xix.
[36] *S. Theol.*, I, xxxviii, 2.

condition in heaven, one continuous offering to the Father, continuously accepted and continuously transformed. At the time of the Ascension the offering was complete in the sense that no more events were to take place in Christ's human life, no more episodes to be added to it; thenceforth it persists as a finished and perfected product, perpetually offered to the Father and perpetually accepted by him. 'All that he said, did and endured,' wrote Denis the Carthusian, 'he did and suffered for our salvation to the glory of the Father; all that he did and suffered was meritorious for our sake. Thus the whole life of Christ on earth was, as it were, one solemn Mass, in which he himself was the altar and the temple, the priest and the victim.'[37] And we can parallel this with some words of the late Fr. P. N. Waggett, written as far back as 1906 but strangely ignored since then:

> We know that the Lord's Sacrifice is an offering of his whole life to the Father, and that it is such that his divinely unbegun life had already this character of presentation to the Father, from whom, as from the Fount of Deity, it springs. So the Incarnation itself is from the first an offering, because it is a bringing of the creature into the great stream of the Son's love towards the Father by the Holy Spirit. Now in the Incarnation the Creature also is offered by the same Spirit to the Father and the whole life of Christ, from the Conception to the end, is one effectual sacrifice.[38]

What, then, is the place in this of the Cross and the death on Calvary? They are, I would affirm, essential

[37] Quoted by F. Clark, S.J., *Eucharistic Sacrifice and the Reformation* (1960), p. 527.
[38] P. N. Waggett, *The Holy Eucharist* (1906), p. 32.

and inevitable when a perfect offering of a human life
was made in a fallen world. We have seen that even in
pagan sacrifices and in those of the Jewish religion the
death of the victim was seen not as its destruction but
as the offering of its life to God. And I have suggested
that the only way in which man, in his fallen and
divided condition, can put his gift entirely and un-
reservedly in God's possession is by removing it totally
from his own. So he slays or burns it, in order that it
may wholly pass into the presence of God. No such
necessity dogged the perfect offering of the sinless Incarnate Son. He gave himself completely in his whole
life; he did not slay himself. But the making of the
perfect offering in a sinful world inevitably drew down
upon itself the concentrated forces of evil in a desperate
effort to destroy it or to mutilate its perfection. The
onslaught had to be allowed to go to the ultimate point
of ferocity, for without rendering his offering imperfect
the Offerer could not meet force with force or hate
with hate. So the life passed through death in a way of
which the death of the victim in the ancient sacrifices
was only the faintest and most remote foreshadowing.
Nevertheless, the death was the offering of the life and
not its destruction, and in the Resurrection it was
accepted by the Father and transformed into a condition of perpetual efficacity. Christ ever liveth to
make intercession for us.

What then is the bearing of this on the Sacrifice of
the Eucharist?

The offering that the ascended Christ makes of himself to the Father in heaven in his glorified manhood is
communicated to the Church, which is his body, by
the descent of the Spirit at Pentecost, and to its mem-

bers, who are his members, by their baptismal incorporation into him. As St. Paul told his Roman correspondents, Christian baptism is an actual participation in the death and resurrection of Christ (Rom. vi, 3–11), and in the words of the Epistle to the Ephesians, God has raised us up and made us sit with him in the heavenly places in Christ Jesus (Ephes. ii, 6). And by this participation we are given back our lost sonship and our life becomes filial once more. This is precisely expressed by St. Paul in the Epistle to the Galatians:

> When the fulness of the time came, God sent forth his son born of a woman, born under the law, that he might redeem them which are under the law, that we might receive the adoption of sons. And because ye are sons, God sent forth the Spirit of his Son into our hearts, crying, Abba, Father. So that thou art no longer a bond-servant but a son; and if a son, then an heir through God (Gal. iv, 4–7).

So our lost sonship is restored through our incorporation into Christ, we are *filii in Filio*, and the Church, which is Christ's body, is also the family, the household of God.

As the Russian Orthodox theologian Dr. Paul Evdokimov writes:

> The formation of Christ in man, man's christification, is neither an impossible imitation nor the application to man of the merits of the Incarnation, but the projection into man of the Incarnation itself, operated and perpetuated by the Eucharistic mystery.[39]

[39] Paul Evdokimov, *L'Orthodoxie* (1959), p. 113.

So it is in the Eucharist that the Church is continually sustained and renewed in her character as Christ's body. By the Eucharist the Church is made what she already is and Christians are made what they already are. And I think it has come to be seen in recent years that the only doctrine of the Eucharistic Sacrifice that is both realistic and tolerable is one that understands the Eucharist as neither a repetition nor a commemoration of the Sacrifice of Christ but as identically the *same* sacrifice, differing only in its mode of presentation. I shall develop the implications of this in our subsequent discussion.

Chapter Five

THE EUCHARISTIC SACRIFICE – I

I SHALL now pass on to consider the relation between the Sacrament of the Eucharist and the sacrifice which, as I have argued in the last chapter, was offered by the Incarnate Son throughout the whole sweep of his life on earth and has now reached its consummation as a permanent and abiding reality in his ascended and heavenly glory. There are many aspects of the Eucharistic Sacrifice, some of them of great importance, which will not be referred to at all or referred to only incidentally. I shall say little or nothing, for example, about the relation of the Eucharist to the Church's ministry, although this is a question of major interest which has received considerable discussion in recent years. The question with which I am here concerned is vital and central, although it has received little attention from Anglicans for nearly three decades. In spite of this neglect there is a great deal that can be profitably said about it as a result of some highly original and penetrating work which has been done by theologians of the Roman Communion. It is because this movement of thought seems to offer at least some prospect of loosening the deadlock which has stultified discussion between Catholics and Protestants for the last four hundred years that I have thought it worth while to engage on the present discussion. Later on we shall see how much development has in fact taken place during the decade that has elapsed since the first edition of this book was published, though it must be regretfully acknowledged that Anglican theologians have played a very small part in it.

I. THE REFORMATION DEADLOCK

When the Catechism of the Book of Common Prayer describes the purpose for which the Sacrament of the Lord's supper was instituted as 'the continual remembrance of the sacrifice of the death of Christ and of the benefits which we receive thereby', it makes a statement from which it is difficult to imagine that any Christian could dissent. If, however, we go on to enquire what precisely is to be understood by the word 'remembrance' in this context and what is in fact the relation between the Eucharist and Calvary, we find ourselves inevitably involved in controversies which have rent Western Christendom for four centuries and are even now very far from resolution.

In the theology of the Eucharist, as in many other matters it may well be the case that the ultimate cause of the deadlock between Catholics and Protestants lies not so much in the points on which they have explicitly differed and of which both parties have been therefore fully aware as in a common assumption which both parties have inherited from the Middle Ages and of which, just because it was a common assumption, both parties have been almost if not entirely unconscious. Fr. Tavard, in his important book *Holy Writ or Holy Church*, has shown how, in the sixteenth century both Catholics and Protestants shared a common belief, which in fact arose only in the fourteenth century, that Scripture and Tradition were two sharply demarcated and parallel sources of revelation, although Catholics accepted both of them and Protestants only one. I have given a number of other examples in the first two chapters of my book *The Recovery of Unity*. In the first edition of the present work I suggested that the method of seeking the unrecognised common assumption might be extremely illuminating in relation to the Eucharistic Sacrifice and, although a good deal of what I said then has been called in question in a recent book by Fr. Francis Clark, I shall repeat the substance of the argument before enquiring how far, if at all, it needs to be modified.

As long ago as 1930 the late Dr. F. C. N. Hicks, in his important if cumbersome work *The Fullness of Sacrifice*, drew attention to the way in which, both during the Reformation period and after, discussions of the Eucharist had been dominated by the mediaeval conception of sacrifice as consisting exclusively in the death of the victim, this being taken in complete isolation from the circumstances which led up to it, accompanied it or followed from it. (Substantially the same argument had been put forward with equal learning but greater brevity by Dr. B. J. Kidd as long before as 1898 in his book *The Later Medieval Doctrine of the Eucharistic Sacrifice*.) The consequence of this was a situation in which each side had an argument which was quite invulnerable to the attacks of the other. The Protestants were in effect incessantly asserting 'Christ being raised from the dead dieth no more; therefore the Eucharist cannot be a sacrifice', while the Catholics as constantly replied 'But the Eucharist is a sacrifice, therefore Christ must be in some sense put to death in it'; and neither side observed the suppressed major premise which was common to both arguments, namely that sacrifice is simply equivalent to death. For Catholics, therefore, the Eucharist was seen as a *repetition* of Calvary, while for Protestants it was at most a *commemoration* of Calvary. (How difficult in fact the Protestants of the Reformation period found it to go even as far as this has been shown by Dr. Brilioth in the discussion which he gives of the Eucharistic doctrine of Luther, Zwingli and Calvin in his work *Eucharistic Faith and Practice*.)[1] Dom Gregory Dix has made the same point in his own way in his great book *The Shape of the Liturgy*.[2] It is true that in actual fact both sides have tended to mitigate the sheer starkness of their initial affirmations. Catholic theologians have generally asserted that, while the Eucharist is a repetition of Calvary, it is not a *literal* repetition, while many Protestant theologians have been anxious to insist that, while it is a commemoration of Calvary, it is not a *bare* commemoration; but what exactly is involved in a repetition which is not literal or a commemoration which is not bare neither side has found it very easy to explain.

There has, of course, been a school of Protestant thought which, while it has considered the Eucharist as simply a commemoration, has seen it as a commemoration not of Calvary but of the Last Supper, the meal at which the Eucharist was instituted and was first celebrated. Such a view, in addition to any other objections which may be brought against it, only

[1] Chh. iv, v.   [2] Pp. 623f.

pushes the problem a stage further back and renders it even more intractable. For it evades the question of the relation between the Eucharist and Calvary only at the expense of raising, as an independent problem, the question of the relation between the Last Supper and Calvary; and this certainly makes things no easier.

When we turn to the great Anglican divines we find ourselves in an atmosphere of thought which is much less clear cut than is that of either continental Protestantism or continental Catholicism. It would be easy to take this as merely an example of the well-known Anglican genius for woolliness and compromise, but I doubt whether such a judgment would be altogether fair. I suspect that their hesitations arose largely from the fact that they had much more respect than the continental reformers for the writings of the fathers; and although they failed to locate the root weakness of late mediaeval Eucharistic theology in its exclusive identification of sacrifice with death, they seem to have realised fairly clearly that the error had lain not in the view that the Eucharist was a sacrifice but in an inadequate and restricted view of sacrifice itself. (It is interesting to notice that Fr. Tavard finds them also as being the only people of their time who had some glimmering of the true relation between Scripture and Tradition.)[3] Many of them repudiate quite clearly the common Protestant thesis that the only sacrifice in the Eucharist is the purely metaphorical sacrifice which consists of the offering which the worshippers make of their own praise and thanksgiving. Thus we find Jewel writing in the Elizabethan period: 'We offer up Christ, that is to say, an example, a commemoration,

[3] Op. cit., p. 242.

a remembrance of the death of Christ. This kind of sacrifice was never denied' (later on we shall see how similar this is to the view of St. Thomas Aquinas[4]); while Laud saw the Eucharist as having a threefold sacrificial character, first in the offering made by the priest of 'the commemorative sacrifice of Christ's death, represented in the bread broken and wine poured out', secondly in the sacrifices made by priest and people, of praise and thanksgiving, and thirdly in the self-oblation of the individual communicant. We might add, as a third example, the words of Bishop Bull: 'In the Eucharist then, Christ is offered, not hypostatically, as the Trent fathers have determined (for so he was but once offered) but commemoratively only.'[5] What, however, such writers understand by a commemorative sacrifice is not at all easy to see.

I must now turn to the criticism of this thesis which has been offered by Fr. Francis Clark, S.J., in his massive work *Eucharistic Doctrine and the Reformation*, which appeared in 1960. His conclusion can be stated quite simply. He has investigated systematically no less than eleven alleged defects in late mediaeval theology which bear upon the Eucharistic Sacrifice and which have been alleged to explain the attitude of the Reformers, and his examination of the relevant writings has led him to conclude that in every case the alleged defect was to all intents and purposes non-existent; it was foisted upon Catholics by the Reformers, who, with their basically anti-incarnational views of grace and justification, had convinced them-

[4] Cf. p. 216 *infra*.
[5] Cf. Stone, *History of the Doctrine of the Holy Eucharist*, II, pp. 230, 269, 446.

selves that these were the sort of things that, in spite of their remonstrances and denials, Catholics must have really believed. Late mediaeval theology turns out to be, if anything, rather old-fashioned and unadventurous, and in particular the famous equation 'sacrifice =death' turns out to be a chimera. So far as it was ever accepted by Catholics, it was by a few in the Counter-Reformation and later, and even then it was in a comparatively harmless form.

Now clearly, the passing of a definitive judgment on Fr. Clark's conclusions would require as lengthy and detailed examination of all his sources as he has himself made; I do not think it has yet been undertaken. It may be said at once that there is no reason whatever to suspect Fr. Clark of carelessness or incompetence, and he has evidently tried to be scrupulously fair. The method which he has followed, however, makes it very difficult to judge whether he has in fact succeeded, in his nearly six hundred closely packed pages, in giving a balanced account of late-mediaeval thought on the Eucharist; as we shall see shortly his fellow-Jesuit Fr. A. A. Stephenson thinks he has not. To assemble quotations in groups in order to rebut eleven distinct criticisms is a procedure of polemical rather than expository value; and, as I shall show, in at least one case the texts which are adduced in order to refute one charge provide fairly strong evidence in favour of another. However, granting the substantial accuracy of Fr. Clark's material, there are three questions which may be usefully asked.

First, had the mediaevals a satisfactory doctrine of sacrifice as such? However much the point may have been exaggerated later on, as by writers of the seventeenth-century French school,[6] the note of destruction was present in St. Thomas's amplifications of the assertion that there is a sacrifice when 'something is done with things offered to God' by the illustrations 'as when animals are killed and burnt, or when bread is broken, eaten and blessed'.[7] There was, to say the least, only a very dim realisation of the truth to which, as we have seen, Canon Eugène Masure has given such eloquent and inspiring expression, that the essence of sacrifice is the offering of God's creature to God, not to be destroyed but to be transformed by his acceptance of it, and that the element of death is strictly relative to the world's actual fallen condition.[8]

Secondly, had the mediaevals a satisfactory doctrine of the sacrifice of Christ? Again, I think no. Fr. Clark does indeed quote one glorious passage from Denys the Carthusian: 'All that he said, did and endured he did and suffered for our salvation unto the glory of the Father; all that he did and suffered was meritorious for our sake. Thus the whole life of Christ on earth was, as it were, one solemn Mass, in which he himself was the altar and the temple, the priest and the victim.'[9] No doubt this passage could be paralleled by others. Nevertheless the general tendency is not merely to see the Cross as central to Christ's sacrifice but as identical with it. Every one of the thirteen passages which Fr. Clark quotes on pp. 391–3 in order to show that Catholics did not assert a *literal* immolation of Christ in the Mass makes this identification; on p. 228 he himself admits that this was true of popular mediaeval devotion. And in his citation of popular devotional

---

[6] Cf. p. 86 *supra*.   [7] *S. Theol.*, II II, lxxxv, 3 *ad* 3.
[8] Cf. p. 88 *supra*.   [9] Quoted on p. 527.

passages on p. 288 he quite groundlessly takes the mediaeval habit of meditating on different events of Christ's life at different moments of the Mass as indicating a theological understanding of the inclusive nature of Christ's sacrifice; all it shows is that, instead of uniting themselves with the action of the Mass, the faithful were merely using it as a convenient stimulus for edifying individual meditation. In consequence, the question of the relation of the Eucharist to Christ's sacrifice becomes simply the question of the relation of the Eucharist to Calvary. And in spite of his drastic criticisms of Hicks, Fr. Clark has to admit that this particular feature of mediaeval piety was propagated rather than repudiated by the Reformers.

So then, thirdly, had the mediaevals a satisfactory doctrine of the relation of the Eucharist to the sacrifice of Christ? Fr. Clark assembles a great many passages to prove that they did not explicitly teach that Calvary is *repeated* in the Mass. Indeed, he argues that their dominant thought was one of *commemoration* rather than of *repetition*. If this is so, we should have a case of the Reformers uncritically (as I should say) inheriting an inadequate assumption from the late mediaevals rather than reacting against them, and we may well have here an illustration of the thesis which Dr. T. M. Parker has argued in his eagerly awaited Birkbeck Lectures, that most of the issues and concepts which we think of as characteristic of the sixteenth century had already been discussed in the fourteenth century or even earlier. My suggestion that, because of their identification of sacrifice with death, Catholics thought of the Mass in terms of repetition of Calvary and Protestants in terms of commemoration may need revision; it may be that both Catholics and Protestants thought in terms of commemoration, though Protestants could not persuade themselves that Catholics did so. However, I have been at pains to point out that, when Catholics thought in terms of repetition, it was hardly ever *literal* repetition. And in fact the word 'repetition' itself needs clarification. When we speak of 'repeating a performance' we do not normally mean that anything is done to the performance, as when, for example, we speak of 'interrupting a performance' or 'applauding a performance'; we do not mean that the original performance is witnessed again (though, paradoxically, I shall argue below that if we did mean this, *in a carefully defined sense*, we should have found the key to the deadlock in Eucharistic doctrine). We mean that a new performance is enacted which, in its appearance and circumstances, closely resembles the original one. And in chapter v and elsewhere in his book Fr. Clark seems to show that this was the mediaeval and Tridentine view: Christ was offered with shedding of blood on Calvary; he is offered in an unbloody way in the Mass. That is to say, although the Victim is the same there are two different offerings, whether the second offering is better described as a 'repetition' or as a 'commemoration'. In chapter xii, on the other hand, we are told that the late-mediaeval (and Catholic) doctrine is that the sacrifice of the altar is simply *identical* with that of the Cross;[10] St. John Fisher said so and so, more significantly, did Pope Leo XIII. So too did Jeremy Taylor and the Archbishops of Canterbury and York in 1897. Now Fr. Clark very reasonably remarks that 'these propositions cannot be

[10] Op. cit., p. 247.

simultaneously true: that the Reformers repudiated the Mass because the prevailing Catholic view had made it a realistic immolation, a repetition of the slaying of Christ on Calvary; and that they repudiated the Mass because the prevailing Catholic view had taught them to see it as a mere commemoration of Calvary'.[11] What Fr. Clark fails to see is that he himself has in two different places argued that the late mediaevals held (and, in his view, rightly held) both these points of view, however irreconcilable they may seem to be. In effect, they first of all asserted the absolute identity of the Sacrifice of the altar with the sacrifice of the Cross and then, when they realised that this would seem to imply an actual slaying of Christ in the Mass (as seems, for all Fr. Clark's attempts to explain them otherwise, to be the plain implication of the visions of bleeding hosts), they then substituted for identity the notion of commemoration. We have, I think, here an example of the fact, which has many exemplifications in the history of Christian doctrine, that positions which are unbalanced or unstable have a disconcerting way of toppling over into their opposites.

One of the most useful features of Fr. Clark's book is provided by the quotations which he has gathered from Catholic divines of both the late-mediaeval and the Reformation period; one is sometimes left wondering why the thoughts which they express have been so much neglected since. There is a splendid passage from Schatzgeyer about the sacrifice of the Whole Christ:

> The sacrifice of Christ to God the Father belongs not to

[11] *Eucharistic Sacrifice and the Reformation*, p. 328.

Christ himself alone but also to the Church, which is his mystical body, and to every member of that body – that is, to every believing Christian.... It is one who offers the sacrifice: Christ the head and his body the Church together with the members.

In this and similar passages, from Pighius and Latomus, we see the Middle Ages at their best and we are reminded of the magnificent exposition of the three births of Christ – in eternity, at Bethlehem and in the Church – given by Isaac of Stella four centuries before and rescued for us by Père Bouyer in his book *The Cistercian Heritage*.[12] And the quotations from popular sermons and manuals of devotion, like the anthologies of R. H. Benson and Miss Frances Comper,[13] bear witness to a deep and simple devotion which, unbalanced as it no doubt was from the standpoint of strict theology, is deeply moving as the medium in which so many of our forefathers adored their Redeemer and found their way to heaven.

A very striking reply to Fr. Clark has appeared from the pen of Fr. Anthony Stephenson, S.J., in the American periodical *Theological Studies*.[14] Fr. Stephenson holds that St. Thomas's view of the Eucharistic Sacrifice, which he himself holds and which he believes to be favoured by the Council of Trent, is in fact a 'commemoration' view and that Anglicans and others can therefore hardly be blamed if they held it, especially in view of the fact, as Fr. Stephenson believes it to be, that many late-mediaeval theologians

[12] Pp. 178f.
[13] *A Book of the Love of Jesus* (1918); *Spiritual Songs* (1936).
[14] Vol. xxii (1961), pp. 588f. This has been reprinted in the English periodical *Reunion*, VI (1962), pp. 233f.

had come to hold an objectionable 'repetition' view, largely through a misunderstanding of a key-word in St. Thomas. As will appear in the sequel, I myself hold that neither the 'commemoration' nor the 'repetition' view is adequate, but I think that Fr. Stephenson may very well be right about St. Thomas, and his argument, however paradoxical it may appear at first sight, is certainly of great interest.

Briefly, Fr. Stephenson's thesis is as follows. St. Thomas, in concession to the long-standing usage of theologians of his time, gives an affirmative answer to the question whether Christ is 'slain' (*immolatur*) in the Sacrament.[15] When, however, he goes on to explain what he means by this, it turns out that, if 'slain' is taken in the ordinary sense, his 'Yes' really means 'No'. For he explains that this 'slaying' means two things. First that the Mass is 'a sort of representation or portrayal' (*imago quaedam repraesentativa*) of the Passion, and secondly that in the Mass we partake of the fruits of the Passion and so *opus nostrae redemptionis exercetur*. And neither of these is a literal 'immolation'. Furthermore Fr. Stephenson is at pains to affirm that *repraesentare* in this context simply means 'represent' in the ordinary sense of that word and not, as some later writers have alleged, 're-present' in the sense of 'make present again'. He quotes from St. Thomas the passage *Sacrificium autem quod quotidie in ecclesiae offertur non est*

---

[15] *S. Theol.*, III, lxxxiii, 1. I am not sure that Fr. Stephenson is right in saying on p. 590 that in this article St. Thomas describes the Mass as *vera immolatio*; it seems to me that he applies that phrase to the Passion. But he certainly says that in the Mass Christ is 'immolated'. The suggestion has, however, been made that for St. Thomas *immolare* may simply mean 'offer' and that his unambiguous word for 'slay' would be *mactare*.

aliud a sacrificio quod ipse Christus obtulit, sed eius commemoratio,[16] and he comments '"Its commemoration, and therefore the same!" This is surprising use of language, to say the least.'[17] We may indeed agree. In a later chapter of this book I shall discuss St. Thomas's Eucharistic theology in some detail and, while I shall be less approving of it than Fr. Stephenson is, I shall not see any reason to question his interpretation, which is that 'St. Thomas, instead of protesting against the unsatisfactory and dangerous ambiguity of the traditional language, adopted the phrases, while emphasising that Christ is *not* actually immolated (slain) in the Mass, and that the Mass is *not* (in the obvious sense of the phrase) the same sacrifice as Calvary.[18] 'But', he continues, 'plain as St. Thomas made his real meaning, his refusal to protest against the misleading character of the traditional expressions appears to have had important consequences.'[19] And those consequences are stated in the following passage:

It would appear, therefore, that in the course of the Middle Ages there did emerge – though perhaps not at the higher theological levels – one development of the greatest importance in respect of the Eucharistic sacrifice. Namely, St. Thomas's admirable theology of the Mass underwent a subtle transformation – just as, given the terminological situation, could almost have been predicted – and became the very different 're-presentation' theory. Just such a type of theory, Fr Clark tells us, was actually one of the two dominant theories of the Mass in the Late Middle Ages. According to this general type of theory, the Mass is not a mere representation of Calvary,

[16] *S. Theol.*, III, xxii, 3 *ad* 2.
[18] Ibid., p. 598.
[17] Art. cit., p. 598.
[19] Ibid., p. 599.

but 'its actual *re*-presentation.... As by transubstantiation there is brought about another "real presence in place" of Christ's one glorious body in heaven, so by the sacramental separation of the species in the twofold Eucharistic consecration there is brought about another "real presence in time" of Christ's one redemptive sacrifice of Calvary.'[20] This theory, therefore, clearly teaches that in the Mass Christ is, quite literally, crucified, that in the Mass there is a 'Bloody mactation'. This theory of the literal identity of the Mass and the cross does not, of course, teach a *new* slaying of Christ; nevertheless, a sound Christian instinct rejects it. Moreover, the theory leaves no room for a proper theology of the Resurrection; indeed, it impairs the all-important function of the Risen Christ in the sacramental economy of salvation. There is also the practical objection that it would be extremely difficult to make the less educated faithful grasp and remember the subtle distinction between the numerical identity of the Mass and the cross, which the theory asserts, and a specific identity, which would make the Mass a *repetition* of Calvary. In any case, the Reformers objected to *any* 'bloody mactation' of Christ in the Mass. The admission, therefore, that such a theory was current in the Late Middle Ages virtually concedes the substance of the Anglican contention in its moderate form.[21]

II. A FALSE TRAIL

Whatever may be the truth about the late mediaevals, there can be no doubt that the general tendency of post-mediaeval Roman Catholic theologians down to our own time has been to think of the relation between the Eucharist and Calvary in terms of repetition, and

[20] Clark, op. cit., pp. 256–7.
[21] Stephenson, art. cit., pp. 604–5.

this has led them almost inevitably to seek for some action in the Mass which can be considered as an equivalent of the slaying of our Lord which took place once for all on the Cross. They have, of course, done their best to avoid any suggestion that in the Mass there is a *literal* slaying of Christ by the officiating priest; nor has there been any marked tendency to revive the view, held perhaps by a few mediaeval thinkers, that Calvary was the sacrifice for original sin and the Mass is the sacrifice for actual sin,[22] or that Calvary was the sacrifice for the sins committed before Christ's death and the Mass is the daily sacrifice for the sins committed each day. They have emphasised rather the contrast between Calvary as a bloody sacrifice and the Mass as an unbloody one; they have tended to speak of Calvary as involving a real immolation and the Mass as involving a mystical one. Nevertheless, the domination of their thought by the idea of repetition has caused them to look for some ceremonial act, included in the celebration of the Mass, which depicts and, as it were, re-enacts the slaying on Calvary, and they have conceived the sacrificial character of the Mass as residing in this act. They have viewed the Mass rather as a kind of passion-play, differing from other passion-plays simply in the facts that it has been instituted by Christ and that he himself takes the role of the victim. Thus Melchior Cano, to take but one example, saw the *fraction* of the host as the essentially sacrificial act, re-enacting the breaking of Christ's body on the Cross; with the start-

----

[22] This was alleged by Melanchthon, in the Augsburg Confession, to be the common Catholic teaching. The allegation is argued against in detail by Fr. Clark, op. cit., ch. xxi.

ling consequence that a Mass in which the fraction was omitted would be no sacrifice at all.[23] Others, such as Salmeron, Vasquez and Lessius, have located the essential sacrificial act in the *separate consecration* of the Body and the Blood, typifying the separation of Christ's body from his blood in his death.[24] Others again, such as de Lugo and Franzelin, have conceived the transubstantiation as inflicting a kind of humiliation upon the glorified Christ, as reducing him sacramentally to a lower condition (*status declivior*), as producing a kind of kenosis (*desitio*) of the risen Lord.[25] Whatever its weaknesses, and they are many, this last view has at least the advantage that it associates the sacrificial character of the Mass with the consecration of the elements and not with something done to them after they are consecrated. But all these views have the inherent defect that they locate the sacrificial character of the Mass in some feature of it which is alleged to re-enact, in however 'mystical' or symbolic a way, the slaying of Christ on Calvary. They all envisage the Mass as a *repetition*, even if an 'unbloody' repetition, of Calvary. They naturally tend, in spite of the efforts of their exponents to avoid this conclusion, to make the Mass a sacrifice *numerically different* from Calvary, even if dependent on it.[26] And the paradoxical consequence follows that when these theologians go on to consider how the Mass is related to Calvary they come re-

[23] Stone, *History of the Doctrine of the Holy Eucharist*, II, pp. 356f.
[24] Ibid., pp. 359f.
[25] Ibid., pp. 373f.
[26] Billot is even quoted by Masure as having maintained the sacrifice of the Cross and the sacrifice of the Mass as different not only numerically but even specifically (*The Sacrifice of the Mystical Body*, p. 19).

markably near to the Protestant theory of commemoration. For they see the Mass as related to Calvary simply through the fact that (as they allege) some ceremonial act in the Mass pictures the death of Christ; though they differ from most Protestants in holding that this ceremonial act is performed with the Body and Blood of Christ and not simply with bread and wine. Thus, although (or perhaps it would be more accurate to say *because*) they consider the sacricial element in the Mass as consisting in something, namely a ceremonial act, which is other than the death on Calvary, they can restore the link with Calvary only by seeing this ceremonial act as, so to speak, a *symbolic imitation* or *picture* of the death on Calvary. There is moreover the further drawback that when we consider it as a *picture* of Calvary the Eucharist is not in fact a very good one, not nearly such a good one, for example, as the Oberammergau Passion Play. It is surely very doubtful whether a visitor from Mars who had read the account of Christ's Passion in the Gospels and then found himself present at the Sacrament of the Lord's Supper in either a Catholic or a Protestant church would derive the impression that there was any connection between the two unless he listened very carefully to the words of the rite; and even then he would probably be quite baffled as to what the connection was. So far as what was being *done* was concerned, if the ceremony struck him as resembling anything at all it would be the Last Supper rather than Calvary, and even so the resemblance would be difficult to discern unless the church was of a very consciously 'evangelical' type. In short, however firmly we may be convinced that the Eucharist was instituted for the continual remembrance of the Sacrifice of the death of Christ, it seems clear that any attempt to conceive the relation between the Eucharist and the death of Christ as being simply one of *resemblance* is quite misdirected. And in fact the fundamental ceremonial features of the Eucharist – the taking, blessing, breaking and giving of the bread, and the taking, blessing and giving of the cup – do not appear to derive from any deliberate prefiguring of the Passion by our Lord at the Last Supper, but from the normal ceremonial of a Jewish religious meal. What Christ in fact deliberately added, and what invested the meal with a sacrificial significance, was not anything that he *did* but certain words that he *said*, his declaration that the bread was his body and that the cup was the new covenant in his blood, and his command that the rite should be repeated as his *anamnesis*. It is highly significant that in recent years some Roman Catholic theologians have shown a tendency to abandon the attempt to find in the ceremonies of the Mass some action which can be looked upon as an equivalent of the immolation of Calvary simply in virtue of its external structure; it is not, however, always recognised that that attempt was the natural outcome of the view that the Eucharist is, in however qualified a sense, a *repetition* of Calvary.

There is clearly no logically necessary connection between a 'destruction' theory of sacrifice in general and a 'repetition' theory of the Eucharist, but in the post-Reformation period the two certainly were both held by representative Catholics, while the former was common to Catholics and Protestants alike. The opening that they offered to an unsympathetic critic can be well illustrated by a passage in Daniel Brevint's *Missale Romanum, or the Depth and Mystery of Roman Mass laid open and explained for the use of both Reformed and Un-reformed Christians*, which was published at Oxford in 1672. Brevint, who became Dean of Lincoln in 1681, was anything but temperate as a controversialist, as the passage shortly to be quoted will show, but another side of his character is shown by the fact that he was also the author of a devotional work on the Holy Communion which his biographer in the *Dictionary of National Biography* has commended for its beauty. The passage in question occurs in chapter vi of his book, which bears the recalcitrant title 'Concerning *Masse* as pretending to sacrifice Christ; and what a horrid Mystery *Masse* were, if it were true.' It is based largely upon references to Suarez and Bellarmine and runs as follows:

> Nevertheless rather then to be put to a stand, and want a Sacrifice, they [*sc.* the Roman theologians] will put all these acts together, and order one way or other the whole matter so dextrously, that, before their Masse be over, the Son of the living God (here both *Melchisedek* and *Aaron* may rent their clothes) shall lye under hands, *mortuo modo*, that is, in the most pittifull condition of a dead man: and though the priest doth not radically destroy his life, when by his Consecration, he sets the Body in one place and the Blood in an other, because Concomitancy prevents that actual *separation*, which otherwise would be to him an actual *death*: yet he takes from him so perfectly, all sense and use of life, that without a continual Miracle, as long as He is in his hand, or in his *Pix* (that is a box which they keep Him in) he can neither breath, nor feel, nor move, so much as one finger. All his internal senses and faculties are so mortified and bound up, that he

apprehends nothing, nor can make any ordinary use of his understanding or reason. This poor victim can see neither the hand that holds him up, nor the poor people that kneel about him, nor the Altar he lyes upon: a Church or a dunghill is all one as to his knowledge. He can not so much as see himself; or if it be imagined he doth, by vertue of the feigned Concomitancy; 'tis to make him so much the worse, by seeing and feeling this sad condition, which Masse pretends to bring him to. He hath no manner of strength left to help himself.... To this passe comes the best & highest Service of Roman Church, and thus is Christ honoured at Masse.[27]

Needless to say, the more extreme conclusions of Brevint's argument were disowned by his opponents. Nevertheless, however much one may regret the intemperance of his language, they seem to follow naturally from the doctrine that Christ is reduced to a *status declivior* in the Mass and this doctrine was highly influential at the time. That it persisted in high-level popular preaching for at least another two centuries is shown by the following passage which Dr. E. B. Koenker quotes from a sermon on the Mass preached by Père Monsabré in Lent 1884:

What power, my God, thou hast given to thy priests.... Their word has become an instrument more pointed and trenchant than the knife which slaughtered the victims of the ancient law.... They introduce divine life where there had been nothing before except inert matter, and, at the same stroke, they inflict death.... [Christ] continues to live beneath the mortal blow, and yet he gives expression, so far as in him lies, to the state of death and destruction proper to sacrifice. He gives expression to this

[27] Op. cit., pp. 53–4.

by the total eclipse of his glory, *by the captivity* of his sacred members and of his movements *under the eucharistic species*, by the cessation of natural functions which are proper to his senses: obscurity, immobility, silence, annihilation, which place him at our disposition to such an extent that we can treat him as inert matter, a mysterious state which he has only assumed that he might become our nourishment, and results, therefore, in the destruction of his sacramental being, which is the consummation of the sacrifice.[28]

III. DA LA TAILLE AND OBLATION

The first clear instance of the abandonment by a modern Roman Catholic theologian of the repetitive view of the Eucharistic sacrifice would seem to be provided by the distinguished Jesuit theologian Père Maurice de la Taille, whose great work *Mysterium Fidei* was completed in 1915, though faint adumbrations of it have been traced in Thalhofer and Lepin. Logically if not chronologically, de la Taille's teaching forms a natural sequel to that of F. C. N. Hicks. Hicks maintained that in the Old-Testament sacrifices the essentially priestly and sacrificial act was not the slaying of the victim, which might in fact be performed by a lay person, but the offering upon the altar to God of the blood, which in Jewish thought was identical with, or was at least a divinely ordained symbol of, the victim's life. The slaying was merely an indispensable

---

[28] *The Liturgical Renaissance in the Roman Catholic Church* (1954), p. 100. The passage is taken from an article by A.-M. Roguet, O.P., in *La Maison-Dieu*, XI (1947), p. 181. As recently as 1955, in a book bearing the *Imprimatur* of the Cardinal Archbishop of New York, the statement could be made: 'According to Catholic belief, in every Mass God himself is offered as a sacrifice repeating the sacrifice on the Cross' (Zsolt Aradi, *The Popes*, p. 108).

preliminary by which the life was set free to be offered. So, wrote Hicks, applying these considerations to the work of Christ, in whom all the Old-Testament types are fulfilled, 'the Sacrifice is not the death alone; nor the pleading with the blood alone; nor the offering upon the altar "in heaven"; nor the act of Communion alone.... Each stage is sacrificial. All together make the one Sacrifice.'[29]

Following a somewhat similar line of thought, de la Taille sees a sacrifice as consisting of three elements, namely a ritual oblation, an immolation, and a divine acceptance. In the case of the one true Sacrifice of Christ, these are realised respectively at the Last Supper, on Calvary, and in the entrance of Christ into the heavenly places. What, then, is the Mass? It cannot be a new *immolation*, for Christ cannot die again; and if he did die again in the Mass, the Mass would be a different sacrifice from that of Calvary, whereas it is actually the same. It must therefore be a new *oblation*, one made by the Church after the immolation, an *oblatio hostiae immolatae*, as the Last Supper was an oblation made by Christ before the immolation, an *oblatio hostiae immolandae*. The Mass brings about no change in Christ and inflicts no humiliation upon him; he is a victim, but a glorified victim, and is present in the Mass as such. Substantially the same view as this was developed independently by the Anglican theologian Sir Will Spens in his essay on the Eucharist in *Essays Catholic and Critical*, which was published in 1926, and in subsequent articles in the journal *Theology*; he used a slightly different terminology from de la Taille and referred to the three elements

[29] Op. cit., p. 251.

as oblation, immolation and consecration respectively.
For him, 'the Last Supper and the Eucharist are not
separate sacrifices from that of Calvary, but supply a
necessary element in the sacrifice of Calvary, by ex-
pressly investing our Lord's death before God and
man with its sacrificial significance.'[30]

The strong points of this line of approach to the
Eucharistic Sacrifice are obvious. By making the death
of Christ and the Eucharist two distinct elements in
the one Sacrifice, it avoids any suggestion that the
Eucharist is a repetition of Calvary. So far from the
Eucharist doing again, in however 'mystical' or
symbolic a manner, what was done on Calvary, it does
something essentially different. In de la Taille's
terminology, the Eucharist *offers* what Calvary *immolated*, and it offers *after* the immolation the victim
which the Last Supper offered *before*. Furthermore, this
view altogether avoids that exclusive identification of
sacrifice with death which we have seen to be the root
cause of the deadlock between Catholics and Protestants. The death is only one element in the sacrifice;
and although it is a necessary element and is indeed the
element in which the sacrifice comes to its climax of
self-giving in obedience to the Father's will, nothing
prevents us – though neither de la Taille nor Spens
seems to have taken this step[31] – from viewing the
sacrifice as one great and all-inclusive activity of filial
homage which begins with the Incarnation – *Verbum
supernum prodiens nec linquens Patris dexteram* – and
reaches its consummation when the risen victim makes

[30] *Essays Catholic and Critical*, p. 436.
[31] It was clear from discussion which I had with Spens shortly
before his death in 1962 that he was in fact definitely opposed to it.

his triumphal entry into the heavenly realms, bearing with him for the Father's glory the spoils which he won by the shedding of his blood.

Nevertheless, this view would seem to demand careful qualification. We may well agree that the death of Christ is only one constituent of the Sacrifice and at the same time hesitate to describe the Eucharist as a further constituent of it. We may well envisage the Sacrifice as including the whole sweep of the incarnate life of Christ – birth, childhood, temptation, ministry, death, resurrection and ascension – without feeling able to add the Eucharist as a further item in the list. Nobody, I think, would be prepared to say that the Eucharist is something which *happens* to Christ,[32] in the sense in which we may quite legitimately say that the Passion, Resurrection and Ascension were things which happened to him. Both de la Taille and Spens seem to have had a lurking awareness of this difficulty, for each of them hesitates to consider the Eucharist as a distinct element of the sacrifice in separation from the Last Supper. For de la Taille the Last Supper and the Eucharist *together* provide the element of oblation; while Spens writes that 'the Last Supper and the Eucharist ... supply a necessary element in the sacrifice'[33] (not, we must observe, *two* necessary elements) and that '*at the Last Supper and in every Eucharist* he consecrates that his most holy death to be a sacrifice.'[34] The only writer, so far as I know, who has explicitly affirmed that the Eucharist, as distinct from

[32] But I am not quite sure about Père Monsabré!
[33] Loc. cit.
[34] 'The Christian Sacraments', in *Theology*, XVIII (1929), p. 15, italics not in original. Spens goes on to suggest that the Eucharist is necessary in order that we shall take part in the consecration.

the Last Supper, is necessary for the completeness of
the Sacrifice is the Roman Catholic Bishop of Victoria,
British Columbia, Dr. Alexander Macdonald, who
wrote in his book *The Sacrifice of the Mass* (1924) as
follows: 'Without the ceremonial offering in the Mass,
the Sacrifice finished on Calvary would have been
ritually incomplete.... Our Lord's Sacrifice of himself
attained its *actus primus*, or complete essence, on Calvary: it attains its *actus secundus*, or complete operation,
on our altars.'[35] Even here, however, the contrast
between Calvary as *actus primus* and the Mass as *actus
secundus* suggests that the Mass cannot enter into the
constitution of the sacrifice in the same way as that in
which the events of our Lord's incarnate life enter into
it. Nevertheless, in whatever degree these writers may
have been conscious of the difficulty, none of them
seems really to have faced it; in each case we are left
with the suggestion that without the Eucharist the
sacrifice of Christ would be incomplete. If the Catholic
theologians of the Counter-Reformation tended to
make Calvary and the Mass into numerically distinct
sacrifices, the theologians of the school which we are
now considering tend to make neither Calvary nor the
Mass a sacrifice at all. For them, when we celebrate
Mass we are either adding an element which *is*
necessary to make the sacrifice complete or else re-
enacting *ex post facto* the act of the Last Supper, which
was necessary to make the sacrifice complete. If we
take the former alternative, neither the offering which
Christ makes of himself in the incarnate life nor the
offering which the Church makes of him in the Mass
can be properly described as a sacrifice, though each

[35] Op. cit., pp. 105, 108.

might be described as, in a broad sense, sacrificial; it is only the two together that form the sacrifice by their conjunction. If we take the latter alternative, then the incarnate life is perhaps to be described as a sacrifice, in view of its consecration at the Last Supper (since the Last Supper is itself an event in the incarnate life), but the Eucharist, so far from being a sacrifice, is only an imitation of the act by which the incarnate life was so consecrated.

It goes without saying that probably none of the writers mentioned would in fact admit the consequences which have just been drawn. All of them were anxious to assert that the Mass is a genuine sacrifice and that it is identical with Calvary. What we are concerned with here, however, is not whether this last assertion is correct, but whether the theories which these writers held about the nature of the sacrifice provide an adequate basis for it; and it seems fairly clear to me that they do not. These writers avoid making the Eucharist a repetition of Calvary only at the expense of making both it and Calvary something less than a sacrifice. However near they come to propounding an adequate theory, they fail to achieve complete success. Something is still lacking.

IV. VONIER AND SACRAMENTAL SIGNIFICATION

The missing factor can, I believe, be found in the work of another Roman Catholic writer, Abbot Anscar Vonier, whose book *A Key to the Doctrine of the Eucharist* was published in 1925. For Vonier, the fundamental fact about the Eucharist is the fact that it is a *sacrament*; and the fundamental fact about a sacrament is the

10

fact that it is a *sign*, albeit a sign of a very special kind.
Now, the purpose of a sign is to represent; and the
purpose of that particular kind of sign which is a sacrament is to re-present, to make present, to effect, that
which is represented. (Fr. Stephenson would, as we
have seen, dissent from this assertion.) A sacrament is a
sign which has effective causality, a sign which brings
about that which it signifies. Furthermore – and this
is Vonier's special contribution to the discussion –
sacramental efficacy is an altogether unique type of
effective causality and it must not be confused with
other types. It is, of course, supernatural, but not all
supernatural causality is sacramental. 'If', writes
Vonier, 'the priest at the altar brought down Christ
from heaven in his natural state as a full-grown man,
this would not be a sacrament in the least, as it would
lack the very essence of the sacrament, representative
signification.'[36] And again,

> The sacramental world is a new world created by God,
> entirely different from the world of nature and even from
> the world of spirits. It would be bad theology to say that
> in the sacraments we have here on earth modes of spiritual
> realities which resemble the ways of the angels. We have
> nothing of the kind. If we spoke with the tongues of angels
> and men it would not help us in the least to express the
> sacramental realities. Sacraments are a new creation with
> entirely new laws.[37]

For Vonier, then, the Eucharistic Presence of Christ
is entirely real, but it is of an altogether different type
from his presence on earth before his Ascension and his
presence in heaven after it. These presences are, so to

[36] Op. cit., p. 32.   [37] Op. cit., p. 35.

speak, presences in their own right, while the Eucharistic Presence exists because and only because Christ, by his institution and promise, has attached it to certain sensible signs. It exists simply because it has a sacramental sign ordained by God and through no other cause whatever. In Vonier's words, 'the sacramental world is an unknown world with a well-known inhabitant.'[38] A surprisingly similar statement has been made more recently by the Presbyterian theologian Dr. J. K. S. Reid, who writes as follows:

> The virtue of ordinary water or bread and the virtue of sacramental water and bread are strictly incommensurable. The effectiveness of the first is the result of causal sequence; the effectiveness of the second is the result of the operation of Christ himself working according to a pledged word of appointment and promise. The water and bread might by themselves be bare signs; they become sacramentally efficacious signs in virtue of the use made of them by the Lord of the sacraments to convey himself.[39]

It must, I think, be admitted that Vonier is inclined, in the mediaeval manner, to identify sacrifice too exclusively with death, but this is an emphasis which can easily be corrected without detriment to his special contribution. What is of primary importance is his recognition that the Mass is not to be thought of as something that *happens* to Christ in the sense in which

[38] Op. cit., 92. Vonier was to a remarkable extent anticipated in the middle of the nineteenth century by R. I. Wilberforce; see, e.g. his *Doctrine of the Incarnation*, p. 289, and his *Doctrine of the Holy Eucharist* (3rd ed.), pp. 96f.

[39] *Essays in Christology for Karl Barth*, ed. T. H. L. Parker (1956), p. 203. I do not of course suggest that the whole of Reid's view would coincide with Vonier's.

the events of his incarnate life in general can be thought of as happening to him, as the last event in a series of which the other chief members are his conception, birth, infancy, temptation, ministry, death, resurrection and ascension. The sacrificial character of the Mass does not consist in its being an event which happens to Christ after his Ascension and which in some way repeats or imitates his death, but in its being the means by which the whole sacrificial action of Christ, centred in the Cross and culminating in the Ascension, is made sacramentally present in the Church. It is not a repetition of the sacrifice, or an imitation of the Sacrifice or the completion of the Sacrifice; it is simply the Sacrifice itself, present in the unique mode of a sacrament, present, that is, simply and solely because the sacramental species are the divinely ordained effective signs of it. The inner reality which the sacramental signs contain – namely, the whole redemptive act of Christ – does not *happen* historically and physically in the Mass; it is simply *there*, sacramentally. As something done by the Church, as the saying of certain words and the doing of certain things with the sacramental species, each Mass is, of course, a new event; but it is not a new event in the life of Christ.[40] Calvary was, of course, an event in the life of Christ and so was his entry into heaven; if we ask what Jesus is doing now, the answer is that he is reigning in glory and interceding for us with the Father, not that he is dying on our altars. In the physical, chronological order the Mass is simply some-

---

[40] It is, of course, a new event in the life of Christ's mystical body the Church, in the life of the *totus Christus*. More will be said about this later.

thing done by the Church with the sacred elements. It is in the sacramental order that the Mass is a sacrifice. That is to say, it is a sacrifice not because Christ is dying at a particular time on a particular altar as he died once at a particular time on a particular cross, but because the elements of bread and wine which are at that time on that altar are the divinely appointed signs of the sacrifice. And in the sacramental order the Mass contains and communicates the whole redemptive activity of Christ, the whole sweep of filial self-oblation that extends from his incarnation in the womb of Mary through his death on Calvary to his heavenly glorification. The Mass is therefore neither a new sacrifice nor a part of the one Sacrifice; it *is* the one Sacrifice in its totality, present under a sign. We may legitimately inquire what part is played in the one Sacrifice by the various events in our Lord's incarnate life; how, for example, Calvary is constituted as a sacrificial reality, and is made something more than a legal execution, by the events of the Last Supper, and whether Calvary can be considered as a sacrifice apart from the Resurrection and the Ascension. But we cannot legitimately inquire what part is played in the sacrifice by the Mass, for the Mass is not part of the sacrifice; it just *is* the sacrifice – sacramentally. Its efficacy consists not in its being an operation performed upon, or an action performed with, the crucified and glorified Body and Blood of Christ, but in the fact that, by divine ordinance, the Eucharistic species are the sacramental signs of the Body and Blood. Nothing happens to Christ in the historical order as a result of the Eucharistic consecration. What happens in the historical order as a result of the Eucharistic consecration happens to the bread and wine; which become, not by a change of physical properties but by sacramental causality, the Body and Blood of Christ, so that the one Sacrifice is made present in the Church as the ground of the Church's existence and the source of the Church's life.

V. MASURE AND THE EFFICACIOUS SIGN

A very important step forward in this whole movement of thought was taken in the remarkable work of Canon Eugène Masure, the Director of the *Grand Séminaire* at Lille. This can be found in two outstanding books, *Le Sacrifice du Chef*, of which the second edition appeared in 1932 and of which an English translation by Dom Illtyd Trethowan appeared in 1940 under the title *The Christian Sacrifice*, and *Le Sacrifice du Corps Mystique*, which was published in 1950 and of which the English translation by Anthony Thorold appeared in 1954 under the title *The Sacrifice of the Mystical Body*. Reference may also be made to an article by Canon Masure in the *Downside Review* of 1947 and to discussions of his views by various writers in the same journal. Masure opens his discussion in his earlier book with an examination of the nature of sacrifice in general, and castigates with some violence the view which has been predominant for the last three centuries, according to which the essence of sacrifice lies in the destruction of the victim.[41] The responsibility for this view he attributed to de Lugo, though, as I have already suggested, it would seem to go back into the Middle Ages; incidentally, it is very prominent in the dis-

[41] Cf. pp. 119f. *supra*.

cussions of the Anglican Sir Will Spens.[42] Masure places the whole notion of sacrifice upon the widest possible basis and goes back to the famous sentence of Augustine; *Verum sacrificium est omne opus quod agitur, ut sancta societate inhaereamus Deo, relatum scilicet ad illum finem boni, quo veraciter beati esse possumus,*[43] with St. Thomas's variant: *Omne illud quod Deo exhibetur; ad hoc quod spiritus hominis feratur in Deum.*[44] But Masure sees still more significance in another passage in St. Thomas: *Sacrificia proprie dicuntur quando circa res Deo oblata aliquid fit ... Et hoc ipsum nomen sonat: nam sacrificium dicitur ex hoc quod homo facit aliquid sacrum.*[45] The root idea of sacrifice, therefore, is not *death* (though the death of the victim may indeed be necessary when sacrifice is offered in a fallen world); still less is it *destruction*, but *transformation* – the transformation, by the divine acceptance, of a gift offered by man in homage to God. For a fuller discussion of this all-important point I would refer the reader to the previous chapter. Here our main concern is to see how, in the light of this doctrine, Masure answers the question 'In what does the Sacrifice of Christ consist?'

First [he answers] in the return of the Son to the Father with his religion of adoring love, accomplished in the hard

[42] *Essays Catholic and Critical*, pp. 433f.

[43] *De Civ.*, X, 6: 'A true sacrifice is every work which is performed in order that in holy fellowship we may cleave to God, that is, which is related to that end of goodness in which alone we can be truly blessed.'

[44] *S. Theol.*, III, xxii, 2: 'Anything which is presented to God in order that the spirit of man may be carried to God.'

[45] *S. Theol.*, II II, lxxxv, 3 *ad* 3: 'There are sacrifices properly so called when something happens in connection with things offered to God.... The very name shows this; for "sacrifice" is derived from a man making something holy.'

conditions which our sins imposed; then in the acceptance granted by the Father with all the depth of his eternal love to this homage of the incarnate Son; so as a result in the meeting of the Son with the Father, conditioned – for our sakes – by previous immolation, and one which went, solely through man's wickedness, *usque ad mortem, mortem autem crucis....*

Thus the Christian sacrifice did not lie only in the immolation of the Cross, although it appears there to our eyes in full relief and in all its force. That would be too narrow a conception.... We must keep the whole, from the kiss of Judas to the Father's welcome....

This sacrifice had nothing ritual about it, if by ritual we mean figurative liturgy. But since all the stages of this divine tragedy correspond to the great metaphysical adventure, the toilsome return and the triumphant welcome, which the ancient holocausts tried in vain to picture on their unsubstantial altars, we must say that Christ's death and Resurrection constitute the Christian sacrifice, the only sacrifice.[46]

But how can we share in this sacrifice, the sacrifice of him who is our Head? How can it be communicated to us? Through our participation in the Sacrament of the Eucharist, Masure replies, and this leads him to consider the meaning of *sacrament*. And he points out that, however much the point may have been neglected by modern Catholic theologians through fear of the misuse which had been made of the notion by Protestants, the fundamental meaning of sacrament is *sign* or *symbol*.

[46] *The Christian Sacrifice*, pp. 185–6. It is interesting to notice that M. J. Scheeben, who anticipated so many of the insights of later theologians, in his *Mysteries of Christianity* (2nd ed. 1887) made a skilful combination of the 'transformation' view of sacrifice with the conventional 'destruction' view (E.T., pp. 433f.).

Our controversies with Protestants [he writes] have as it were broken the force of this vocabulary into pitiable fragments. When we speak of symbols we think nowadays of deceptive appearances, empty signs and mystical illusions. That is why we no longer dare to say that the Eucharist is the symbol of Christ's body.

But our forbears put into the word all the meaning figured externally before their eyes. And they considered that man can possess the same reality in two ways, as such in its historical actualisation – as with the Passion according to the four Evangelists – and in its bare meta-physical nature, veiled by a symbol which makes it at once real and present, and pictured at the same time by our ritual figures – and so is the Saviour's Passion on the Altar.[47]

Masure is quite explicit that the Mass must not be looked on as a further event which *happens* to Christ in the historical order:

We must not make a contrast between Calvary and the Eucharist by adding them together like two distinct quantities similar in kind, for we are not faced here with mere copies of a single reality, but with efficacious symbols of a previously existing mystery.[48]

This authentic tradition, that the whole sacrifice is contained and communicated under the sacramental symbols, Masure asserts to have been fully operative in

[47] *The Christian Sacrifice*, pp. 212–13.
[48] Ibid., p. 214. Cf. the remarkable statement of J. H. Newman as long ago as 1870: 'First and above all is the Holy Mass in which he who once died for us upon the Cross, brings back and perpetuates, by his literal presence in it, that one and the same sacrifice which cannot be repeated' (*Grammar of Assent*, ch. x, Image Books ed., p. 376).

both St. Thomas Aquinas and the Council of Trent, and to have become obscured only in later writers under the stress of their controversies with Protestants. We may perhaps suspect that in forming this estimate Masure has been too much influenced by respect for the exalted position which the Angelic Doctor and the Tridentine definitions hold in his own communion, and that in fact the debasement of the tradition which Masure rightly deplores can be traced back into the Middle Ages. But of the degeneration itself there can be no doubt. I referred at the beginning of this chapter to the widespread interpretation of the Eucharist by Counter-Reformation Catholic theologians as some kind of *repetition* of Calvary. Masure subdivides this interpretation into two varieties. 'One group of theologians', he says – and he includes among these Vasquez, Lessius, and, in general, those of Flanders and the Spanish Netherlands – 'had rightly sought a symbolic reference to Calvary in the sacramental signs, but they had made the new sacrifice consist exclusively in this, as though a resemblance could of itself produce reality.... Then under the pressure of the theory itself, which could develop only by exaggeration, the ground suddenly shifted. Now it is not only because it contains an image of Calvary that the Eucharist is a sacrifice, but because it is itself physically another immolation. Lessius had spoken of an image which would transform itself, if it could, into reality. De Lugo thought that this virtuality actually existed: there is a new immolation at the altar. There is a death upon the corporal: *semper moriens ad interpellandum pro nobis.*'

But, Masure continues, 'at this final stage of the

vicious circle, other theologians, more sensitive, protest. "It is too much" they cry, struck to the heart at the vision of their Saviour's corpse laid upon the altar at their Mass each morning.' And so, as in the case of de la Taille, they take refuge in the saving gesture of *oblation*. 'Some find it at the end of the mystery of the Redemption, in Heaven, where Christ still offers himself, and so bring this upon the altar; others see it at the beginning, at the Supper, where Christ delivered all his Body and his Blood as a holocaust ready for offering to his Father's glory.' Nevertheless, Masure continues, 'there is another interpretation possible of sacramental immolation – the doctrine of the efficacious symbol. A sign instituted by Christ is rich enough to contain within it the reality which it resembles. Its extraordinary power comes to us not precisely from this resemblance, however moving this may be for us, however exquisite our Lord's selection, but from the fact of institution by him. It is a sign possessing, in virtue of its author, the value which it signifies.'[49]

It will, I hope, be clear from this exposition of Masure's doctrine how important is the approach which he opened up. The very remarkable movement in Eucharistic theology which has been evident among Protestant theologians during the last decade must, I think be largely attributed to his direct or indirect

[49] *The Christian Sacrifice*, pp. 223–5. It is important to remember that not only are the Eucharistic elements the effectual signs of the body and blood of Christ, but also that the Eucharistic action is the effectual sign of his redemptive act. The Real Presence is for the sake of the sacrifice, not *vice versa*. Cf. the remarks below concerning Journet, also Masure, *The Sacrifice of the Mystical Body*, pp. 121f., and G. Dix on 'Consecration' in *The Liturgy* (ed. K. D. Mackenzie), pp. 93f.

influence; I shall refer to it in detail later on. In particular his second and shorter work, *The Sacrifice of the Mystical Body*, is remarkable for its clarity, its penetration and its power of synthesis.

Before leaving Masure, there is one further point on which I think it will be well to touch. We have seen that for Masure it is not the *resemblance* of the Mass to Calvary that constitutes it as a sacrifice, but its institution by Christ. 'The sacramental sign', he writes, 'is not efficacious because it symbolically resembles the mystery to be produced by it. It is efficacious because it has been instituted by our Lord.'[50] But he goes on to assert that 'it has been chosen and instituted by him by reason of this resemblance', and that therefore 'its causality derives in the last analysis both from its author and from its resemblance to the effects.' I cannot but think that this concession very much weakens Masure's position: I have pointed out earlier that in fact the ceremonial features of the Eucharist do not derive from any deliberate prefiguring of the Passion by our Lord but from the normal ceremonial of a Jewish religious meal; it was the utterance of certain words in connection with the ceremonial that constituted it as sacrifice and related it to the forthcoming Passion. Masure himself writes:

> It is not because the ritual sign of the consecration of bread and wine was already a sacrificial rite that the Eucharist of the body and blood of Christ is a sacrifice; on the contrary, it is because the Eucharist of the body and blood of Christ is a sacrifice that the Jewish rite of the eucharist of bread and wine has become a sacrificial one,

[50] *The Christian Sacrifice*, p. 225n.

entailing the substantial consecration of the elements which in this way become the oblata.[51]

And Masure has in fact shown considerable vacillation in his views as to how the resemblance between the Eucharist and the Passion is to be understood, even in the secondary place which he assigns to it. When he wrote *The Christian Sacrifice* he took what he was later on to describe as 'the easy view, falling in with the common opinion that the sign of immolation is the separation of the bread and wine, and, after the Consecration, the separation of their species.'[52] This view, which Masure described as having 'hypnotised' Lessius, Billot and Vonier, he himself later came to abandon. (Incidentally, I ought to confess to having succumbed, at least partially, to this hypnosis myself, as can be seen by a reference to page 184 of my book *Christ, the Christian and the Church*.) In 1947 he expressed himself as follows: 'This mystery is wholly present under the species of bread; it is present again under the species of wine. Both species are expressive. The bread by its solidity and mass represents the immolated body – and so Christ's death. The wine, poured forth like Christ's blood, puts before our eyes the same single victim.'[53] But even here Masure feels it necessary to

[51] *The Sacrifice of the Mystical Body*, p. 147.

[52] 'The Mass: Sacramental Immolation', in *Downside Review*, LXV (1947), p. 203. Cf. *The Christian Sacrifice*, p. 204.

[53] *Downside Review*, art. cit., p. 205. It is interesting to compare the following passage, written by Dr. A. M. Farrer in 1937: 'Certainly Blood was not added to Body because these two are complementary constituents of one substance; that would have required Flesh rather than Body. Rather, the two suggest different trains of thought about the one substance – Body the wholeness and reality of the person, and its continuity here and hereafter: Blood the sacrificial death, that which is poured out, given, and not

find *some* resemblance between the Eucharistic species and the crucified victim, though now he sees the resemblance in each species and not in the two considered together; however, Mgr. H. F. Davis, in a discussion of Masure's new position, appears to have overlooked this point and to have understood Masure as holding that the essential symbolism is provided simply by the transubstantiation.[54] Be this as it may, in his second book *The Sacrifice of the Mystical Body*, the original of which was published in 1950, Masure apparently reverts to the earlier view, possibly under the influence of the encyclical *Mediator Dei* of December 1947, for he writes as follows: 'The twofold matter of the sacrament, the bread and the wine, each with its separate consecration, placed apart, side by side and opposite each other, does evoke the image of the body drained of its blood, and of the blood shed to its very last drop at the moment of Christ's death: *exivit sanguis et aqua.*' And again: 'The separation of the species is the image of the death of Christ; their oblation is the symbol of a sacrifice.'[55] In any case, I cannot help feeling that the whole attempt to see the sacrificial character of the Mass as constituted, even in a secondary way, by a *resemblance* between some feature of the sacramental rite and the death on Calvary is devoid of theological content, however edifying it may be from a devotional point of view; it seems to me to be in this respect comparable with some of the

---

recovered, the discontinuity and the break' (*The Parish Communion*, ed. A. G. Hebert, p. 88).

[54] *Downside Review*, LXVII (1949), pp. 1f.

[55] Op. cit., pp. 40, 48; quoted by Dom Illtyd Trethowan in *Downside Review*, LXVIII (1950), p. 402.

more artificial mystical interpretations of Holy Scripture. The performance of the Eucharist does not provide at all an obvious picture of Calvary. As I have already urged and as Masure himself maintains, what ultimately constitutes the Eucharist as a sacrifice is its institution by Christ. It was not, I would suggest, necessary that the sacramental species should be bread and wine in order for the Eucharist to be a sacramental sign of Christ's sacrifice; some quite different elements might have been equally appropriate, if Christ had chosen to invest them with sacramental character. It would, however, seem to be necessary that they should be bread and wine (or at any rate some articles of food and drink) if the Eucharist was to be also a means by which we could feed on the sacrifice; or, to put the matter slightly differently, if the Eucharist was to be that kind of sacrifice (which, for example, the Jewish whole-burnt-offering was *not*) which is consummated in communion. What bread and wine naturally picture is food and drink, not sacrifice.[56] Masure himself seems to recognise this when he writes:

> We may add, or rather we must add, using another suggestion made by P. Sage that the sign [*sc.*, in the Eucharist] by presenting itself before our eyes as food and drink in their most human and necessary forms, shows us throughout its sacramental development that the body and blood of Christ are given to us as a *life-giving* victim. For the normal conclusion of a sacrifice is the consumption of the victim by the assistants, and the species of

[56] It may be for this reason that some Protestants, considering only the external form of the Eucharist, have looked upon it as nothing but a Christian fellowship meal, 'no sacrifice, but a life-giving feast'.

bread and wine enable us to accomplish with the body and blood of Christ, which they represent, precisely this supreme efficacious rite – efficacious, this time, of super-natural grace.[57]

VI. JOURNET AND THE PRESENCE OF THE SACRIFICE

The result of the previous discussion might be summed up by saying that the most satisfactory doctrine of the Eucharistic Sacrifice which it has so far been possible to achieve is a synthesis of the views of de la Taille, Vonier and Masure, a view according to which Christ's sacrifice, although it culminates on Calvary, includes his whole human life from the first moment of the Incarnation to its present heavenly glorification and is made present in its entirety, under the sacramental signs and by the altogether unique mode of sacra-mental signification, in the Sacrament of the Altar. It is perhaps remarkable that Vonier does not appear ever to have seen his teaching as a necessary supple-ment and corrective to that of de la Taille, but rather as excluding it. Since the publication of the first edi-tion of the present work the thought has been carried a stage further by one of the most esteemed theologians of the Roman Communion today, Mgr. Charles Journet. No one could describe Mgr. Journet as a wildly unconventional theologian – such a description could hardly apply to someone who has written a vast ecclesiological treatise in which the four successive volumes deal with the Church under the respective headings of the four Aristotelian causes – but in his

[57] *Downside Review*, art. cit., p. 208.

recent book *La Messe*, published in 1958, the very sub-
title – *Présence du Sacrifice de la Croix* – shows how deeply
these newly recovered insights have affected his
thought.

> The doctrines of transubstantiation and the real presence
> [he writes] had already reached the stage of explicit
> statement when they were rejected by Protestantism. The
> doctrine of the sacrificial character of the Last Supper and
> the Mass, on the other hand, although firmly taught and
> believed, was still in the implicit stage. The Council of
> Trent . . ., in defining the first two points adopts what is in
> its essence a doctrine already made precise. In defining
> the sacrificial character of the Supper and the Mass, on
> the other hand, it can be said that, while it utilised the
> previous theological elucidations – notably those of
> Cardinal Cajetan – it was forced to proceed in a certain
> degree towards a first explicitation . . .
>
> The explicitation begun by the Council of Trent seems
> to be as yet unfinished. It calls for the work of theo-
> logians.[58]

The Mass, Journet insists, in language markedly
reminiscent of Vonier,

> is a true and proper sacrifice: not another sacrifice than
> the unique redemptive sacrifice, but another presence, a
> sacramental presence, to us of that unique sacrifice.[59]

And again:

> If there is only one redemptive sacrifice under the New
> Covenant, that of the Cross, how can the *Last Supper* be a
> sacrifice? There is only one answer: the Supper is not

[58] Op. cit., p. 15.
[59] Ibid., p. 11.

11

another sacrifice than the sacrifice of the Cross, it is the sacrifice of the Cross itself, *already begun at that time* and made present, as it will be later on, under the appearance of bread and wine.

And if there is only one redemptive sacrifice under the New Covenant, that of the Cross, how can the *Mass* be a true sacrifice? There is again only one answer: the Mass is not *another* sacrifice than that of the Cross. The sacrifice both here and there, is substantially and essentially identical; for both here and there the priest is identical and the victim is identical. It is different only accidentally, modally, that is to say, in its mode of presentation; for in the one case Christ, present under his natural and proper appearance, offered himself by shedding of blood and without making use of any minister, while in the other case Christ, present under sacramental and strange appearances, offers himself without shedding of blood, utilising the ministry of priests. It is impossible that the sacrifice of the Mass should compete against that of the Cross; the whole work of the Mass is to represent and to make present to us the sacrifice in which there was shedding of blood and to apply to us its saving power for the remission of the sins which we commit each day.[60]

Furthermore, although he makes use of the conventional phrase 'the Sacrifice of the Cross', Journet explicitly states that it is more inclusive than that term would suggest.

The Passion of Christ [he writes] was only the end of his pilgrimage, it was not the end of his life. It was a death containing in advance the Resurrection, a suffering containing in advance felicity, an apparent defeat containing in advance a manifest victory. And it is as such, that is to say as uniting in itself all these contrasts, that it is

[60] *La Messe*, p. 54.

the cause of our salvation. To speak truly, the Passion, the Death, the Resurrection and the Ascension were, in the strictest sense, the moments of a single act, begun in pain and completed in glory, by which the Saviour descended into the realm of captive humanity in order to lift it to the heights.[61]

We may note, however, that Journet does not here explicitly trace the redeeming act back to its beginning in the conception of the Word in Mary's womb.

Journet is determined to maintain not only that the Body and Blood of Christ are present in the Mass, but that his sacrifice is present too. He is much more clear about this than is St. Thomas, who allows himself on one occasion to say that Christ is immolated in the Sacrifice in the sense in which 'the images of things are called by the names of the things of which they are images, as when we look on a picture or a fresco and say, "That is Cicero"'.[62] It is not, however, easy within the framework of Aristotelian philosophy to give an account of the sacramental presence of an act, any more than to give an account of the sacramental presence of an object. Journet introduces the distinction between what he calls 'substantial presence' and 'operative presence', and he insists that in both cases the word 'presence' is used in a true and proper, not in a metaphorical, sense, while on the other hand the two uses of the word are not univocal but analogical.

> Christ is glorified [he writes]; how can he be present to us *as priest and victim*? The unique redemptive sacrificial act is *past* in relation to us, how can it be efficaciously *present*

[61] *La Messe*, p. 30.
[62] *S. Theol.*, III, lxxxiii, 1c.

to us, as it was to the Apostles at the Last Supper, and to the Virgin and St. John at the Cross? That is the problem.

If it can be solved, the Mass will be, like the Supper, a true and proper sacrifice, bringing to us under the sacramental appearances, without shedding of blood, simultaneously the *substantial* presence of Christ and the application, the contact, the *operative* presence of his redemptive sacrificial act.

The Mass will then be not *another sacrifice* than the unique redemptive sacrifice, but *another presence*, an operative presence – when we are concerned with an act and not a substance, an operative presence is the only one which can be involved – of the unique redemptive sacrifice, a sacramental presence, without shedding of blood, of the unique sacrifice which was with shedding of blood. We can say: just as each consecrated host is Christ substantially, because it multiplies the substantial real presence of the one Christ, so analogically each Mass is a true and proper sacrificial act, because it multiplies the operative real presences of the one redemptive sacrifice.[63]

I do not think we need concern ourselves here with the adequacy of Journet's application of scholastic concepts to the matter in hand, but it is, I think, important to recognise and welcome his determination to maintain that each Mass is not a new sacrifice, but a new and genuine sacramental presentation of the one and unique sacrifice of our redemption.

VII. CASEL AND THE CULT-MYSTERY

For the sake of completeness some words should be added at this point about the theory of the 'Cult-Mystery' (*Kultmysterium*) which is specially associated

[63] Op. cit., p. 86.

with the name of Dom Odo Casel. Casel was a monk of
Maria Laach of great holiness who died on Easter
morning 1948, having collapsed immediately after
singing the threefold *Lumen Christi* of the Paschal
liturgy. He was one of the most original and influential
of German Eucharistic theologians and his influence
does not seem to have declined during the fourteen
years that have elapsed since his death. His work has
provoked enthusiastic support and also violent criticism; some implications of it have generally been supposed to have been disowned in the great Eucharistic
encyclical *Mediator Dei* of December 1947, though in
the gentlest possible way. Sympathetic but critical
discussions of it can be found in chapter seven of Père
Bouyer's *Life and Liturgy* and in chapter twelve of Fr.
Jungmann's *Early Liturgy*; a thorough and laborious,
but not very penetrating, account of the whole movement is given in chapter eight of Dr. Ernest B. Koenker's *Liturgical Renaissance in the Roman Catholic Church*.
Discussions in periodicals are numerous, notably one
by Dom Burkhard Neunhauser in the *Downside
Review*.[64] At the time of writing the only book of
Casel's which has appeared in English is *The Mystery of
Christian Worship*, which comprises a short treatise 'The
Christian Mystery' (*Das Christliches Kultmysterium*) and
two essays compiled from fragmentary material mainly
written for spiritual exercises; his unfinished work *Das
Christliches Opfermysterium* is being prepared for publica-
tion in German.

Casel's approach to the Eucharist really involved
two distinct theses, though they were linked by the
common concept of the Christian 'mystery'. The first

[64] LXXVI (1958), pp. 266f.

thesis, which has aroused much disquiet and has been
questioned on both theological and historical grounds,
does not bear very directly on our present concern; it
introduces the Hellenistic mystery religions as providing the key to the meaning of the Christian mysteries.
Casel had, of course, no use for the old-fashioned
'mystery-religion' hypothesis of the origin of the
Christian sacraments, which saw the whole structure
of Catholic sacramentalism as an alien importation
into the primitive Gospel by St. Paul or some other
early Christians. On the other hand, no fault can well
be found with his insistence that the sacramental
system of the Church meets all those needs, human and
religious, which the Hellenistic mystery-cults in-
effectually tried to meet. The debatable territory in his
thought lies between these two boundaries, and he has
been attacked both by theologians, for the precise way
in which he has envisaged the relation between the
Christian and the pagan mysteries, and by historians,
as regards his account of the pagan mysteries themselves. It is here that the controversy still continues.

The other element in his theory touches much more
closely our present interest, for it involves the relation
of the Eucharist to the redemptive sacrifice of Christ.
Jungmann describes it as follows:

> The central point in Casel's theory is that in the cult
> action – hence certainly in the sacraments and in the Mass
> – it is Christ's saving act itself that becomes present and
> not merely the effect and fruit of this saving act. Accord-
> ingly we must say that Christ's passion and death and
> resurrection are made present, and not merely the grace
> that these acts won for us. Casel admits that this is a
> rather difficult concept, for how can a past happening

become present again? He confesses that this is a mystery, and like all the mysteries of faith, a concept which our limited intellect cannot grasp. But he tries to prove that this mystery is to be found in ecclesiastical tradition he gathers a large number of passages from the Fathers and other early and mediaeval authors which seem to substantiate his theory. His critics, however, have contended – and generally established – that though individual ecclesiastical writers use expressions that can be interpreted in the sense that Casel maintains, there can be no question of a common tradition. This point in Casel's theory, therefore, central though it be, must be dropped.

Gottlieb Söhngen, accordingly, presents a modification of Casel's theory by explaining its meaning in terms of sacramental reality. According to Söhngen the saving act of Christ, the Redemption, becomes present in so far as an image of the Redemption is created in those participating in the sacraments or in the Mass. The Church's external ritual is a figure and memorial of Christ's saving act, and since that ritual is an effective sign, it contains the reality which it signifies. A person baptised is buried with Christ and permitted to rise with him. One who takes part in the Mass and communicates is offered up with Christ and is thus sanctified, etc. According to many theologians who view Söhngen's theory favourably, this theory is a really progressive development in theological thought. If the theory means anything, it means that the image of the Redemption, the symbol produced in the participant, is not the redemptive act itself but its effect, namely, grace; but here grace is viewed as an effect not only in the line of efficient causality but also in the line of exemplary causality. The teaching of the mystery has been under constant attack, but if it endures it will probably do so in this modified form.[65]

[65] *The Early Liturgy* (1959), pp. 161–2.

With all respect to the great authority of Fr. Jungmann, I cannot agree that Söhngen's modification of Casel's view is an improvement. I would agree that Casel's theory needs more careful statement of a strictly theological kind than he appears to have given it, but that statement seems to me to be perfectly possible along the lines of Vonier's doctrine of sacramental signification, supplemented perhaps by such a discussion as that of Journet, though, as I have said, I am not convinced that Journet's application of the Aristotelian concepts, ingenious as it undoubtedly is, is altogether adequate. The strong point of Casel's theory is, in my opinion, precisely his insistence that the Mass contains sacramentally the whole sweep of the Lord's incarnate life, and not merely an image of Redemption; incidentally, there does not seem to be any truth in the assertion that Casel held that the various events of Christ's earthly life are severally present in the liturgy at the corresponding seasons of the Church's year, a view which would hardly be possible to anyone who had even the sketchiest knowledge of liturgical history.[66] We must now turn from the remarkable movement in Eucharistic theology which we have traced in the Roman Communion to consider an equally remarkable convergent movement outside.

[66] For an extremely comprehensive, up-to-date and discriminating discussion of the relation between the pagan mystery-religions and Christianity which includes some very balanced remarks about the views of Casel I would refer the reader to the first part of Fr. Hugo Rahner's fascinating work *Greek Myths and Christian Mystery*. And for a most lucid and penetrating discussion of the Eucharistic Sacrifice which is in many, though not all, respects very similar to that which I developed above I would warmly commend the pamphlet of Père G. de Broglie, S.J., published as a mimeographed typescript by the Institut Catholique de Paris under the title *Pour mieux comprendre le Double Sacrifice du Christ*.

Chapter Six

THE EUCHARISTIC SACRIFICE – II

1. RECENT DEVELOPMENTS IN PROTESTANTISM

I HAVE already referred[1] to the remarkable *rapprochement* that has taken place in quite recent years between Catholic and Protestant theologians on the subject of the Eucharistic Sacrifice, and, although the degree of this *rapprochement* ought not to be exaggerated it is, I think, of the greatest importance that it should be recognised and promoted. We have studied in the last chapter the movement of thought on this question on the Roman Catholic side. In the present chapter I shall consider the teaching of some representative theologians in the Protestant and Anglican communions. And I shall begin with Professor J. D. Benoit.

Professor Benoit, in his striking little book *Liturgical Renewal: Studies in Catholic and Protestant Developments on the Continent*, has some remarkably trenchant criticisms of the traditional Calvinist French liturgy, which he compares to its great disadvantage with the recently introduced new rite, whose first draft appeared in 1948. He describes it as catechetical, sermonising, polemical, sombre and joyless, dominated by the shadow of the Cross, unillumined by the light of the Resurrection: 'it was unlike any other form of worship,

---

[1] Cf. p. 82 *supra*.

155

quite unrelated to the great ecumenical tradition of Christendom, like a boulder in the midst of a stream.'[2] The Eucharist, he says,

> is more than just a memorial – the memory, that is, of a past event. The Lord's supper is a re-presentation of the event. It actualises it; it makes it something that is happening now, so that its effects may be made operative, now and always.[3]

And the event in question is the crucifixion, the Sacrifice of Calvary. St. Augustine, he tells us,

> affirmed the necessity of [the] sacrifice of ourselves in union with the unique sacrifice of Jesus Christ.... It is not a case of my offering myself individually to Jesus Christ. I offer myself in and with the community. It is, then, the community, the Church itself which offers itself to God as a living and holy sacrifice, a sacrifice which is renewed at each celebration of the Lord's Supper, in communion with the sacrifice of Christ.[4]

The late D. M. Baillie, in his book *The Theology of the Sacraments*, has a chapter headed 'The Eucharistic Offering'. Recognising, as does Benoit, that the violence of much of the language of the sixteenth-century Reformers was due to their reaction against late mediaeval abuses, and asserting that the only offering that we can make to God is *the offering of ourselves*, he nevertheless insists that 'we can only make an offering in union with Christ's eternal sacrifice'. He approves such Catholic theologians as Masure for not minimizing the sacrifice of Christ but rather building everything on it, and insists that 'in the sacrament we plead

[2] Op. cit., p. 36.   [3] Ibid., p. 44.   [4] Ibid., p. 41.

the sacrifice of Christ and in union with him offer ourselves to God'.[5]

Much more radical than either Benoit or Baillie, however, is Dr. J. Leenhardt, in his essay entitled, 'This is my Body', which, together with Dr. Cullmann's essay 'The Meaning of the Lord's Supper in Primitive Christianity', is published in the booklet *Essays on the Lord's Supper*. 'I see a positive advantage', he writes, 'in the use of expressions which Protestants were once obliged to repudiate because of the times in which they lived. That reason is precisely that we live no longer in their times.' Again, he writes:

> I know certain Roman theologians who work with a sincere ardour and not without effect to remove from historical Catholicism its inexact expressions and its choking overlay. Some of them react against certain errors which the Reformers condemned in the papist mass and against eucharistic superstitions.... Who can say what would have been the attitude of our Reformers if they could have found, to reply to their disquiet concerning fidelity to the Word of God, men such as these who today run a risk in an attempt to rediscover what is authentic Catholicism?[6]

At the Last Supper, he tells us, assuming that the Last Supper was in fact the Passover meal, 'Jesus Christ, at the moment when he should have spoken of the lamb, mentions his body'.[7] 'At the instant of leaving his disciples, he wishes that, after the arrest and all that follows, his presence shall continue to be real and

---

[5] Op. cit., pp. 115f. A fuller discussion of Baillie's Eucharistic theology may be found in my book *The Recovery of Unity*, pp. 23f.

[6] Op. cit., pp. 26, 27.

[7] Ibid., p. 41.

active as before. The Paschal rite is intended to assure this permanent actuality of the redemptive acts of God.'[8] Leenhardt explicitly asserts the sacrificial character of the Eucharist. 'When we speak of the Lord's Supper as a sacrifice – in the correct sense of the term – we wish to do justice to that intuition of faith that the redemptive action of God in Christ, which culminated in the sacrifice of the Cross, has not ceased to be efficacious and is prolonged in order to reach every generation.'[9] He insists that, in the thought of St. Paul, with its Hebrew background, *anamnesis*, 'remembrance was not for him mental recollection, an evocative thought. Remembrance was for him the restoration of a past situation which has for the moment disappeared. To remember is to make present and actual.'[10] 'What happens [in the Lord's Supper] is what took place during the ministry; it is what is going to happen on the Cross; it is the same gift under different forms, it is the same sacrifice which accomplishes the same service, which realises the same ministry.'[11] Here in different words we have almost the exact teaching that we have already found in Journet; to have effected such a *rapprochement* is indeed an achievement.

We might note one odd feature of Leenhardt's discussion. His discussion of the Eucharist is entirely confined to the bread and the Body; there is not a single mention of the cup or the Blood, except in an incidental reference to the manner of conducting the service.[12] When we think of the emphasis which Protestantism has placed upon the restoration of the

[8] Ibid., p. 48. [9] Ibid., p. 58. [10] Ibid., p. 61.
[11] Ibid., p. 62. [12] Ibid., p. 76.

chalice to the laity, it is astonishing to find a Protestant theologian who can build up his whole theology of the Eucharist upon the bread, as if the rite did not contain the cup at all; this is a feat that no Roman theologian has achieved, and I think it must be admitted that it introduces a certain lack of balance into Leenhardt's discussion.

In Dr. Geddes MacGregor's book *Corpus Christi: The Nature of the Church according to the Reformed Tradition* there is a discussion of the Eucharist which, if he does not go as far as some of the Continental writers, is remarkable for its readiness to reopen the whole question of the Sacrifice.

> It is by no means improbable [he writes] that [the Reformers'] rejection of the mediaeval doctrine that Christ's sacrifice was 'repeated' or 'renewed' in the Mass coloured their thought on the subject of eucharistic sacrifice so as to cause them to overlook certain theological questions of considerable importance for the Reformed tradition. That the Eucharist was from the earliest times accounted in some sense a sacrifice is abundantly plain.[13]

Again MacGregor writes:

> What is unfortunate in the wording of the *Westminster Confession* is that it makes it appear as though nothing really happens in the Eucharist because everything has happened already, so that we are not to be allowed to do anything but pay homage to the memory of this. The Westminster divines, in guarding against the danger of reversion to the attitude that had engendered the Mass ..., used language that fails to draw attention to the indubitable need and duty of the Church to participate

[13] Op. cit., p. 188.

in the work of its Lord, according to the peculiarly
intimate relation in which, at his bidding, it stands to
him.[14]

Thus,

> while it is a truism, according to the Reformed tradition,
> to say that we have nothing to offer to God that is worthy
> of him, it is not to be denied that God, notwithstanding,
> desires us to bring our offerings of prayers, such as they
> are, and what greater offering and oblation can we bring
> than the Eucharist which he has commanded us to 'do'?[15]

And, once more:

> Because Christ, in surrendering himself completely, has
> offered up the only worthy sacrifice, there is no sacrifice
> or oblation or gift that a Christian may dare to offer to
> God *except* by participation in the Church, the Body of
> Christ, which, being united to Christ its Head, partici-
> pates in the sacrifice since he has graciously willed to
> unite it to himself as his Body.... The Church, in receiving
> Christ in the Sacrament, offers itself with Christ.[16]

By far the most significant of these modern Protestant writers is Frère Max Thurian of the Community
of Taizé, whose book *L'Eucharistie* appeared in 1959;
he describes it as a work of 'liturgical theology'. The
greater part of the book consists of an extremely
detailed study of the sacrificial language of the Old
Testament, as providing the key for the understanding
of the redemptive work of Christ and of the Eucharist.
Arguing for a basic interchangeability and identity
of meaning between the Hebrew words *zikkaron* and

[14] Ibid., p. 247.　　　　　　　　　[15] Ibid., p. 191.
[16] Ibid., p. 247.

azkarah and their Septuagint counterparts *anamnesis* and *mnemosunon*, he sees Christ's command 'Do this as my *anamnesis*' as constituting the Eucharist as a memorial before God.[17] We may compare with this the rather different nuance of Dr. Joachim Jeremias's rendering 'Do this that God may remember me';[18] both writers exclude any idea of commemoration before men or of psychological 'calling to mind'.

> In the Eucharist [Thurian writes] the Church wills to recall to God the unique sacrifice of the sole Righteous Man, Jesus Christ; the Lord, faithful to his promise, and because of the perfection of this sacrifice, replies to the Church by filling it with blessings in the Body of his Son.[19]

The 'once-for-all' of Christ's sacrifice, he tells us, must not be interpreted in a past or static sense: 'The expression signifies rather the absolute, definitive and perpetual character of the sacrifice of Christ; it does not imply a unique instant with no repercussion (except for repetition) under the diverse modes which

[17] *L'Eucharistie*, pp. 36f.; cf. p. 57. The translations given are my own and the page references are to the French original. An English translation of this book has appeared under the title of *The Eucharistic Memorial*.
[18] *The Eucharistic Words of Jesus*, pp. 159f.
[19] Op. cit., p. 61. Cf. Neville Clark: 'For Biblical thought the Greek *anamnesis* and the Hebrew *zekher* have the sense of re-calling or re-presenting before God an event in the past so that it becomes living, powerful and operative' (*An Approach to the Theology of the Sacraments*, p. 62). Clark also quotes N. A. Dahl: 'La commémoration n'était pas quelque chose qui se passait essentiellement dans l'âme des fidèles, dans leur mémoire subjective. La célébration elle-même – en grec: mystérion – était une commémoration, une anamnesis de la mort de Jésus et de sa résurrection, où l'histoire du salut devenait à nouveau présente par la commémoration sacramentelle' (*Studia Theologica*, I (1947), pp. 82–3).

recall and actualise it'; it is explained by the *eis to dienekes* of the Epistle to the Hebrews, and is equivalent to 'for eternity'.[20] We are reminded that in Hebrew thought, God is blessed by the recalling and recitation of his favours; hence presentation before God is the essence of Eucharist.[21] The Eucharist, Thurian tells us:

> is not an independent sacrifice, having its efficacity in itself. It draws all its power from the unique oblation of Christ, which it represents, presents and makes present. The Eucharist is a sacrifice in the sense that it is the presence of Christ crucified, glorified and interceding, who presents for us today his unique sacrifice before the face of the Father. The Eucharist is a sacrifice because it is one with the heavenly intercession of Christ, which is itself the perpetual continuance of the sacrifice of the Cross. The Eucharist presents to the Father the unique sacrifice of the Son on the Cross, in communion with Christ's own heavenly intercession. Thus there is one sole oblation of the Body of Jesus Christ under three aspects:
> (a) The unique and perfect sacrifice of Christ on the Cross, a historical act, the foundation of salvation.
> (b) The heavenly and perpetual sacrifice of Christ in intercession, an eternal act, the continued existence (*actualisation*, French) of salvation.
> (c) The memorial and sacramental sacrifice of Christ in the Eucharist, a liturgical act, the sacrament of salvation.[22]

And the Eucharist itself is a sacrifice for three reasons:

> It is the sacramental *presence* of the sacrifice of the Cross by the power of the Holy Spirit and the Word, and the liturgical *presentation* of this sacrifice of the Son by the

[20] Op. cit., p. 143.   [21] Ibid., p. 35.   [22] Ibid., p. 148.

Church to the Father, as a *thanksgiving* for all his blessings and in *intercession* for their continuation.

It is the *participation* by the Church in the intercession of the Son before the Father in the Holy Spirit, for the *application of salvation* to all men and the coming of the *Kingdom* in glory.

It is the *offering* which the Church makes of herself to the Father, united to the sacrifice and the intercession of the Son, as her supreme *adoration* and her perfect *consecration* in the Holy Spirit.[23]

The *anamnesis* made in the Eucharist is all-inclusive:

> The Eucharistic memorial is a recall (*rappel*) made to us, a recall made by us to the Father, and a recall made by the Son to the Father for us. Thus the Eucharistic memorial is a proclamation *to* the Church, a thanksgiving and an intercession *of* the Church, and a thanksgiving and an intercession of Christ *for* the Church.[24]

The Eucharist is seen as fulfilling the Rabbinic tradition that of all the sacrifices of the Law the sacrifice of praise would alone continue in the Kingdom of the Messiah.[25] And Thurian is a strong advocate of the Catholic practice of offering the Eucharist with special intentions:

> To name a being in a *memento* at the Eucharist is to unite it to Christ, in order to present it with him under the eyes of the Father; it is to place it, in some way, at the foot of the Cross, so that it may receive freedom and blessing. In this sense, the celebration of the Eucharist with specific intention has a profoundly Biblical significance.[26]

[23] Ibid., p. 219.
[24] Ibid., p. 173.
[25] Ibid., p. 221. Cf. U. E. Simon, *Heaven in the Christian Tradition*, p. 270.
[26] Op. cit., p. 76.

12

Thurian has the strongest conviction of the communion of Saints in the one Body of Christ. He distinguishes sharply between our prayer *for* the living and our prayer *with* the saints, even when the same form of words is used for both; but he does not seem to distinguish between the Church expectant and the Church triumphant. Commenting on the formula 'Let us pray for ...' in the fifth-century document called *The Testament of our Lord Jesus Christ*, he writes:

> The formula 'Let us pray for...' has three meanings here: to pray for peace, faith, unity or patience is to pray in order to obtain these graces; to pray for the Apostles, prophets and confessors is to make a memorial of them, to ask that we may share the graces which they received and to be 'rendered worthy of their heritage'; to pray for the bishop, priests, deacons etc. is to intercede for them, to ask for them the graces necessary for their life, their ministry and the Church.[27]

And again:

> The memorial of Mary and of all the saints, their consecration in faith, charity, works and prayer, is thus as it were an intercession which the Church presents with her own, as her own, by reason of the communion of the Body of Christ. The commemoration of the saints in the Liturgy is thus not primarily or solely a reminder in order to stimulate the faithful by their example; it is first and foremost a communion, in one praise and one intercession, of the departed saints, whose memorial of faith, charity, works and prayer subsists before God, and of the Church, which presents this memorial with its own

[27] Ibid., p. 161. Cf. N. Cabasilas, *A Commentary on the Divine Liturgy*, ed. J. M. Hussey and P. A. McNulty, pp. 108f.

prayer.... This memorial of the saints finds its place most specially at the moment when the Church, celebrating the Eucharist, presents the memorial *par excellence*, that of Christ. It is in Christ, taken into the Eucharistic memorial of Christ, that the memorial of the saints, united to the prayer of the Church, rises as an adoration and an intercession to the Father.[28]

And once more:

In presenting the Body of Christ [the Church] includes therein all the members of that Body, all the saints who have lived and died in the hope of that return of Christ which was promised them.[29]

Though himself a Calvinist, Thurian is extremely critical of Calvin's Eucharistic theology, with its quasi-local conception of the heavenly exaltation of Christ.

In his exposition of the real presence, Calvin seems to have too carnal a conception of the Body of Christ. Attached firmly to the human nature of Jesus Christ, Calvin does not see adequately the difference of state between the living and suffering Christ from the Annunciation to Calvary and the risen and glorious Christ from Easter to the Ascension and in eternity. He identifies too much the state of the crucified and of the glorified Christ.[30]

In consequence of his restricted notion of the Body of Christ, Calvin localises the Body in heaven, in a very anthropomorphic way, inviting us to 'lift our hearts on high to heaven' to find there our Saviour who cannot be 'lowered to us, to be enclosed in corruptible elements' [31]

[28] Op. cit., p. 165.
[30] Ibid., p. 262.
[29] Ibid., p. 167.
[31] Ibid., p. 265.

Thurian contrasts a 'Protestant extremism' which 'situates the fact of salvation in a historic past to which we have to return by faith' with a 'Catholic extremism' which 'holds to the power transmitted to the Church in the apostolic past, a power which allows it an infinite series of acts of redemption'. 'In these two extreme theological positions', he significantly remarks, 'we find the same notion of salvation as a past history, to which we must either return by faith (Protestants) or which is transmitted by the sacrament (Catholics). A balanced Christian theology holds that in Christ the historic redemption is made present (*s'actualise*) in both faith and the sacrament. The Church, uniting itself by the Eucharist to the heavenly intercession of Christ, unites itself to him as crucified and so makes present (*actualise*) the historic act of redemption in order to apply it to present-day man, who receives it in faith and by faith.'[32]

Indeed we may note that Thurian recognises that the Eucharistic doctrine of the Council of Trent itself excluded the chief errors of late-mediaeval Eucharistic doctrine and practice, and he approves of Du Moulin's readiness to accept Trent's description of the Eucharist as a propitiatory sacrifice.[33] He emphatically accuses Protestant theologians of often falling into the very errors which they professedly reject.

> Even expressions such as 'sacrifice of thanksgiving' or 'sacrifice of praise' can sometimes give the impression that our thanksgiving and our praise have some value in themselves. Those who use them with a polemical intention against the doctrine of the Mass do not always

[32] Ibid., p. 247.   [33] Ibid., p. 232.

recognise that they may well defeat their own purposes. To avoid or combat the idea of a repetition or a complement of the sacrifice of Christ, they may find themselves entertaining the idea of a Christian sacrifice which is possible as a simple response to the gift of God; whereas not only are we incapable by ourselves of giving anything of value to God but we are also, on account of our weakness, incapable of responding to his gifts as we should.[34]

Finally it is of interest to note that Thurian sees a much closer connection than the other Protestant writers whom we have considered between the Body and Blood of Christ and the Eucharistic elements. Benoit, commenting on the new Calvinist liturgy, writes: 'The descent of the Holy Spirit is invoked not upon the bread and wine, but on the faithful, as living people. The bread and wine remain bread and wine, and have nothing to do with the divine action. The Holy Spirit acts upon persons and not upon things.'[35] Baillie, while acquitting the doctrine of transubstantiation as defined by St. Thomas of teaching any crudely localised presence, himself conceives the Eucharistic Presence as being 'presence to the faith of the receiver'.[36] Even Leenhardt writes: 'This bread is truly the body of Christ in the celebration of the rite, because it is as such that Christ presents it at that moment; it does not remain such outside this active presentation.'[37] And again: 'This bread is the Body of Christ because Christ makes use of this bread. Outside

[34] Ibid., p. 221.
[35] Op. cit., p. 42.
[36] Op. cit., pp. 100f. Cf. my discussion in *The Recovery of Unity*, pp. 125f.
[37] Op. cit., p. 53.

this action it is only bread.'[38] Thurian is far less dogmatic, when he writes:

> After the Eucharistic celebration, completed by the communion of all the faithful, and even the sick among them, the real relation between Christ and the Eucharistic species which remain is a mystery which must be respected.
>
> The end of the Eucharist being the communion ('Take, eat ... Drink ye all of this....'), I cannot allow myself to define the nature of the relation of Christ with the Eucharistic species which remain after the communion has taken place. It is not for us to pronounce upon the persistence of the real presence, any more than upon its cessation. The mystery must be respected. In this attitude of respect, it is fitting that the Eucharistic species should be consumed after the celebration. Neglect in this matter compromises faith in the real presence, while a balanced attitude of respect is a sign that one believes truly in the presence of the Body and Blood of Christ, and that at least the material support of this presence has a right to our respect. If we believe in the efficacy of the Word of Christ, we must believe that it does not leave in a state of indifference the creatures to which it extends.[39]

Although it was written earlier than Thurian's book, it will, I think, be useful to conclude this section of our discussion with some reference to a volume by the well-known Swedish theologian Dr. Gustaf Aulén, formerly Bishop of Strängnäs, which was published in Swedish in 1956 and appeared in an English translation in America in 1958 under the title *Eucharist and Sacrifice*. Aulén begins by describing in terms of warm appreciation the new insights that have been brought to bear

---

[38] Ibid., p. 54.　　　　　　　　[39] Op. cit., p. 272.

in recent years, especially by Roman Catholic and Anglican theologians, upon the nature of sacrifice in general and the relation between the sacrifice of Christ and the sacrament of the Eucharist. He then re-examines the teaching of the Reformers, and in particular of Luther (he is himself, of course, a Lutheran), after which he reconsiders in detail the evidence of the New Testament. He insists that 'what the New Testament primarily wants to say is that the sacrifice of Christ was finished in his death',[40] and he is very suspicious of those theologians, some of whom are Anglicans, who speak of Christ's sacrifice as continuing in heaven or say that in the Eucharist 'we offer Christ's sacrifice'.

> We are indebted to the Anglican theologians [he says] for their strong accentuation of the high priestly perspective, which has not always been given due recognition. It is also proper that they have emphasised the connection between the eternal priesthood of Christ in heaven and the celebration of the Eucharist on earth. However, there may be some risks connected with this interpretation of his office as High Priest in heaven. The conception of Christ as the One who continually serves at the heavenly altar tends to suggest that the heavenly 'offering' is of the same type as his sacrifice here on earth 'in the days of his flesh', that it is a continuation of this sacrifice, and that it has the same significance.... Through the exaltation God has spoken his 'yes' to the sacrifice made once for all. He does not continue to offer his Son, and the Son does not continue as the Suffering Servant of the Lord to give himself as he did during his earthly life.[41]

[40] Op. cit., p. 190.   [41] Ibid., p. 191.

I may perhaps remark in passing that this criticism does not seem to me to be in the least valid against the view which I have myself defended and to which Aulén himself refers favourably,[42] according to which in the Eucharist nothing whatever is *added* to the earthly sacrificial work of Christ but the whole of that sacrificial work is *made sacramentally present.* Indeed something very like this seems to be asserted in a remarkably eloquent passage in which Aulén expounds his own teaching:

If the sacrifice offered once for all is eternally valid and relevant, and if it is one with Christ who is himself the sacrifice, then the presence of Christ in the sacrament includes the effective presence of his sacrifice. It is not a question of recalling something which happened two thousand years ago on Golgotha. The past is here, too, the present, as the Lord himself makes the past and eternally valid sacrifice contemporaneous with us. As the Lord on that last evening of his life presented the sacrifice which was momentarily to be made, and which signified the last act in his total sacrificial activity, and as he included his disciples in his sacrifice and united them with it, so also he includes his present disciples in the sacrifice which is eternally valid and eternally effective, and makes them partakers of the blessings flowing from the sacrament. It is significant that the effective presence of the sacrifice of Christ in the eucharist has been emphasised in the ecumenical discussions, not least by the Anglicans. In view of this fact we must insist that the presence of the sacrifice is inseparably connected with the presence of the living Lord. The real presence and the sacrifice belong together. *This sacrifice is present because the living Lord is*

[42] Ibid., pp. 47f.

present. But the living Lord cannot be present without actualising his sacrifice.[43]

This is quite admirable. But, Aulén adds, 'the Anglo-Catholic theologians do not want to speak only of the presence of the sacrifice in the sacrament; they want to connect this sacrifice of Christ with our action by formulas such as: with the eucharistic elements we "offer Christ" or "offer his sacrifice", so that we thus participate in that sacrifice which he himself offers at the heavenly altar.'[44] And while he exonerates such theologians as Dr. A. M. Ramsey and Fr. Gabriel Hebert from any suspicion of belittling the sufficiency of Christ's death, he plainly holds such formulas to be totally illegitimate, and he somewhat weakly suggests that they are prized from a belief that they are, in some emotionally charged sense, 'catholic'.

Now I must admit that I am not myself particularly enamoured of the phrases complained of, for they seem to me to result, not indeed, as Aulén appears to think, from a belittling of Christ's death, but from something equally undesirable, namely forgetfulness of the union between Christ and his members. As I shall argue in the concluding section of this chapter, the correct formula seems to me to be that the Whole Christ offers the Whole Christ. I am not, however, at all sure that this formula would be any more acceptable to Aulén than those which he explicitly rejects. There may be a real stumbling-block here which did not appear in some of the Protestants whom we have already considered, and I believe it is connected with the fact that

[43] Ibid., p. 192 (italics in original).
[44] Ibid.

their background is Calvinist, while Aulén's is Lutheran. Nevertheless, Aulén asserts without quali-fication that

> the Lord's Supper is the church's eucharist, its great service of thanksgiving, in which the church of Christ on earth unites its humble offering of praise with the great paean of praise in heaven. The Lord's Supper is the church's incomparable act of prayer in which we include our prayers in the intercession of our great High Priest.[45]

And his Lutheran emphasis upon the real presence in the elements, while he dislikes the term 'consubstantia-tion', brings him in some respects closer to the Catholic tradition than are some of the Calvinists whose views I have examined. There is at any rate no doubt of the thoroughly irenical intention which his book manifests from its first page to its last; as he says in the Preface, its purpose is 'not to close doors but to open them'.

It will, I think, be clear from the foregoing discussion that in recent years there has been a very striking *rapprochement* between the most vigorous and open-minded theologians in the Catholic and Protestant communions on the subject of the Eucharistic Sacrifice. The movement has come from both sides. From the Catholic side there has been a most welcome anxiety to discard finally any suggestion that the sacrifice of Christ is repeated in the Eucharist and instead to insist that in it the one Sacrifice is sacramentally present. From the Protestant side there has been an equally welcome readiness to admit that the Eucharist is really a sacrifice, and that what is offered is something

[45] Ibid., p. 199.

more than the prayers and thanksgiving of the worshippers. It is true that not all the Protestant theologians whom we have considered have gone as far as Thurian, between whom and such Catholic thinkers as Masure there would seem to be hardly any distance at all; and I shall later on suggest one or two lines of possible further advance.

II. THE EUCHARIST AND THE ORDER OF CREATION

The preceding discussion of the Eucharistic Sacrifice has been almost exclusively concerned with the relation of the Eucharist to the sacrifice of the Incarnate Lord, the sacrifice of the New Covenant. It may therefore be well to recall the fact on which stress was laid at an earlier stage of our argument and which in fact provided Masure with the starting-point for his subsequent exposition, namely that sacrifice is an almost universal element in human religion and to inquire into the relation between the Eucharist and sacrifice as such. This inquiry will, I think, bring out certain aspects of the Eucharist which have not so far been indicated and will throw light upon some puzzling features of the Eucharistic rite. It may also suggest some practical consequences for liturgical practice.

Our discussion will begin not with the order of redemption but with the order of creation, though, since creation itself has been redeemed, it will not stop there. The starting-point will be the place that man holds in the created universe.

Man alone, so far as we know, among God's creatures has the privilege of belonging to two realms, the realm of matter and the realm of spirit.[46] Above him are the angels, the holy incorporeal powers; below him is the material creation, both animate and inanimate. He himself belongs to both realms at once. He is not, as Descartes held and as much pietistic modern Christianity, both Catholic and Protestant, has assumed, a pure spirit, temporarily confined in a body but destined for an incorporeal eternity. He is one being, made up of two elements, soul and body, spirit and matter, each made to fit the other, and united in a most mysterious and complicated way. His ultimate destiny is not the immortality of the soul, but the resurrection of the body. Although in the order of grace he is exalted above the angels, in the order of nature he is not at the top of creation but in the middle of it. And that is a very good place to be. But it is one which involves considerable complications, even if we leave sin out of account; so many complications, in fact, that men are always tempted to give up the exhilarating but elaborate business of living as men in favour of the simpler business of being either animals or angels. Man is, however, neither an animal (in the sense of an irrational living being) nor an angel, and the attempt to live as something that he is not inevitably leads to frustration or disaster. What man is is man, and this involves him in all the complexities of living in two realms at once. It also – and this is the point with which we are here concerned – confers upon him a unique privilege, for it means that

[46] For some reflections on the possibility of there being somewhere in the universe other rational corporeal beings than man, reference may be made to my *Christian Theology and Natural Science*, pp. 36f.

he is the focal point in which the material world becomes articulate; he alone, so far as we know, can
make a physical noise intelligently; he alone of
material beings can praise God with the intellect and
the will. This is what is meant by the common phrase
that man is nature's priest. Nourished by material
food, thinking with a material brain, communicating
his thoughts and receiving his knowledge by means of
material lips and eyes and ears, man is the agent and
the instrument through which the lower creation
becomes articulate and praises God.[47] Man and the
lower creation, however, have alike been spoilt by sin.
Even were man himself fit to offer the lower creation
to God, the lower creation is not fit to be offered.[48] It
needs, no less than man himself, to be brought into the
sphere of divine redemption, to be re-made by Christ
and in Christ. And this is surely what happens in the
Eucharist. For the Eucharist does not only perpetuate
the sacrifice of Christ in the Church's midst under the
sacramental signs; it also offers to God material objects, bread and wine, that they may become part of
Christ's sacrifice, that, being offered to God, they may
be transformed by the divine acceptance. It was
frequently pointed out by Archbishop William Temple
that the matter of the Eucharist is not just wild corn
and grapes, but bread and wine; that is to say, not
just the fruits of the earth, but those fruits as produced
through, and worked upon by, the hands of man, as
passing through the hands of nature's priest. Our
thought must not, however, stop there; for the fruits

[47] Cf. my *The Importance of Being Human*, ch. ii.
[48] On the effect of pre-human sin on the material creation, cf.
Christian Theology and Natural Science, pp. 299f.

pass not only through the hands of nature's priest but through the hands of the supernatural priest, the Incarnate Lord, acting through the organs of his mystical priestly body the Church. They are presented to the Father not only by the race of the Old Adam, which has received from God the privilege of co-operating with him as his creature in bringing to its full expression the work of creation; they are also presented to him by the race of the New Adam, which has received from him the privilege of co-operating with him in bringing to its full expression the work of redemption. Thus the Eucharist is not only the sacramental and eschatological representation of the redeemed community; it is also the sacramental and eschatological representation of the restored and transfigured universe.[49] And this provides us with the explanation of something which is at first sight very puzzling. The sacrifice which is sacramentally made present in the Eucharist is the sacrifice of Christ; it is that which we bring before the Father and that by which alone we claim salvation. That and that alone is the full, perfect and sufficient sacrifice, oblation and satisfaction for the sins of the whole world. And yet, if we examine carefully the canon of any one of the ancient liturgies, that of the Roman rite for example, what the Church appears to be offering to God is not the Body and Blood of Christ but simply bread and wine, though it dignifies these by the most exalted terms. 'Therefore, most merciful Father' the canon

---

[49] By 'eschatological' here I mean to indicate that the Eucharist mysteriously but really brings about an anticipation of the final consummation of all things in Christ which, from the standpoint of ordinary history and chronology, is a future event.

begins 'we humbly pray and beseech thee, through Jesus Christ thy Son our Lord, that thou wouldest vouchsafe to accept and bless these gifts, these presents, these holy unspotted sacrifices which in the first place we offer thee for thy holy Catholic Church, that thou wouldest vouchsafe to keep it in peace, to preserve, unite and govern it throughout the whole world ...' Is it really as a result of the offering to God of bread and wine that the redeemed community is perpetuated? And yet the same theme runs throughout the canon. 'Therefore this oblation of our service, as also of thy whole family, we beseech thee, O Lord, graciously to accept, and to dispose our days in thy peace and to preserve us from eternal damnation and to number us in the flock of thine elect ...' And it is well known that the words which the canon ends referred originally not to the Body and Blood of Christ but to the fruits of the earth: 'through Christ our Lord, by whom, O Lord, thou dost ever create, sanctify, quicken, bless and bestow on us all these good things.' What the canon offers to God seems, therefore, to be simply bread and wine, though from this offering the most tremendous results are expected. Can we solve this problem?

I think that the solution lies in a phrase in the canon which I have not yet quoted, a phrase which immediately precedes the narrative of the Institution: 'which oblation do thou, O God, vouchsafe in all respects to make blessed, approved, ratified, reasonable and acceptable, that it may become unto us the Body and Blood of thy most dearly beloved Son Jesus Christ our Lord.' All that the Church can do of her own initiative, if the phrase may be allowed, is to bring to God the fruits of the earth as they have passed through the hands of man, the priest of the natural order. She brings them to God as his Son brought them to him at the Last Supper, and in obedience to the command that he there gave; she brings them to God to be transformed and made a sacrifice by God's acceptance. And if man was unfallen Adam that would be the whole story. Man is not, however, unfallen Adam; he is fallen and is redeemed by and in the New Adam, who at the Last Supper declared that the bread was his Body and the wine was his Blood. Man's sin-stained gifts of bread and wine are totally ineffective, but they are all he has to offer. He cannot bring a worthy offering of the fruits of God's creation, yet he must bring what he can. He brings his bread and wine into the realm of redemption and does with it what the Redeemer has commanded him to do. He speaks of it as if it were in that pristine state in which unfallen Adam might have offered it. He puts it into the hands of God to be transformed by God's acceptance. And lo! when God accepts it, it is transformed into the one offering which *is* unstained and worthy, the offering of the Body and Blood of Christ. God has, as it were, slipped underneath man's stained and inefficacious offering the pure and altogether sufficient offering of his Son. Taking the fruits of creation from the hands of his Church he has re-created, redeemed and restored them. So, in the Eucharist not only the redeemed community but also the redeemed material order is offered to God the Father in the ascended Christ.

If what I have said is true, certain practical consequences would appear to follow. I venture to suggest that we ought to reconsider the extreme prominence that has been given to the offertory procession in many churches that have been influenced by the Liturgical Movement. That prominence is the outcome of the view that the offertory is the Church's solemn offering to God of bread and wine, the typical fruits of the created order. It would be widely held that there are three great moments in the Mass: (1) the offertory, in which bread and wine are solemnly given to God by the Church; (2) the consecration, in which they are transformed into the Body and Blood of Christ; and (3) the communion, in which they are given back to the Church as her supernatural food. It is the view of the offertory here expressed that I feel bound to question. I would not describe it as an *offering* of bread and wine, in the strict sense of an offering made to God. If we go back to the Last Supper and consider the four actions of our Lord – he took, he blessed, he broke, he gave – we see that the first of these was not an act of offering, but of reception: he *took*. And in the primitive liturgies, such as that of Hippolytus, the 'offertory' is simply the bringing of the elements to the altar for the sacramental rite. It is a highly impressive act, as how should it not be, in view of what is just about to occur. The Church is bringing the fruits of God's creation to God that they may be offered to him and in being accepted by him may be redeemed and transformed. But, strictly speaking, she is not offering them'– yet. It is significant that in the rite of Hippolytus the celebrant has no part in this act; it is the deacons who bring up the bread and wine to him, he merely receives them. The offering begins with the canon, when the celebrant offers the bread and wine to God as Christ offered them at the Last Supper and

13

identifies what he is doing now with what Christ did
then. The Father accepts the plea that is made in the
name of his Son, and accepting what is offered he
transforms it. What began by being an offering of
creatures of bread and wine has been transformed into
the offering of the Body and Blood of Christ; the
sacrifice of the Church has become the sacrifice of
Christ. 'God makes these holy offerings so much his
own' writes the fourteenth-century Greek theologian
Nicholas Cabasilas 'that he transforms them into the
Body and Blood of his only-begotten Son. Surely it is
not possible to conceive of anything to equal such an
appropriation, nor to set a measure to the way in
which these gifts are accepted.'[50] And when the faithful come up to the altar to receive Holy Communion,
the truth is not so much that the Body and Blood of
Christ are being given to them for their sanctification
as that they are being drawn up into Christ for the
building up of his Body; the Sacrament does not dis-
perse Christ among the faithful, it unites the faithful in
Christ. And so, in the words of St. Augustine, it is
shown to the Church that in that which she offers she
herself is offered.[51]

I do not, of course, wish to deny that the offertory
is, as its name implies, in some sense an offering, a
'bringing up'. It is. But it is the bringing of the
elements for the sacrifice; it is not the first stage of the
sacrifice itself. Père Bouyer has made this point with
some emphasis:

[50] *Commentary on the Divine Liturgy*, ed. J. M. Hussey and P. A.
McNulty, p. 105.
[51] Some further discussion of the offertory will be found in my
book *The Recovery of Unity*, pp. 146f.

Let us note carefully at this point that the offering of man, even of man now regenerated, would have no value unless it were made through Christ, through his own perpetual offering. What man presents at the altar is properly only the material for the sacrifice. But the sacrifice itself is only performed through the consecrative power of the Eucharist, of the *prex sacerdotalis*, in which Christ himself takes man's offering and makes it his own, so that it is no longer man's bread and wine, but his [*sc.*, Christ's] Body and Blood.... The offertory, in other words, is not in itself the sacrifice: the Mass is not, as we too often hear it explained, our own sacrifice coming to be united to Christ's own sacrifice. In Christianity there is not and cannot be any sacrifice other than Christ's own sacrifice.[52]

Thus there is not first of all an offering to God of bread and wine at the offertory and then a second offering to God of the Body and Blood of Christ in the canon after the consecration. There is one offering, an offering of bread and wine which, being transformed by the divine acceptance, *becomes* the offering of the Body and Blood; and it takes place in the canon. This seems to me quite obvious if we examine carefully what our Lord did at the Last Supper. It was a thanksgiving to God for bread and wine that was the basic material of his eucharistic prayer; but he converted it into something far greater when he identified the bread and wine with the Body and Blood in which he was offering the one perfect and sufficient sacrifice to the Father. Cirlot seems to me to make the point quite clear. 'In

[52] *Life and Liturgy*, p. 170. Bouyer goes on to add that 'both the sacrifice of Christ and our being joined to it have a further purpose. This is the completion of Christ's risen body by the full participation of all the elect in its eternal life, in its divine life given to men' (p. 171).

the *Apostolic Tradition*' he writes 'the only "offering" mentioned in reference to the unconsecrated elements is the "offering" of them by the deacon to the bishop. They are offered *to God* for the first and only time by the bishop by means of the consecratory thanksgiving prayer.' And again: 'The primitive Eucharistic prayer was already in and of itself, at one and the same time, *implicitly* both a consecration of the elements and an oblation of them, long before it was *explicitly* either.'[53] The point is plain: it is that the essence of the Eucharist is the one great action of the Eucharistic canon, which is able to offer the Church's gifts to God solely because it consecrates them into things that are worthy to be offered. There is not first an offering and then a consecration, for not until the consecration are the gifts fit for offering. But neither, on the other hand, is there first a consecration and then an offering, for the consecration is simply the transformation by God's acceptance of the gifts that are offered to him. There is one prayer, the great Eucharistic Prayer, which simultaneously consecrates and offers in one action; which offers by consecrating and consecrates by offering and does both by giving thanks.[54]

[53] F. L. Cirlot, *The Early Eucharist* (1939), p. 105.
[54] Speaking of the different sections of the early liturgies Dr. G. A. Michell wrote: 'On any showing it is obvious that the most important of these sections are the Consecration and Communion, and there is no reason to suppose that in the earliest times either the Offertory or the Fraction were accorded the prominence which they subsequently attained' (*Landmarks in Liturgy* (1961), p. 41).

III. WHO OFFERS WHAT?

In discussing the relation of the Eucharist to the order of creation I have perhaps run rather ahead of my argument and have bypassed a very important question which has given rise to violent controversies.

Clearly the fundamental question about any sacrifice is 'Who offers what?', and in the case of the Eucharist a variety of answers have been given explicitly or by implication. Does Christ offer Christ, or does Christ offer us, or do we offer Christ, or do we offer ourselves? Or, perhaps, do we merely offer bread and wine? Writers could be quoted in support of each of these alternatives, and their answers would pretty obviously range them on the Catholic and Protestant sides. I would, however, suggest that the very possibility of listing the alternatives in this way as mutually exclusive is one of the results of the disintegrated condition which characterised late-mediaeval theology and which persisted in both its Catholic and its Protestant heirs. It presupposes an artificial and perverse separation between the Incarnate Lord and his members, a morcellation or atomisation of the Body of Christ. If we whole-heartedly recognise, as Mersch insisted throughout his writings, that the Whole Christ is the Head and his members as one mystical Body, through the hypostatic union of the Incarnation and the adoptive union of baptism – *Totus Christus membra cum capite: unum corpus multi sumus* – we shall, I suggest, be simply content to say that in the Eucharist the Whole Christ offers the Whole Christ, and leave the matter at that.

Dr. C. W. Dugmore, in his recent book *The Mass and*

the English Reformers, has made a most learned and
interesting attempt to discover just what it was that
happened to Eucharistic theology at the Reformation
and in particular what happened to it in the Anglican
Church. He is fully conscious of the disadvantages
under which Cranmer and his associates laboured.
'The emphasis upon the *death* of Christ', he writes,
'was part of the late mediaeval eucharistic theology
which all the reformers inherited from their "unre-
formed" days.'[55]

And again:

> The tragedy was that in casting off the mediaeval notion
> of a daily pleading before God of the sacrifice of Christ
> by the celebrating priest, they also jettisoned the wholly
> scriptural belief in the High Priestly work of Christ, him-
> self pleading before God his sacrifice upon the Cross.
> Though they believed in the mystical union betwixt
> Christ and his Church, they were, therefore, unable to
> see that this belief must logically include the idea of the
> Church as the mystical Body of Christ, through Christ its
> Head, pleading in the heavenly places the sacrifice once
> offered upon the Cross. This theological blind spot was to
> mar the Reformed Catholic position in England until
> after the danger of a papal Counter-Reformation under
> Elizabeth had passed, and the Caroline divines had
> recovered something of what was lost.[56]

And again: 'Cranmer failed to retain any idea of
presenting or pleading before God in the Eucharist the
sacrifice of Christ once offered upon the Cross as a
ground of our acceptance with him.'[57]

Concerning Jewel, whose Eucharistic teaching has

[55] Op. cit., p. 133.   [56] Ibid., p. 137.
[57] Ibid., p. 194.

always been something of a puzzle, Dr. Dugmore
writes:

> With regard to the sacrificial aspect of the Eucharist, he
> says that the sacrifice once offered on the Cross 'is
> revived, and freshly laid out before our eyes, in the
> ministration of the holy mysteries', and, in this sense,
> 'we offer up Christ, that is to say, an example, a com-
> memoration, a remembrance of the death of Christ', but
> the 'unbloody sacrifice' in the Eucharist is properly to be
> understood as a sacrifice of prayer, praise and thanks-
> giving. . . .
>   He is clearly trying to express a real belief in the sacra-
> mental presence of Christ in the Eucharist. There is
> something *there* quite apart from the faith of the worthy
> receiver, yet it can only be apprehended by faith. And
> he cannot bring himself to identify the presence with the
> elements, or attach it specifically thereto, because he
> cannot get away from the characteristically Calvinist
> notion of lifting up our hearts to heaven where Christ is in
> his bodily form. Yet he does not go the whole way with
> Calvin or the *Consensus Tigurinus*, and talk about Christ's
> body being present in the sacrament merely in virtue,
> force or efficacy.[58]

All this is very illuminating, but I cannot see that
Dr. Dugmore is very helpful in his main thesis. For his
avowed aim is, in the words of Mr. Peter Brooks, 'to
depict the English Reformation as not merely a
reaction against Ambrosian realism (as it became distorted in the later mediaeval doctrine of eucharistic
sacrifice), but as a conscious revival of the more
spiritual Augustinian tradition'.[59] He argues that from

[58] Ibid., p. 231.
[59] *Theology*, LXII (1959), p. 160.

very early times there were two views of the nature of
the Eucharist, an Augustinian or 'realist-symbolist'
view, according to which the Eucharist is a *commemoratio* of the Passion and a self-oblation of the Church,
and an Ambrosian or 'realist' view, according to which
the emphasis is upon the change of the elements by
consecration and in which the thought is not so much
of the Church's offering of itself in union with Christ,
as of the priest's offering of the sacrifice of Christ on
behalf of the people.[60] I cannot help wondering
whether the two views were either as sharply defined
or as mutually antagonistic as Dr. Dugmore suggests; I
suspect that they represented two elements in a whole
rich complex of Eucharistic thought and that neither
can be abandoned without impoverishment.[61] Dr.

[60] Op. cit., pp. 17, 21.
[61] Dr. J. N. D. Kelly (*Early Christian Doctrines*, pp. 446f.) remarks that Augustine's 'thought about the Eucharist, unsystematic
and many-sided as it is, is tantalizingly difficult to assess. Some, like
F. Loofs, have classified him as the exponent of a purely symbolical
doctrine; while A. Harnack seized upon the Christian's incorporation into Christ's mystical body, the Church, as the core of his
sacramental teaching. Others have attributed receptionist views
to him. There are certainly passages in his writings which give a
superficial justification to all these interpretations, but a balanced
verdict must agree that he accepted the current realism.' Again:
'There can be no doubt that he shared the realism held by almost
all his contemporaries and predecessors. It is true that his thought
passes easily from Christ's sacramental to his mystical body.' Dr.
Kelly adds, however, that 'there is no suggestion in [Augustine's]
writings of the conversion theory sponsored by Gregory of Nyssa
and Ambrose'. Dr. T. M. Parker, in a very searching review of Dr.
Dugmore's book (*J.T.S.*, N.S., XII (1961), pp. 132f.) has accused
him of two errors. The first, regarding Cranmer, does not concern
us here. The second, regarding Augustine, is a failure to recognise
that for the Fathers, whose philosophical background was mainly
Platonic, the term 'symbol' would imply a real identity between
the symbol and the thing symbolised.

Dugmore further points out how preponderant the
Ambrosian emphasis became in the later Middle Ages
and how unbalanced Eucharistic thinking and devotion became as a result; he also argues that in reaction
from this the Reformers, and especially the Anglican
Reformers, adopted an equally unbalanced emphasis
upon the Augustinian view. However, as a result of his
own preference for the Augustinian view, he appears
to look upon this as a thoroughly good thing, and only
criticises the Reformers, as we have seen, for their
failure to get entirely free of their late-mediaeval
heritage.

> If [he writes] the mediaeval Church took hold of the realist
> Ambrosian tradition and developed it into a logical
> system of sacramental theology, it was the merit of the
> English Reformers that they restored to the Western
> Church the other, equally ancient, realist-symbolist
> Augustinian tradition and enshrined it in a vernacular
> liturgy which has profoundly affected the whole English-
> speaking world.[62]

Dr. Dugmore does indeed deny that 'Augustine or
Ambrose were the only representatives in the early
Church of the doctrines associated with their names,
or that the two traditions were fully developed in their
day. The complete parting of the ways only came later,
with the Lateran definition of 1215.'[63] Again, he tells
us, 'Catholicism, in the pre-scholastic period, was able
to embrace both traditions'.[64] What he fails to see is
that they can be no less fully embraced, and more
profoundly reconciled, when their development is

[62] Op. cit., p. 247.   [63] Ibid., pp. 246, 247.
[64] Ibid., p. 247.

carried beyond the stage reached by the Lateran Council and the later Middle Ages. And then we shall say, not that the Church is offering herself or that the priest is offering Christ, but that the Whole Christ – Head and members in one mystical unity – is offering the Whole Christ. And we shall also see that, since man is nature's priest and Christ is God and man, the whole material order, over which man was placed as God's vicegerent, is offered in the Whole Christ by the transformation of the elements of bread and wine into the Body and Blood of the Incarnate Word.

Dr. Dugmore quotes the late F. E. Brightman as describing the Canon of the Prayer Book of 1549 as

> an eloquent paraphrase and expansion of the Roman Canon adjusting it clearly to the conception of the Eucharistic Sacrifice as threefold: viz. (*a*) as a commemoration of our Lord's *historical* self-oblation in his death upon the Cross; (*b*) as a sacrifice of praise and thanksgiving for the benefits of redemption so secured; and (*c*) as the offering of the Church, of ourselves, our souls and bodies.[65]

Is it not clear that these three very different offerings – so different, indeed, that left to themselves they would almost seem to make the Eucharist into three sacrifices rather than one – are drawn into a real unity and supplement one another if we see them all as subsumed into the offering of the Whole Christ by the Whole Christ, that *totus Christus* which, as St. Augustine tells us, *caput est et corpus*?[66]

Again, I would suggest that another false antithesis

[65] *The English Rite*, p. cvi, cit. Dugmore, p. 160.
[66] *In Psa.* lvi, 1.

is presented by the question whether *anamnesis*, in its Eucharistic context, implies a recalling of Christ's sacrifice to God or to man. On the purely linguistic point I think that Jeremias and Thurian have made good the claims of the former alternative, but from the theological point of view I cannot see that the two interpretations are mutually exclusive. For, if *anamnesis* means not a psychological act of remembering but a genuine recalling into the present of an act which is past as an event of history but is eternalised in the heavenly places, the act when recalled will be recalled before God and man alike, and for the matter of that before the angels and the devils as well. It is not a recalling before this or that spectator; it is simply a *recalling*, a re-presentation, a sacramental instantiation, of the tremendous act and event itself.

Furthermore, it should be noted how sadly the whole notion of the Eucharistic Sacrifice has been weakened through a mistaken interpretation of the notion of a sacrifice of praise and thanksgiving. Whatever those who employ the so-called 'interim rite' may do in the way of crossings and elevations, it cannot be doubted, I think, that the prayer of oblation in the English Prayer Book meant by 'this our sacrifice of praise and thanksgiving' a sacrifice in which praise and thanksgiving are what we offer, and this interpretation is often supported by the exhortation in Hebrews xiii, 15, 'Through him then let us continually offer up a sacrifice of praise to God, that is, the fruit of lips that acknowledge his name'. However, the phrase 'sacrifice of praise', *thusia aineseos*, is used in the Septuagint of Leviticus for the sacrifice of the peace-offering, the *thusia soteriou*, which occurs also a verse or two later in the combined form 'peace-offering of praise'; we may note that in the Hebrew text the word is not 'praise' but 'thanksgiving' (*todah*). [Lev. vii, 2, 3, 5, LXX; vii, 12, 13, 15, E.VV.] What Hebrews, then, is telling Christians to offer up with their lips is not their own praises but the sacrifice of the peace-offering, the one sacrifice which would continue in the Messianic kingdom;[67] and this in its Christian context is nothing other than the sacrifice of Christ, who is 'our peace'. But if Christ is our peace-offering, he is our sin-offering too: and Dr. F. C. Synge has ingeniously argued that this is implied by a famous verse in Hebrews which comes shortly before that just quoted.[68] According to him, xiii, 10, 'We have an altar whereof they who serve the tabernacle have no right to eat', means 'Our altar is an altar of sin-offering', for it was precisely the sin-offering of the Day of Atonement of which the priests were not allowed to partake and which was, as the next verse of Hebrews says, burnt outside the camp. Synge would therefore seem to be correct in asserting that the altar mentioned in Hebrews xiii, 10 has no eucharistic reference, but he misses altogether the eucharistic reference of the passage as a whole, which includes the peace-offering as well.

Some remarks will not, I think, be out of place at this point on a very original, and indeed somewhat audacious, work by a priest of the American Episcopal Church, Dr. F. Hastings Smyth. Dr. Smyth's early

---

[67] It is relevant to observe that 'thanksgiving' (*eucharistia*) is the Christian appellation of the Eucharist. Dr. Kelly remarks (op. cit., p. 197) that Justin 'uses the term "thanksgiving" as technically equivalent to "the eucharistised bread and wine"'.

[68] *Hebrews and the Scriptures*, pp. 39f.

background was provided by chemistry, geophysics and the tactics of chemical warfare; after ordination he became Superior of the Society of the Catholic Commonwealth, a body whose concern with the social aspects of Christian doctrine is indicated by its motto *Metacosmesis mundi per Incarnationem.* His first book, *Manhood into God,* is less well known on this side of the Atlantic than it deserves to be. His second book, *Sacrifice: A Doctrinal Homily,* is an exposition of Eucharistic theology, based upon two premises, one theological and the other metaphysical. The former premise is a view of sacrifice which is very similar to that which I have expounded in chapter four of the present work; it is summarised by Dr. Smyth as 'the *conveyance* of substances offered under material forms out of their natural world of origin and into the supernatural world which a spiritual god inhabits'.[69] In accordance with this notion the one genuinely effectual and successful sacrifice is 'our Lord's conveyance of the substance of a unit of created human nature [sc., his own humanity], perfected in its every aspect and potentiality within this world, through to its proper eternal destiny'.[70] It has, however, a 'dynamic continuation in time' in the survival and persistence in history of his socially extended Body the Christian Church. The second postulate is that of a dynamic metaphysic, according to which the past history of an object is part of its present constitution: 'the substance of a particular object is the structure of its actual total history ... it *is* the temporal-spatial connection which the object both has in the present and out of which it has grown in the past'.[71] The consequence is that the

[69] *Sacrifice,* p. 22.   [70] Ibid., p. 38.   [71] Ibid., p. 18.

Eucharistic elements, brought to God by the Church at the Offertory, 'are not "ordinary" bread and wine', but 'substances which have been formed within the ever-growing social Body of the Incarnate Lord'; they are 'historical substances which are additions to his earthly Incarnate Body and Blood'.[72] To use the rather strange term which Dr. Smyth has invented, by the action of the offertory the elements are *ensubstantiated* into Christ's body. Offertory is not, however, the whole of sacrifice, and the final stage is the passage of the ensubstantiated elements into the heavenly realm by *transubstantiation*: 'the ascended Body of the Incarnate Son ... "grows" even in eternity by the movement into it by transubstantiation of the ensubstantiated liturgical Offertories of his natural social Body, of his Church, as these Offertories are continuingly and successively gathered in by the redeemingly active lives of baptised Christians who remain in the time process'.[73] No lesser term than 'transubstantiation' will satisfy Dr. Smyth to denote this process, but he condemns the Thomist doctrine as not being really a doctrine of transubstantiation at all; it is purely static, a mere *replacement*, a *desubstantiation* of the bread and wine combined with a *substantiation* of the Body and Blood. 'The Transubstantiation of our present argument, on the other hand,' he writes, 'refers to a true movement of our Lord's ensubstantiated natural Body and Blood into the supranatural Body and Blood of the Resurrection and Ascension.'[74] But Dr. Smyth has still less use for the Eucharistic doctrine of the six-

[72] Ibid., p. 44.
[73] Ibid., p. 48.
[74] Ibid., p. 58.

teenth-century reformers, and the rite of the Book of Common Prayer, in both its English and American forms, is pronounced to be gravely inadequate. He therefore gives in an appendix a slightly modified translation of the mediaeval English rite 'according to the Use of the Society of the Catholic Commonwealth'.

There are points which I should be prepared to dispute with the author, in particular his formulation of the relation between the ensubstantiation at the offertory and the transubstantiation at the consecration. I should rather wish to say, following Cirlot,[75] that there is one action, that of the great Eucharistic Prayer, which offers by consecrating and consecrates by offering and does both by giving thanks. And, while agreeing with Dr. Smyth's exposition of the impersonal humanity of our Lord, I am surprised at his suggestion that the hypostatic union was broken between Christ's death and resurrection.[76] And when he writes: 'Human persons incorporated by Baptism into the social Body of Christ are to their liturgical Offertories of Bread and Wine as the Person of the Son of God Incarnate is to the natural Body and Blood of his individuated Incarnate humanity placed for sacrifice upon the Cross',[77] I find it necessary to remind myself rather vigorously that analogy of proportionality consists in a likeness, and not an identity, of proportions. Again, it seems to me to be a defect in his treatment that it contains no adequate discussion of the *sacramental* character of the Eucharist, that is to say, of its character as an effectual *sign*. Nevertheless, Dr. Smyth's book provides an example of that combination

[75] Cf. p. 182 *supra*.   [76] Op. cit., p. 62.   [77] Ibid., p. 55.

of orthodoxy with audacity which is so necessary for really constructive theological advance. And his exposition of the revolutionary social implications of a truly Catholic doctrine of the Eucharistic sacrifice, while it was written with the American situation of 1953 primarily in mind, has a good deal to teach us in Europe in 1965 as well.

'The Whole Christ offering the Whole Christ' – this, then, I would suggest as the most adequate brief answer that we can give to the question 'Who offers what?' concerning the Holy Eucharist, and it is an answer which if accepted might draw the sting from most of the post-Reformation disputes. Once it has been accepted it is, I think, then possible to ask a number of subsidiary questions, whose formulation does not break the unity of the basic formula or lead to unnecessary oppositions. We can ask in what sense Christ, the Church, the priest and the communicant can be understood as 'offerers', and Christ, the Church, the priest, the communicant and the elements as 'offerings', for all these will find their legitimate place within the great inclusive act by which Christ draws into his one oblation once offered his members, their gifts and the whole material universe. I will sum up this discussion with two quotations. The first is from Scheeben.

> He [sc., God the Son] became the representative of the race by taking human nature from its midst, by proceeding from it. Thus it was from the midst of the race that he took the body and the blood which he was to sacrifice to God. The flesh and blood that he immolated and that, glorified by the fire of the Holy Spirit, he gave over to

God, was at the same time our flesh and blood. Therefore, it was not alone Christ himself, but the whole human race that in Christ's flesh and blood took from its own substance and offered to God the pledge of an infinite worship and sent it up to heaven.

On the other hand, the human race not only can and should offer Christ in his own body as a sacrifice to God, but conversely Christ can and should consummate the sacrifice of himself both in himself as the head, and likewise in his entire mystical body. His entire mystical body is to be sacrificed through his power and according to the model of his real body. As his sacrifice is by no means purely symbolic in character, but is utterly real, so too, when considered as the sacrifice of the community, it must not merely represent what the community of itself could and should achieve for the honour of God, but should be the efficacious ideal of the real sacrifice which the community ought actually to offer.

This is why Christ continues the immolation and glorification of his own body in his mystical body. By their union with him the bodies of his members attain to a higher, mystical consecration. Furthermore, they receive thereby a freedom from death in virtue of which they undergo death not so much as a natural necessity or punishment, but rather, after the example of their head, take death upon themselves for the honour of God. This they do by allowing Christ, to whom henceforth their life belongs, to immolate that life. The bodies of Christ's members have necessarily the destiny to be one day awakened from death as his own body was and, transfigured by the fire of his glory, to be stationed by him before the face of God for all eternity....

After the general resurrection the whole Christ, head and body, will be a perfect holocaust offered to God for all eternity, since Christ himself, not only in his personal being, body and soul, but also in his entire mystical body, will be a truly universal, total holocaust offered to God through the transforming fire of the Holy Spirit.[78]

I have already referred to the fact that Scheeben, in advance of his time as he was, nevertheless did not altogether shake himself free of a 'destruction' view of sacrifice, and it is perhaps significant that this passage comes from the section on the activity of the God-Man and not from the section on the Eucharist, which is in fact far more typical of its period. Nevertheless, when the suggestions of such words as 'immolate' have been adjusted it would be difficult to find a more eloquent expression of the true nature of the Eucharistic action than is provided by it.

My second quotation is from the present-day Flemish theologian, Fr. E. H. Schillebeeckx, O.P. He is discussing the sacraments in general, but he would be the first to acknowledge that the Eucharistic provides the supreme example of sacramental efficacy.

> The whole redeeming mystery of Christ [he writes], not in some way or other in its historical content, but as the act of God, becomes actively present in the sacraments, so that in these sacraments we are immediately encompassed by the redemptive efficacy of the 'redeeming Incarnation'. It thus becomes clear that the core of the sacramental efficacy is the eternally-present act of redemption of the Son of God; and that this is *identical* with both the mystery content of the saving activity of the living, glorified *Kyrios* and, finally with the mystery content of the saving power of the Sacramental Church....
>
> It is only this encounter with Christ in and through the actual presence in the sacraments of the eternally-present redemptive act of the living Christ (and of the redeeming

[78] *The Mysteries of Christianity*, E.T., pp. 438–9.

Christ himself in the Eucharist) which explains the historical perspective in the sacraments insofar as they are: (1) an *Anamnesis* (commemoration) or celebration in mystery of the past sacrifice of the Cross (*signum rememorativum*), because precisely at the sacrifice of the Cross the eternally-present redemptive act of the Son of God amounted to really giving up his life; (2) *actual bestowal of grace* (*signum demonstrativum*), because the receiving subject is here and now really drawn into the eternally-present redemptive act; (3) an *anticipation*, in germ, of the eschatological Parousia (*signum prognosticum*), because they are the sacramental act of rendering the *Eschaton* itself present (in the Eucharist) or at least of making present the eternally-actual redemptive act of the Son of God in his efficacy as the glorified *Kyrios* (in the other six sacraments); they allow our own time to be grasped in a visible way by the *Eschaton* itself. The sacramental encounter of man with Christ in the Church is, therefore, on the basis of the historically-past redeeming event, the beginning or the *arrha* (pledge) here and now of eschatological salvation; and the supporting substratum of all this is the permanence of the redeeming man Jesus, who is God and who, through his sacraments, receives us into his redeeming mercy.[79]

This passage, with its extremely 'existentialist' language, reads very differently from those previously quoted from Roman Catholic theologians; yet its content seems to me to be substantially the same, and it will, I hope, provide a fitting conclusion to our present discussion. Clearly the dialogue between Catholics and Protestants concerning the Eucharist has not yet reached the point of complete agreement and it would

[79] 'The Sacraments: An Encounter with God', in *Christianity Divided* (1962), ed. D. J. Callahan *et al.*, pp. 261–2.

be neither wise nor honest to exaggerate the degree of agreement that has been achieved. Nevertheless, when we reflect on the polemical violence and the lack of mutual comprehension which has characterised the debate for four hundred years, this recent *rapprochement* is a matter for both astonishment and thankfulness. Nor is it solely, though it is no doubt largely, the result of a more cordial and charitable attitude of mind in those whose predecessors were bitterly and joyfully at variance; it is also the result of genuine theological advance and development on both sides. And the extent of that advance and development is quite remarkable even in the decade that has elapsed since the publication of the first edition of the present work.

Chapter Seven

THE EUCHARISTIC PRESENCE

I PROPOSE in this chapter to discuss the significance of the fact that the sacred gift which is received by the faithful in the Holy Eucharist is the Body and Blood of Christ. I have previously discussed[1] the significance for the Eucharistic Sacrifice of the fact that in the Sacrament the Body and Blood are exhibited in separation from each other; the Body as the host on the corporal, and the Blood in the chalice. I shall not repeat that discussion, but it may perhaps make for clarity if I summarise briefly the view which is there expounded. I do not believe that the Eucharist is constituted as a sacrifice by the separate consecration of the bread and wine as two separate objects, separated by an interval of space. Nor do I believe that it is constituted as a sacrifice by anything that is done to the consecrated elements in the course of the rite, such as, for example, the fraction of the consecrated host or its reception in communion. Such views would, so far as I can see, make every Eucharist a numerically different sacrifice from every other one, and all of them numerically different from the sacrifice which was offered by Christ in his earthly life. What I believe constitutes the Eucharist as a sacrifice is the fact that in the Eucharist Christ identifies the bread and wine respectively with his Body and his Blood, which latter were separated in

[1] See ch. v *supra*.

199

his death on the Cross. The *separation* of the Body from the Blood took place on Calvary; there, and there only, did the death of Christ occur as an event in history. What takes place in the Eucharist is not a new separation of the Body from the Blood, not a new *immolation*, but the *identification*, by that unique mode of efficient causality whose name is sacramental signification, of the bread and wine with the Body and Blood. Thus every Eucharist is the *same* sacrifice as every other one, and all of them are the *same* sacrifice as that which was offered by Christ in his earthly life.

My present question is a different one from that outlined above, and my discussion of it will not presuppose the view which I have just stated about the Eucharistic Sacrifice, though it will be thoroughly compatible with it. I am now concerned not with the separation of the Body and the Blood but with their unity. And, just as the separation is peculiarly connected with the Sacrifice, so the unity is peculiarly connected with the communion; for what we receive when we kneel at the altar is not the dead Christ but the living and ascended Saviour, whose Body and Blood shall never be separated again, since he lives for evermore in the unity of his glorified humanity.

It has sometimes been maintained that a distinction ought to be drawn between Christ himself on the one hand and his Body and Blood on the other. Such a distinction was suggested by the late Dr. E. S. Talbot at the Farnham Conference on Reservation in 1925.[2] But, as Dr. Quick and Dr. Goudge then pointed out, such a distinction is difficult to sustain;[3] in St. John's Gospel the phrases, 'He that eateth my flesh and

[2] *Reservation*, p. 65. [3] Ibid., pp. 68, 70.

drinketh my blood' and 'He that eateth me', appear to be used indifferently. And indeed, in Hebrew idiom, which provides the background of the phraseology of the New Testament, 'flesh and blood' or 'body and blood' (for there is no difference between the words for 'flesh' and 'body' in Hebrew[4]) simply means human nature in its entirety. The Jews did not think of a man as the Greeks did, as an immortal soul temporarily condemned to inhabit an alien physical organism. Although, at any rate in later Judaism, they distinguished between the soul and the body and believed that the soul survived bodily death, they looked upon man as consisting of body and soul together and placed their emphasis quite as much upon the body as upon the soul. Thus, when they thought of man's final condition, it was in terms of the resurrection of the body rather than of the immortality of the soul. It has been well remarked that, whereas the Greeks looked upon a man as an embodied soul, the Jews looked upon him as an ensouled body. For them, man was essentially a material creature, although one upon whom God had conferred a unique destiny which had set him over the rest of creation as God's vice-gerent, and into whom God had breathed the breath of life. In consequence, for the Jews the term 'flesh and blood' was practically synonymous with 'human nature'. It denoted man in his totality, and not merely the lower physical part of him as contrasted with a spiritual immaterial soul which was the real man. Thus, when at Caesarea Philippi our Lord said to Peter, with reference to Peter's acknowledgment of him as the Christ, 'Flesh and blood hath not revealed this unto thee, but my

[4] Cf. J. A. T. Robinson, *The Body*, p. 12.

Father, which is in heaven,' the meaning was simply
'No human agency has revealed this'; the contrast is
not between body and soul, but between the creature
and the Creator. Again, when St. Paul writes to the
Galatians 'I conferred not with flesh and blood, neither
went I up to Jerusalem to them which were apostles
before me, but I went into Arabia', his meaning clearly
is that he took counsel with no human beings, not even
those who were of most eminence in the Church, but
withdrew to commune with God.[5] The point has often

[5] A note on certain New-Testament linguistic usages may help to
remove misunderstanding. (1) 'Flesh' (*sarx*), just like 'flesh and
blood', often means simply human nature in its entirety: 'The
Word became flesh and dwelt among us' (John i, 14). But 'flesh'
is also taken as meaning human nature in its fallen sinful state, in
contrast to 'spirit'. In this case 'spirit' (*pneuma*) seems primarily or
mainly to refer to the Spirit of God, or to the spirit of man as
indwelt by the Spirit of God: 'the flesh lusteth against the Spirit,
and the Spirit against the flesh, for these are contrary the one to
the other' (Gal. v, 17). This double use can be paralleled in the
case of the word 'world' (*kosmos*), which sometimes simply means
God's creation as such ('God so loved the world ...', John iii, 16)
and sometimes means that creation in its fallen state, especially the
human part of it ('Ye are not of the world ...' John xv, 19). (2) In
I Cor. ii, St. Paul contrasts the 'soulish' (*psychikos*, 'psychic', A.V.
and R.V. 'natural') man with the 'spiritual' (*pneumatikos*, 'pneu-
matic') man. The 'soulish' man is the man who is living simply on
the level of animal life ('soul' =*psyche* = *anima*), in contrast with the
'spiritual' man, whose human spirit is indwelt by the Spirit of
God. 'Soul' here thus plays practically the same role in contrast to
'spirit' as is played by 'flesh' in the former case; so far from 'soul'
being contrasted with 'flesh', it is practically identical with it. (3)
In I Thess. v, 23, St. Paul prays that 'your spirit and soul and body
may be preserved entire'. Here he is adopting a current contemporary trichotomy of man into mind (*nous*), soul (*psyche*), and body
(*sōma*), and, since he is writing to Christians, substituting 'spirit'
for the more coldly intellectual term 'mind'. In none of these cases
is there any suggestion that religion is concerned exclusively with
one part of man, whether 'soul' or 'spirit', the other part or parts
being outside the concern of religion. So far is spirit as such from

been made, but I do not think its implications for Eucharistic theology have been fully appreciated. And indeed I wish to suggest that both Catholic and Protestant theology have been frequently vitiated by a false spirituality in regard to the Eucharistic gifts.

In the sixth chapter of St. John's Gospel, our Lord said 'Except ye eat the flesh of the Son of man and drink his blood ye have no life in you. Whoso eateth my flesh and drinketh my blood hath eternal life, and I will raise him up at the last day.' Here he is quite clearly not telling his disciples that they must enter into a spiritual relation with him by faith, that they, as spiritual creatures, must commune with him who is uncreated Spirit. What he is saying is that they, as living men of flesh and blood, must feed upon him who is a living man of flesh and blood. How they were to do this they would discover at the Last Supper, but the fact is plain. This is not soul communing with soul, it is men feeding upon a man. If this phrase sounds shocking, it is relevant to observe that our Lord's own words shocked his hearers; but he was not prepared to

---

being unconnected with the realm of flesh or body that St. Paul can describe the resurrection body as a 'spiritual body': 'It is sown a soulish body (*sōma psychikon*), it is raised a spiritual body (*sōma pneumatikon*)' (I Cor. xv, 44). It is only in this sense of 'spiritual' that we can justify the use of such well-established phrases as 'the spiritual life', 'Christian spirituality', and the like. These must not be taken as implying the cultivation of one part of man, his 'soul' or 'spirit', to the exclusion of his 'body' or 'flesh', but as the raising of the *whole man* from the purely natural or animal or 'soulish' level, to the supernatural or spiritual level; from the realm of the fall, to the realm of redemption; from servitude under sin and death, to the liberty of the sons of God. And it is only in this sense that we can say with Article XXVIII that 'the Body of Christ is given, taken and eaten, in the Supper, only after a heavenly and spiritual manner'.

mitigate their force, even when many of his disciples went back and walked no more with him. In spite of this, theologians have shown a recurrent tendency, in their discussions of the Eucharist, to fall into a false spirituality, sometimes merely as regards their language but also sometimes as regards their thought. They have frequently separated man into soul and body, then assumed that it is only the soul that matters, and finally concluded that the Eucharist is solely concerned with the sanctification and salvation of the soul. And I shall reluctantly have to draw an example of this from the Book of Common Prayer.

'What,' asks the Catechism, discussing the Sacrament of the Lord's Supper, 'are the benefits whereof we are partakers thereby?' And the answer is: 'The strengthening and refreshing of our souls by the Body and Blood of Christ, as our bodies are by the Bread and Wine.'[6] The thought is perfectly clear, however extraordinary the consequences may be. I am made up of two parts, a body and a soul. Each of them needs to be fed. My body is a material thing and needs for its food material things, such as bread and wine. That is one half of the picture, and it makes perfectly good sense. But here is the other half. My soul is a spiritual thing and needs for its food spiritual things, such as — what? The Body and Blood of Christ? But the Body and Blood of Christ are not just spiritual things. Clearly the parallel has broken down. The human soul of Christ is a spiritual thing, and so (if, *salva reverentia*,

[6] Almost the same phrase appears in Calvin (*Inst.*, IV, xvii, 10). Cf. Ridley: 'The true substance and nature of bread and wine remaineth: with the which the body is in like sort nourished, as the soul is by grace and Spirit with the body of Christ' (*Remains*, Parker Soc., p. 275).

the word 'thing' may be used in this connection) is his divine Person; but the Catechism does not tell us that in the Lord's Supper we receive Christ's human soul or his divine Person. It tells us that we receive his body and blood; and this, in Biblical usage, means manhood in its entirety. Obviously something has gone badly wrong with the thought, and it is something that is altogether independent of the view that is held about the nature of the Eucharistic presence. The difficulty is precisely the same whether we believe in transubstantiation, consubstantiation, receptionism or even virtualism. It arises out of the assumption that what the Eucharist imparts is merely spiritual sustenance for our souls, and this is an assumption that the words 'body' and 'blood' simply will not bear. However unintentionally, in this unhappily worded question and answer the Catechism has managed to suggest both an inadequate view of man and an inadequate view of the Eucharist. It has divided man into two parts, a body which needs merely natural nourishment and a soul which needs supernatural nourishment, thus removing the body from all direct contact with the supernatural realm. In consequence, since the Eucharistic food is clearly supernatural, the Catechism has had to restrict the operation of the Eucharist to the soul and, in doing so, to treat the Body and Blood of Christ as purely spiritual objects. The material is treated as purely natural, and the supernatural as purely spiritual; this is an assumption which is highly congenial to the modern world and which has had remarkable and devastating results in other spheres than those of Eucharistic theology. The Theological Committee of the Church Union commented on it in connection with the Report of the Lambeth Conference of 1948. Referring to the sections of the Report which dealt with the Christian Doctrine of Man and with the Church and the Modern World, the Committee said:

> For the Catholic duality of the natural and supernatural they [i.e., the Lambeth fathers] tend to substitute a duality of the material and spiritual, or a duality of the earthly and the heavenly, and indeed they oscillate indecisively and uncomfortably between these last two. The doctrine that man's fulfilment consists in a supernaturalisation of his nature by divine grace, a supernaturalisation which includes in a coherent whole every stage and every component of man's activity, from his rebirth in the womb of the Church at baptism to his enjoyment of the beatific vision in the final resurrection, is nowhere either stated or apparently even assumed.[7]

When we get the material equated with the natural, and the supernatural equated with the spiritual, two consequences follow. The first is that the material realm escapes altogether from the over-arching control of religion, and the second is that religion becomes entirely concerned with the culture of the soul. What the Catechism should have told us, and perhaps meant to tell us, but certainly failed to tell us, is that, just as the whole man, in his unity of body and soul, is strengthened and refreshed by bread and wine for the achievement of his natural end as a citizen of this world, so the whole man, in his unity of body and soul, is strengthened and refreshed by the Body and Blood of Christ for the achievement of his supernatural end as a member of the Body of Christ. Had it said this, the Catechism could then have gone on to point out

[7] *Lambeth 1948 Reviewed*, p. 4.

that, just as the bread and wine are the outward signs of the Body and Blood of Christ, which are really present beneath them, so the natural earthly life of the Christian is the outward sign of his supernatural heavenly life, a life which, while it will achieve its culmination in the beatific vision, is already operative here and now. Thus the fatal separation of religion from common affairs, which has so tragically dogged the footsteps of modern man, would have been repudiated.

There is indeed one formula in the Anglican Eucharistic rite which avoids this lamentable dichotomy. Anglicans have frequently pointed with pride to the words of administration, which pray that the Body and Blood of our Lord Jesus Christ would preserve the *body and soul* of the communicant to everlasting life, and they have contrasted it with the unsatisfactory form in the Roman secular rite, *Corpus D.N.J.C. custodiat animam tuam in vitam aeternam.*[8] (Incidentally, we may remark that the Dominican rite contains the much more satisfactory form *custodiat te* and that in the Roman secular rite a decree of April 25th 1964 has substituted the even simpler form *Corpus Christi*, to which the communicant replies *Amen.*) But behind the Anglican formula there lies a very strange history. The *Order of Communion* of 1548 distributed the host with

[8] This form appears to have come into use in the time of St. Gregory the Great (Cf. Addis and Arnold, *Catholic Dictionary*, *s.v.* 'Communion'). It is amusing to notice that a parishioner, defending in a pamphlet the rite introduced into Harborne church in 1938 by a vicar of modernist views, wrote: 'The words of administration are translated from the Roman form and cannot be thought to refer to the Resurrection of the Body.' (They followed in fact the Dominican form: 'preserve thee'.)

the words 'The Body of our Lord Jesus Christ which
was given for thee preserve thy body unto everlasting
life', and the chalice with the words 'The Blood of our
Lord Jesus Christ which was shed for thee preserve thy
soul unto everlasting life'. Here, too, we have a
dichotomy, but it is quite a different dichotomy from
that which, in 1661, was to appear in the Catechism.
According to the Catechism, our bodies are strengthened by the bread and wine, and our souls by the Body
and Blood. But according to the Order of Communion,
our bodies are preserved by Christ's Body and our
souls by his Blood. The Prayer of Humble Access
(which came into the Prayer Book from the Order of
Communion) echoes the latter doctrine when it prays
that 'our sinful bodies may be made clean by his body
and our souls washed through his most precious
blood'; this is not a Reformation doctrine, but goes
right back to St. Thomas[9] and earlier in the Middle

---

[9] Cf. *S. Theol.*, III, lxxiv, 1c. Cranmer's chaplain Thomas Becon
quotes the gloss on a Gelasian canon (*De Consecr.*, Dist. 2, Can.
Comperimus) to the following effect: 'The kind [i.e., species] of
bread is referred unto the flesh, and the kind of wine unto the soul;
when one [presumably, wine] is the sacrament of the blood, in the
which is the seat of the soul. And therefore is the sacrament
received under both kinds, that it may be signified that Christ
took both the flesh and the soul, and that the participation of the
sacrament is profitable as well for the soul as for the body; so that,
if it should be taken only under one kind, it should be signified
that it profiteth unto the tuition and preservation of the one only'
(*Catechism*, Parker Soc., p. 243). A passage attributed throughout
the Middle Ages to St. Ambrose runs as follows: *Caro enim salva-
toris pro salute corporis, sanguis vero pro anima nostra effusus est, sicut prius
praefiguratum a Moyse. Sic enim ait, Caro, inquit pro corpore vestro
offertur, sanguis vero pro anima* (*In I Cor.*, cap. xi). St. Anselm writes:
'We place bread and wine upon the altar to represent each [sc.,
the Body and the Blood], that we may believe that by bread made
Body, and worthily received by us, our body will be conformed to

Ages. It is certainly less open to objection than the wording of the Catechism, for it is free from the implication that the material is purely natural and the supernatural purely spiritual; in fact it does not mention man's natural end at all. But it makes a similar separation between the human body and the human soul, and it makes an even more remarkable contrast between the Body and the Blood of Christ. Christ's *Body* feeds our *bodies* – well and good. But Christ's *Blood* washes our *souls*. The Body of Christ is thus related to the material realm, but his Blood to the realm of spirit. This is a dichotomy which, on any showing, it must be impossible to maintain.

The highly realistic – we might almost say, materialistic – nature of the Eucharistic discourse in the sixth chapter of St. John was pointed out as long ago as 1940 by the late Sir Edwyn Hoskyns. 'No room', he wrote,

---

the Body of Christ in immortality and impassibility; and similarly that by wine turned into Blood, and received by us, our souls become conformed to the soul of Christ' (Ep. cvii). The passage from Pseudo-Ambrose was quoted by Peter Lombard and hence the idea expressed by it became general in mediaeval thought.

The earlier teaching is found in Tertullian, who writes *Caro corpore et sanguine Christi vescitur, ut et anima de Deo saginetur* (*De carnis resurr.*, 8). It is laudably echoed by Thorndike: 'The Body and Blood of Christ in the Sacrament turns to the nourishment of the body, whether the Body and Blood in the truth turn to the nourishment or the damnation of the soul' (*Works*, iv., p. 82). And Jewel in one place writes 'The Communion of the Body and Blood of the Lord ... is through faith wrought in the souls of the faithful, whereby not only their souls live to eternal life, but they surely trust to win their bodies a resurrection to immortality' (Homily 'Of the Worthy receiving of the Sacraments', cit. Dugmore, *The Mass and the English Reformers*, p. 232).

I am indebted to Dr. F. L. Cross for drawing my attention to the appendix on 'The Prayer of Humble Access' in John Dowden's *Further Studies in the Prayer Book*.

'is left for any "spiritualising" interpretation. The eating and drinking of the Flesh and Blood of the Son of man involve a real physical eating and drinking, although the Flesh and the Blood are altogether misconceived if they be thought of, as the Jews are determined to think of them, as the mere material of the human Body of Jesus, instead of being rigorously defined in terms of the significance wrought out and manifested in his sacrificial death.' 'The Eucharistic food and drink', he continued, 'are physically bread and wine, spiritually the Flesh and Blood of the Son of man; together they constitute the true food and drink of the faithful: the true food and drink because they effect the sacred union of the Son of God with those who believe on him, and thus communicate eternal life and guarantee immortality.'[10] Hoskyns had clearly seen the essential point, but even he capitulated, perhaps unconsciously, to the inaccurate terminology which had become almost universal. For, having said that there is no room left for any 'spiritualising' interpretation, he almost immediately asserted that the Eucharistic elements are 'spiritually' the Flesh and Blood of the Son of man. I am not, of course, pleading for a crude 'Capharnaite' view, for which Christ would be present in the Eucharist under the same mode and in the same condition as he was present on the roads and in the fields of Galilee. It is the ascended Christ, Christ as he is *now*, that we receive in Holy Communion, and we receive him under sacramental signs. But the best word for the mode of the Eucharistic presence does not seem to me to be 'spiritual' but 'supernatural', or, better still (since, as has been

[10] *The Fourth Gospel*, 2nd ed., p. 297.

pointed out in an earlier chapter,[11] it is a narrower term than 'supernatural') 'sacramental'. It is the whole Christ, in his ascended glory, who is present in the Eucharist, and he is present as the food of the whole man. He is present there simply because, by his institution and promise, the bread and wine have become the effectual signs, the *sacramenta*, of his Body and Blood.

[11] Cf. p. 132 *supra*.

Chapter Eight

THE EUCHARISTIC THEOLOGY
OF ST. THOMAS

THE strong points of St. Thomas's Eucharistic theology are so obvious as hardly to need mention. His clear recognition that the Eucharist, while it is a real sacrifice, does not involve a literal slaying of the divine victim, and his insistence that the Eucharistic presence, while it is a real presence, is not a crudely material one which would subject the ascended Saviour to the limitations of spatio-temporal existence, have been of quite inestimable importance, and it can be plausibly argued that many of the defects from which subsequent Eucharistic theology has suffered are due not to the extent to which the main direction of the Angelic Doctor's teaching has been followed but to the extent to which it has been ignored or abandoned. Nevertheless I shall suggest that in some respects St. Thomas's discussion of the Eucharist is inadequate, and I shall not feel that in doing so I am casting any slur upon his greatness. For St. Thomas, while he towers above his age, is none the less a child of his age, and we lesser children of a later age, while we shall have our own defects which may very well be greater than his, are not on the whole likely to have the same ones. We are in a better position than he was in to see where he was wrong, even if we must leave it to our successors to perform the same service for us.

I

It is impossible to glance at St. Thomas's treatment of the Eucharist in either the *Contra Gentiles* or the *Summa Theologica* without recognising how very much the question of the Eucharistic Presence predominates in his thought over the question of the Eucharistic Sacrifice. This fact, which he shares with other mediaeval theologians, does not, of course, mean that either St. Thomas or mediaeval Christians in general had any doubts that the Eucharist was a sacrifice; the whole elaborate system of requiems and chantries is sufficient to show this. It may well be that St. Thomas treats the Eucharistic Sacrifice so sketchily precisely because everyone believed in it; it was only under the pressure of the Protestant denials that the Catholic theologians of the Counter-Reformation gave it such a detailed – and, we may add, such a wrong-headed – discussion. Nor, we must remind ourselves, does the emphasis upon the Presence mean that mediaeval religion was centred around the reception of Holy Communion; communion, except for the clergy, was, as we all know, lamentably infrequent. What mediaeval religion was centred around, so far as the Mass was concerned, was adoration. It was to see the host and to adore it that the people came to Mass; the concentration of mediaeval Eucharistic theology upon the Presence is the natural reflection of this.

It has, in contrast, come to be more and more fully realised in recent times, that a balanced discussion of the Eucharistic must start from the Sacrifice and must see the Presence in relation to this; such works as those of de la Taille, Dix and Masure provide outstanding examples of this approach. That is to say, we must not look upon the Mass as primarily a means of manufacturing the Body and Blood of Christ, which are then to be used for the three more or less parallel purposes of adoration, sacrifice and communion. Rather we must look upon the Mass as primarily the Christian Sacrifice, which, just because it is a sacrifice, requires the presence of the victim, who being present is rightly adored and who by being received in communion imparts to the faithful the benefits of redemption and unites them with himself in the mystical Body which is the Church. St. Thomas would of course deny none of these truths, and indeed they can all be found expressed in his writings. But what we are concerned with is a question of emphasis, and I think it must be admitted that St. Thomas places his emphasis upon the Presence rather than upon the Sacrifice, and that in consequence, while his discussion of the Presence is elaborated to the last degree, his discussion of the Sacrifice is brief and almost perfunctory.

The notion of sacrifice in general is treated by St. Thomas not in the *Pars Tertia* when dealing with the Eucharist, but in the *Secunda Secundae* under the virtue of justice. Sacrifice is included in the practice of religion, and religion is a duty arising out of the cardinal virtue of justice: justice, that is, towards God, *giving God his due*. And, as Masure has stressed in his book, *The Christian Sacrifice*, St. Thomas's definition is extremely general and does not include as a necessary element the death or the destruction of the object offered. 'There are sacrifices properly so called,' he writes, 'when something happens in connection with things offered to God, as when animals were slain or when bread is broken and eaten and blessed. And the very name shows this, for "sacrifice" is derived from a man making something holy.'[1] When in the *Pars Tertia* St. Thomas discusses whether Christ's passion was a sacrifice he tells us that 'a sacrifice properly so called is something done that is properly due to God for his honour to appease him',[2] and goes on to quote the famous remark of St. Augustine that 'a true sacrifice is every work which is performed in order that in holy fellowship we may cleave to God, that is, which is related to that end of goodness in which alone we can be truly blessed'. Now Christ, he goes on, 'offered himself in suffering for us, and this very work, that he voluntarily bore suffering, was in the highest degree accepted by God, inasmuch as it proceeded from charity. Hence,' he concludes, 'it is manifest that the passion of Christ was a true sacrifice.'[3] It seems difficult to find very much fault with St. Thomas's doctrine of sacrifice as such, or of the sacrifice of Christ though the note of acceptance and transformation is certainly not as explicit as it is, for example, in Masure. While he recognises that, in a sinful world and as a redemption for human sin, Christ's sacrifice could fittingly operate only by means of his death (though he does not deny that, absolutely speaking, God might have redeemed mankind in some other way[4]), he emphasises the centrality of the fact that Christ's death was above all else a manifestation of his charity. Christ's Passion was a satisfaction for our sins, he tells us, 'in the first place, on account of the greatness of the charity from which he suffered.... The charity of the suffering Christ was

[1] *S. Theol.*, II II, lxxxv, 3 *ad* 3.   [2] Ibid., III, xlviii, 3*c*.
[3] Ibid., xlviii, 3*c*.   [4] Ibid., xlvi, 2.

greater than the malice of those who crucified him.'[5]
When, however, he goes on to discuss in what sense the
Eucharist is a sacrifice and what is its relation to the
Passion, his language becomes somewhat vague. The
Eucharist is 'commemorative of the Lord's Passion';[6]
it is 'something representative of the Lord's Passion';[7]
it is 'a reminder (*rememorativum*) of the Passion which
is past';[8] it is 'a memorial of the Lord's Passion';[9] and
so on. St. Thomas is, of course, quite clear that the
Eucharist is a sacrifice; he says explicitly that it 'is not
only a sacrament, but also a sacrifice'.[10] But how is it a
sacrifice? 'It is called a sacrifice inasmuch as it represents the very Passion of Christ.'[11] What are we to
understand by these ambiguous words, *commemorative*,
reminder, *memorial*, *representative*? Not, it is frequently
said, what Protestants would understand by them:
these words do not imply a bare imitation or dramatic
performance which merely imitates a past event. Does
not the Angelic Doctor quote with approval Augustine's words that Christ is immolated every day in the
sacrament?[12] Yes, indeed. But does he not also add,
again quoting Augustine, that this is because 'the
images of things are called by the names of the things
of which they are images, *as when we look upon a picture
or fresco and say " That is Cicero"*'?[13] And does he not
also say that, 'when Christ was going to leave his
disciples in his proper species, he left himself with them
in the sacramental species, *as the Emperor's image is set
up to be venerated in his absence*'?[14] I am not, of course,

[5] *S. Theol.*, III, xlviii, 2c *et ad* 2.   [6] Ibid., lxxiii, 4c.

[7] Ibid., lxxiii, 5c.   [8] Ibid., lxxiii, 5c.

[9] Ibid., lxxiv, 1c.   [10] Ibid., lxxxii, 4c.

[11] Ibid., lxxiii, 4 *ad* 3.   [12] Ibid., lxxxiii, 1 *sed contra*.

[13] Ibid., lxxxiii, 1c.   [14] Ibid., lxxiii, 5c.

suggesting that St. Thomas did not believe in the Real Presence; 'this sacrament, ...' he writes, 'is called a victim *inasmuch as it contains Christ*, who is the victim of sweetness';[15] and he devotes two questions to discussing transubstantiation. But, clear as he is that in the Mass the divine *victim* is really present, is he equally clear that the *sacrifice* of Christ is really present? He does of course quote with approval the words of the Secret for the Ninth Sunday after Pentecost: 'As often as the commemoration of this victim is celebrated, the work of our redemption is exercised', but he explicitly interprets this as meaning simply that 'by this sacrament we are made sharers in the fruits of the Lord's Passion'.[16] What I am in fact suggesting is that St. Thomas was rightly anxious to avoid any suggestion that there is in the Mass a literal slaying of Christ, a literal repetition of Calvary, and that in consequence he took refuge in the rather vague notion of the Mass as a commemoration, representation or memorial of the Passion. I do not suggest that for him these words had a merely psychological significance, as they have had for the majority of Protestants. St. Thomas was quite clear that Christ is really present in the Mass and that by the Mass the fruits of the Passion are communicated to the Church and to the faithful. But what, in his anxiety to avoid a crude immolationism, he did not, so far as I can see, manage to achieve was an equally clear realisation that the Mass is really and not merely figuratively a sacrifice. To say this is not to blame him for anything that he could very well have avoided; it is merely to say that he could not do in the thirteenth century what de la Taille, Vonier and

[15] *S. Theol.*, III, lxxiii, 4 *ad* 3.   [16] Ibid., lxxxiii, 1*c*.

Masure in conjunction managed, at least in principle, to do in the twentieth. What I suggest was the fundamental cause of this deficiency was an inadequate understanding of the nature of a sacrament.[17]

A sacrament, St. Thomas tells us, is a sign, but not every sign is a sacrament. A sacrament is 'a sign of a holy thing in so far as it makes men holy'.[18] It is a sensible thing, and it requires words for its signification.[19] Furthermore, the sacraments of the New Dispensation contain and confer grace and derive their power from the Passion of Christ.[20] They are instrumental causes of spiritual effects, and therefore, since God is their principal agent, they can be instituted by no one other than God himself.[21] All this is excellent, as far as it goes, but what we miss in St. Thomas is anything like an adequate discussion of the peculiar

---

[17] Fr. A. A. Stephenson, S.J., has pointed out to me that St. Thomas gives not one but two reasons why the Mass is called an immolation of Christ, first that it is an *imago repraesentativa* of the Passion, as I have stated above, but also that in it we are made partakers of the fruits of the Passion (*S. Theol.*, III, lxxxiii, 1c); he has suggested that St. Thomas compensates, as it were, for a 'low' view of the Eucharistic immolation by a 'high' view of the Eucharistic presence. This is, I think, true, but it does not in my opinion render the Angelic Doctor's view of the Eucharistic Sacrifice satisfactory. It should also be noted that the (to me) astounding comparison with the Emperor's image which is 'set up to be venerated *in his absence*' is used to illustrate not the *immolation* but the *presence*. This does not mean, of course, that St. Thomas did not believe in a literal presence in the Mass, but it does suggest that he was unhappy in his choice of illustrations. Fr. Stephenson's own view of the Eucharistic Sacrifice is, as we have seen above (pp. 116f. *supra*) a definitely 'commemorative' one.

[18] *S. Theol.*, III, lx, 2c.

[19] Ibid., lx, 5, 6.

[20] Ibid., lxii, 3, 4, 5.

[21] Ibid., lxiv, 2.

type of instrumental causality which a sacrament exercises. 'There is in a sacrament', says St. Thomas, 'a certain instrumental power for producing the sacramental effect',[22] but I do not find him giving anything like an adequate discussion of the way in which sacramental causality acts. I hasten to add that I am not concerned with that burning question of the schools, whether sacramental causality is physical or moral. Whatever the answer may be to that question, the fundamental question remains: how does sacramental causality differ from non-sacramental causality? If sacramental causality is physical, how does it differ from other physical causality? If it is moral, how does it differ from other moral causality? What precisely is involved in the fact that it is sacramental, that it operates in the manner of a *sacrament*, that is, in the manner of a *sign*? How does a sacramental sign differ from any other divine instrument?

It was, in my opinion, the great merit of Abbot Vonier, in his book *A Key to the Doctrine of the Eucharist*, to realise the truth (I am expressing it in my words, not in his) that the difference between sacramental and non-sacramental causality is not a physical or a moral difference, but a metaphysical one. Sacramental causality is, of course, supernatural, but not all supernatural causality is sacramental. 'If', writes Vonier, 'the priest at the altar brought down Christ from heaven in his natural state as a full-grown man, this would not be a sacrament in the least, as it would lack the very essence of the sacrament, representative signification.... The sacramental world is a new world created by God, entirely different from the world of

---

[22] Ibid., lxii, 4c.

nature and even from the world of spirits.... Sacraments are a new creation with entirely new laws.'[23] That is to say (and here again I am using my own words), sacramental signs do not make present the realities which they signify by spatially enclosing them, in the way in which a gas-cylinder may contain hydrogen, or by being instruments by which they are manufactured, as a sausage-machine produces sausages, or by being channels through which they are communicated, as a water-pipe delivers water, but by being divinely-ordained efficacious signs of them. The word 'efficacious' is, of course, fundamental. Sacraments are not signs of realities which are absent, but signs of realities which are present; and the means by which, as instrumental causes, they make the realities present is by being signs ordained by God. Applying these considerations to the Eucharist, we are not left merely with the alternatives of either viewing the Eucharist as some kind of physical *repetition* of the Passion of Christ or, on the other hand, of viewing it as nothing more than (in the modern sense of the word) a *commemoration* of the Passion. Nor should we regard it, as de la Taille and Spens tended to do, as a kind of complement of the Passion, without which the Passion, as a sacrifice, would not be complete. To put the matter in another way, the Eucharist is not a new event in the messianic biography, not something which *happens* to the ascended Lord, as we may rightly say that his Passion, Resurrection and Ascension happened to him. Everything that *happens* in the Eucharist happens either to the Eucharistic elements or to the faithful who participate in it, but not to Christ. In consequence, the

[23] Op. cit., pp. 32, 35.

relation of the Eucharist to the Passion is not to be found in some resemblance, real or fancied, between certain characteristics of the Eucharistic rite and certain events of the Passion, whether the fraction, the separate consecration or anything else, useful as such resemblances may be for purposes of edification and devotion.[24] It consists in the fact that Christ has declared that the bread is his Body and the wine his Blood; that is, in the fact that, by his institution and promise, he has made the bread and the wine the sacramental signs of the realities which they contain. This, I would maintain, is what establishes the real presence and what constitutes the Mass a real sacrifice. St. Thomas was quite clear about the Real Presence, but I do not think he was equally clear about the real sacrifice; and I have tried to indicate why. I do not suggest that he was wrong to describe the Mass as a commemoration, or a memorial, or a representation of Calvary; our Lord himself commanded that the rite which he instituted at the Last Supper should be done as his *anamnesis*. But I do suggest that St. Thomas failed to understand what was involved in the fact that the commemoration, memorial or representation was a sacramental one. He avoided admirably – as, I think, not all mediaeval religion managed to avoid – the notion that the Mass is either a separate sacrifice from that of Calvary or a physical repetition of Calvary. He also avoided – as I do not think de la Taille and his followers entirely managed to avoid – the notion that the Mass is something additional to the Passion without which the Passion would not be a sacrifice at all. But I do not think, in spite of all that Vonier tried to

[24] Cf. pp. 120f. *supra*.

do for him, that he altogether managed to avoid the notion, which came to its full expression in the theology of some of the sixteenth-century reformers, that the Mass is simply a divinely appointed commemoration of the Passion, much as he differed from them as to what such a divinely appointed commemoration achieves.

II

I shall now go on to suggest that St. Thomas's failure to achieve a full understanding of the nature of sacramental causality has gravely weakened his discussion of the Eucharistic Presence. So long as the discussion is conducted simply in terms of the metaphysical doctrines of Aristotelianism, it is difficult to see how it could lead to any other conclusion than that to which St. Thomas actually comes. And St. Thomas does in fact quite successfully avoid any crude Capharnaite theory about the way in which the Body and Blood of Christ are present under the appearances of bread and wine. The separate consecration of the two elements does not involve a real separation of his Body from his Blood. Under the appearance of bread the Body is present in virtue of the consecration, but the Blood is also present by real concomitance; under the appearance of wine the Blood is present in virtue of the consecration, but the Body is also present by real concomitance.[25] Nor is Christ spatially extended under the sacramental appearances in such a way that part of him is in one part of the host and another part of him in another; he is whole in every part, both before and after the fraction:[26] *tantum esse sub fragmento quantum toto*

---

[25] *S. Theol.*, III, lxxvi, 2.　　　　　　　[26] Ibid., lxxvi, 3.

legitur.[27] Nor is the Body of Christ present in the Sacrament in any way locally, nor, strictly speaking, movably.[28] Nor have the elements lost any of their sensible properties, anything that the word 'substance' implies in the scientific, as contrasted with the metaphysical, sense.[29] In consequence St. Thomas is led to maintain that the accidents of bread and wine, considered as a whole, remain in the Sacrament without any subject whatever, being sustained simply by divine power, while he adds that the dimensive quantity (in modern terms, the extensional properties) of the bread and wine acts as a subject of the other accidents.[30] It is at this point that the difficulty arises. For the result is, not merely that the Eucharist is supernatural, but that every Mass is a kind of metaphysical miracle, in which the divine power has to be invoked at each step of the argument in a way which virtually implies that grace does not only perfect nature but destroys it. It can, of course, be said that transubstantiation does not necessarily involve the destruction of the bread and wine but merely means that, while everything of the bread and wine remains as before, they cease to have the status of substances, since that status is assumed in respect of them by the Body and Blood. It is commonly insisted by scholastic theologians that transubstantiation is not a doctrine of the annihilation of the bread and wine but of their conversion. Nevertheless anyone who has read the discussion of the Eucharistic change in Penido's *Rôle de l'Analogie en Théologie dogmatique* can hardly fail to have noticed how the doctrine of analogy has to be strained to maintain this assertion.

---

[27] *Lauda Sion.*
[29] Ibid., lxxvii, 3, 6.
[28] *S. Theol.*, III, lxxvi, 5, 6.
[30] Ibid., lxxvii, 1, 2.

The contrast between St. Thomas's Eucharistic doctrine and his discussion of the Incarnation is striking in this respect. The difficulty is not that we are here faced with an occurrence which can only be accounted for as the effect of supernatural divine power; everything that happens in the order of grace is that. The difficulty is that we are confronted not with an exemplification or an amplification of our previously accepted metaphysical principles but with a suspension of them. The fact that this is so does not, of course, provide an argument against the reality of the Eucharistic conversion; but it does suggest that the metaphysical principles which have been employed to describe it are inadequate, that they need, if not to be abandoned, at least to be supplemented.

What I am in fact going to suggest is that they need supplementing by the notion of sacramental signification, considered not merely as a moral or a physical principle but as a metaphysical one. What I mean by this is that we need to invoke the notion of sacramental signification not only in order to describe how the Eucharistic conversion is brought about, or what are its effects after it has been brought about, but also in order to describe what it is. It is not, I suggest, an adequate description of the consecrated elements to say simply that the accidents of bread and wine continue to exist by divine power though the substance of bread and wine is no longer there, while the substance of the Body and of the Blood are there although by divine power their accidents are not manifested. We must add that the substance of the Body and of the Blood are there under the appearance of the bread and of the wine because God has ordained that the bread and wine shall no longer have the status of substance but shall be the sacramental signs of the Body and the Blood. The Body and Blood are there not simply by a direct and unmediated act of the divine power, but by a mediated act of divine power using sacramental causality as secondary cause. The bread and wine are thus not destroyed by ceasing to have the status of substance nor when they cease to have the status of substance has anything been withdrawn from them. On the contrary, something has been added to them, namely the status of being the sacramental signs of the Body and Blood. The Body and the Blood themselves have not undergone any change by becoming the substance of the Eucharistic gifts, nor have they on the other hand lowered the metaphysical status of the bread and wine by doing so. On the contrary, they have elevated it, for, if sacramental signification is a metaphysical, and not merely a physical or a moral fact, bread and wine have a higher and not a lower metaphysical reality if they have the status of sacramental signs of the Body and Blood of Christ than if they have the status of substance.

It will, I hope, have been clear, that I have not introduced this doctrine of sacramental signification as a metaphysical principle in order to contradict anything that St. Thomas positively says, but in order to complete it and to save it from metaphysical absurdity. I must add, however, that the introduction of this doctrine does not *necessarily* presuppose the particular explanation of the Eucharistic conversion which St. Thomas adopts. But I would submit that any explanation of the Eucharistic conversion which is not to overthrow the nature of a sacrament must in fact take seriously the metaphysical implications of the fact that the Eucharist *is* a sacrament. It will not do simply to describe the Eucharistic conversion in terms which take no account of the fact that the Eucharist is a sacrament and then to introduce this fact as a kind of after-thought; to use it, for example, to explain how the Eucharist is a sacrifice or how the Blessed Sacrament bestows grace when received in communion, if we have not used it previously to explain how the Eucharist exists at all.

When, then, I ask whether St. Thomas's Eucharistic theology is adequate, I feel bound to answer 'No'. In giving this answer, however, I do not mean to imply that in its main assertions, St. Thomas's doctrine is demonstrably erroneous, but only that it does not go far enough. Both in his doctrine of the Eucharistic sacrifice and in his doctrine of the Eucharistic Presence St. Thomas seems to me to have paid far too little attention to the nature of sacramental signification and in consequence to have come up against a brick wall. I need hardly add that I am sure that, if he had paid attention to it, St. Thomas would have made much better use of it than I have.

Chapter Nine

THE EUCHARISTIC THEOLOGY
OF CHARLES GORE

ALTHOUGH it is now half a century old, it will, I think, be of interest to devote some attention to the late Dr. Charles Gore's book *The Body of Christ*, a work which, in spite of its great intrinsic excellence, has fallen into undeserved neglect. This book appeared in March 1901, and its stimulus was provided by two conferences in which Gore had recently taken part. The former of these was a conference on Priesthood and Sacrifice which met at Oxford in December 1899 under the chairmanship of Dr. Sanday; it consisted of three groups of theologians representing high-church Anglicans, low-church Anglicans, and nonconformists respectively. The second was a 'round-table' conference of Anglicans on the doctrine of the Holy Eucharist; it met at Fulham Palace in October 1900 at the invitation of Dr. Mandell Creighton, then Bishop of London, and under the chairmanship of Dr. Wace.

At the Oxford Conference three notable speeches were made by Fr. Puller, S.S.J.E., which remarkably anticipate the position put forward in 1915 by Père de la Taille and maintained later on by Sir Will Spens. Fr. Puller pointed out that in the Jewish sacrifices the priestly act consisted not in the killing of the victim but 'in the manipulation of the blood, and in placing the body or part of it on the altar to be burned',[1] and he carried over this principle into the consideration of the Sacrifice of Christ. 'I would lay great stress', he said, 'on the thought that while our Blessed Lord's death on the Cross is a most essential and fundamental element in his sacrifice, his priestly work is especially to be connected with his life in glory.'[2] Commenting on the teaching of the Epistle to the Hebrews, Fr. Puller said, 'it would appear that, when our Lord entered the heavenly sanctuary and was about to present himself to the Father, he *became* a High Priest.... The Jewish sacrifices had to be offered in death with no resurrection life in them; while the Christian sacrifice has passed though death and "is alive for evermore".'[3] 'In fact,' he asserted on a later occasion, 'I believe that Holy Scripture teaches that the oblation of the Sacrifice of Christ is not limited to heaven, but that it takes place also on earth in the celebration of the Eucharist.'[4] And in a written statement he said, 'Christ exercises his Priesthood in heaven in his own Person. He exercises it on earth in and through his Church.'[5] The whole discussion is well worth examination; here it will be sufficient to note that Gore, after emphasising that 'the Cross, the instrument of [Christ's] own sacrifice, is to belong to the disciples as well', added, 'I should have thought, however, that the New Testament as a whole required us to draw a distinction between the spiritual meaning and efficacy of our Lord's dying or our Lord's sacrifice, and anything which we, through him, can share.'[6]

The Fulham Conference, which was explicitly

---

[1] *Report*, p. 70. [2] Ibid., p. 100. [3] Ibid., pp. 101–2.
[4] Ibid., p. 134. [5] Ibid., p. 15. [6] Ibid., p. 113.

devoted to the Eucharist, was quite remarkable for the extent to which some of the Evangelical members identified the gift received in Holy Communion with the dead Christ. Just because they held a 'commemorative' view of the relation of the Eucharist to Calvary and so were immune from the danger of viewing the Eucharist as a *repetition* of Calvary, and just because they rejected any quasi-physical identification of the elements with the Body and Blood, they were able to express in the most unqualified way the view that the sacred realities to which, in however symbolic or instrumental a manner, the consecrated elements are related are the Body and Blood of the *dead* Christ. Thus Mr. Nathaniel Dimock roundly asserted: 'The *Res sacramenti* is not Christ as he now is, but Christ's Body and Blood as separated in sacrificial death for our sins.'[7] Dr. W. H. Barlow no less emphatically wrote: 'With Waterland I understand that the feeding on Christ in the Holy Communion, is on the crucified Christ.'[8] Dr. H. C. G. Moule 'urged that it was involved in the terms of Institution that our Lord put forward his body and blood as sacrificed – the body as dead, and the blood as shed – to be participated in as a sacrifice', though he added 'that it is through participation in this sacrifice that we are made partakers of the glorified body of our Lord'.[9] It will be clear from these quotations how these theologians were dominated by the mediaeval identification of sacrifice with death. Gore was provoked to comment that 'it seemed to him difficult to accept the statement adopted from Waterland by Mr. Dimock to the effect that we are made "partakers of the crucified body directly and of the

[7] *Report*, p. 12.   [8] Ibid., p. 12.   [9] Ibid., p. 44.

glorified body consequentially", and he suggested that it might be more correct even to reverse the order thus stated. He could not conceive of participation of the crucified body except as an act of memory. Whereas if we were made partakers of the glorified body, we were of course partakers of the body which had been crucified.'[10] And again, 'He [Dr. Gore] could not separate the sacrificed from the glorified body of our Saviour, and could not conceive of our partaking of the former except through the latter. The latter, he urged, is the only body now existing or that ever has existed; and it is the same body which, once crucified, is now in a glorified state.'[11] This assertion called forth a very remarkable reply from the Chairman, Dr. Wace, who replied 'that, recognising the force of that observation, he wished to meet it directly, by observing that it was precisely in order to meet the difficulty in question that our Saviour appointed the broken bread and the poured-out wine to be the Sacrament of his crucified body and blood – that is, to be to all practical intents and purposes the body which was crucified and the blood which was shed. By virtue of the Sacrament, that crucified body is made present with us for the purpose of our participation in its sacrifice.[12] In other words, for Dr. Wace, the Eucharist is a divinely instituted means of making the Body and Blood of Christ present, not as they now are but as they once were. Certainly we may say that, for Dr. Wace no less than for Abbot Vonier, the sacramental world is a new world and that sacraments are a new creation with entirely new laws. One cannot help regretting that his assertion was not taken up and developed. For the

[10] *Report*, p. 44.   [11] Ibid., p. 5ᵏ.   [12] Ibid., p. 51.

Evangelicals at Fulham were by no means Zwinglians; they were mainly realistic receptionists. But, like most of the members of the conference with the exception of Gore, they made the simple mediaeval equation of sacrifice with death. They would not identify the consecrated elements themselves with the dead Christ, but they were convinced that the gift which they received through the consecrated elements was the dead Christ, and it was this that shocked Gore. The only alternative, however, which Gore seemed able to suggest (though he suggested it less forcibly than Puller would have done had he been there) was that the sacrifice of Christ is not to be located so much on Calvary as in heaven. When one reads its proceedings today in the light of more recent thought, it becomes clear that, like the Conference on Reservation which was held at Farnham Castle almost exactly a quarter of a century later, the Fulham Conference was hampered by two defects. The first defect was the lack of a really inclusive doctrine of sacrifice, which would equate the sacrificial activity of Christ with the whole offering of his incarnate life from his conception to the heavenly session. In consequence of this, there seemed to be only two alternatives: either with Dimock to equate the sacrifice with Calvary and to say that we receive in communion the dead Christ, or with Puller to equate the sacrifice with the heavenly session and to minimise the importance of the Cross. The second defect was the lack of any adequate doctrine of sacramental signification, as a result of which it was impossible to assert intelligibly both that the Christ whom we receive in communion is Christ as he is *now* in his glory, and also that the Eucharist sacramentally makes

present in the Church the whole sacrificial action of
Christ; though, as we have seen, Wace came very near
to seeing what was needed, in spite of his mediaeval
equation of sacrifice with death.

In the preface to *The Body of Christ* Gore explicitly
states that that book was in part the result of an attempt
to clear up his own thoughts in view of the Fulham
Conference, but it can hardly be doubted that the
question of Eucharistic Theology had been in his mind
for a long time. The book is still worthy of attention
and in fact it is in many ways of far greater relevance
today than a good many of the statements about the
Eucharist which have been made by Anglican theologians in the intervening space of time. I shall here
point out those of its features which seem to me to be
of special importance.

In the first place, while placing the Christian sacraments, as Masure does, in the setting of religion in
general, Gore points to the fact that the Christian
Eucharist is inextricably rooted in Judaism. 'As to its
origin, indeed, it was wholly Jewish, not heathen. Any
other suggestion is quite unhistorical. It was developed
out of the rites and associations of the paschal sacrifice
and meal.'[13] This fact, which has been so strongly
stressed more recently by Dom Gregory Dix and others,
provides, of course, the real answer to the 'mystery-
religion' theories of Eucharistic origins, but there were
very few who saw its significance at the time when Gore
was writing. Then, again, Gore was emphatic on the
essentially social nature of the Eucharist and saw it as
the great safeguard against a false spirituality. 'The

[13] *The Body of Christ*, p. 18. (All quotations are made from the
fourth edition, 1907.)

more we dwell on the social meaning of sacraments,' he wrote, 'the more profoundly satisfying an answer does it supply to the difficulties raised by such a false spiritualism as resents the attachment of spiritual gifts to outward conditions.'[14] And again, he urges the social character of Christianity as an argument for the real presence against receptionist or virtualist views: 'Nor does it seem to me difficult', he writes, 'to suggest a reason, both practical and spiritual, why, if the loving purpose of Christ was to communicate to us the spiritual food of his most blessed body and blood, he should, on the institution of his sacrament, have vouchsafed the gift, first of all, as an objective presence in the church, and not conveyed it directly to the individual worshippers in connection with an act of eating bread and drinking wine. For even if the members of the church ate and drank all together at the same meal, yet the act of eating is separate to each individual, and the divine gift would thus have taken the character of an individual communication. But the presence vouchsafed amongst them emphasises unity; as apparently the divine Spirit on the day of Pentecost, when he came to make the church one, symbolised his coming in a fire which appeared first as one and then divided and distributed itself in fiery tongues. In each case that which was to be distributed to all was given first as one object, to make evident the unity and unifying effect of the divine gift.'[15]

'The spiritual in the New Testament', Gore tells us, 'means not what is separated from the material or the bodily, but that in which the spirit rules, or that which expresses a spiritual meaning. Thus from the days

[14] *The Body of Christ*, p. 45.   [15] Ibid., p. 94.

when the first Christian Fathers were fighting their great battle against the false spirituality of Gnosticism it has been the sound argument of Christian theologians that the idea of sacraments – the idea of spiritual gifts given through material means – is of a piece with the whole method of God in the creation and redemption of man; of a piece, to put the matter otherwise, with the twofold nature of man, in which the body is associated most intimately with every spiritual faculty, and in which every spiritual emotion and capacity is made to depend upon external and physical facts. But', he adds, 'the argument is enormously strengthened when the *social* character of sacraments is had in view.'[16]

And it is the whole Christ that we receive in communion. 'It is not merely the Spirit for our spirits, or the teaching for our intellects, that we ask for and receive, but the whole Christ for our whole selves. Nothing less than this ... can satisfy the language of the New Testament.'[17] Furthermore, this whole Christ is the glorified Christ. In words that repeat his assertion at the Fulham Conference he writes: 'It stands to reason that if there be thus, as the Christian Church so constantly believed, a real communication to us of the flesh and blood of Christ, it must be the "flesh" and "blood" of the glorified Christ, for no other exists. These mysterious things are given to us in the eucharist under conditions which recall a past state – the state of sacrificial death.' But, 'the person who now feeds us with his own very life, divine and human, is he who is set before us in a vision of the Apocalypse as a "Lamb as it had been slain", but alive for evermore in the heavenly places.'[18]

[16] *The Body of Christ*, p. 39.   [17] Ibid., p. 60.   [18] Ibid., p. 66.

When he comes to discuss the Eucharistic sacrifice Gore repudiates vigorously any view that Calvary is repeated. 'Consecration ... does not effect any renewal of the sacrifice of the cross – any renewed surrender of Christ to death. Symbolically, no doubt, in the breaking of the bread and the outpouring of the wine, and in the separate consecration of the bread and of the wine [though he remarks in a footnote that this idea is not apparently ancient] there is represented the violation of Christ's body, and the separation of the blood "which is the life" from the body in death,... but the death, or the humiliation which belongs to the death, is commemorated only, not renewed or repeated.'[19] Gore denounces, even more strongly than Masure, the notion that sacrifice requires the *destruction* of the object offered with the corollary that, if the Mass is a real sacrifice, Christ must be in some way destroyed in it.[20] He would, we may imagine, have been very much surprised to know that, fifty years later, almost all Roman Catholic theologians would have agreed with him in disowning what, at the time of writing, he could quote from Einig as being what *communiter docent doctores*! He no less decisively rejects the view held by a number of Anglicans 'according to which there is postulated in the eucharist some real presence of the flesh and blood of Christ as they were when he was dying or dead upon the Cross'.[21] 'It is natural enough' he writes, perhaps with the Evangelicals at Fulham in mind, 'that those who adopt a merely commemorative view of the eucharist should say that it is the dead Christ who is presented to us there, in the sense that a

[19] *The Body of Christ*, pp. 174–5.   [20] Ibid., pp. 180, 306.
[21] Ibid., p. 181.

past event in history is presented to our contemplation. But it seems wholly unintelligible how divines who in any sense believe in a real presence can speak of the eucharistic body – one hesitates even to write the words – as "the corpse" of Christ, or use language which is certainly highly misleading, unless they mean – which God forbid – that there is in every eucharist a body sacrificed afresh and blood shed anew in death.'[22] And he quotes as an example the well-known passage from Lancelot Andrewes in a sermon on (of all subjects) the Resurrection, which culminates in the phrase 'We must repair even *ad cadaver*'.

Gore's own view is that the Eucharist is constituted as a sacrifice by its relation to the offering of the glorified Christ in heaven. 'The sacrifice of the Son of Man once offered in death has been accepted in glory. In the power of that sacrifice Christ ever lives, our high priest and perpetual intercessor, the continually accepted propitiation for our sins unto the end of time. All that we need to do or can do is to make thankful commemoration, in his way and by his Spirit, of his redemptive sufferings, and to unite ourselves to his perpetual intercession, where he presents himself for us in the heavenly places, or as he makes himself present among us in our eucharistic worship.... Meanwhile, if the church has been offering many sacrifices at many altars, whatever value they have or have had must be because the church which offers is a priestly body by union with Christ's unique high priesthood, and what she offers obtains its ratification through union with his sacrifice.'[23]

It is thus clear that, for Gore, the Eucharist is consti-

[22] *The Body of Christ*, p. 182.   [23] Ibid., p. 183.

tuted as a sacrifice by a relation which it bears to the continual offering which our Lord makes of himself in heaven. But what is this relation? Gore traces in antiquity what he describes as 'three, not incompatible attempts to express the truth'.[24] There is the view, expressed in the prayer *Supplices te* of the Roman canon, 'that the human prayers and sacrifices are, by eucharistic oblation and consecration, accepted at the heavenly altar and returned to the church as the spiritual food of Christ's body and blood'.[25] Then there is the view that, by the descent of the Holy Ghost upon the earthly altar the elements become for the Church the body and blood of Christ; 'the "Lamb as it had been slain" – but who is alive for evermore, our perpetual and never-failing propitiation – becomes present in the midst of the worshipping people in his body and blood of sacrifice, and they become present to him .[26] (Incidentally we may note that Gore accepted the now generally abandoned view that an epiclesis of the Holy Ghost was a normal feature of the primitive Eucharist.[27]) Gore remarks that 'the difference [between these two views] is rather imaginative than real. In both views what gives its value to the church's sacrifice is its being offered on the heavenly altar of Christ's perpetual self-presentation.'[28] Both these views 'recognise that the sacrifice is consummated in communion'.[29] But there is a third view, which Gore illustrates by an impressive list of quotations from St. Augustine, according to which we can only offer Christ because, by communion, we ourselves are offered with and in Christ; 'the Church herself [is] the sacrifice of the

[24] *The Body of Christ*, p. 185. [25] Ibid., p. 188. [26] Ibid., p. 192.
[27] Ibid., pp. 76f.   [28] Ibid., p. 198. [29] Ibid., p. 199.

altar, as offered there in and with Christ'.[30] And it is this view which to Gore was clearly the most satisfactory and all-inclusive. 'The sacrifice is the sacrifice of the whole body, and the communion is the communion of the whole body.'[31]

It is impossible not to be impressed by the scope and power of Gore's discussion. Nevertheless his basic assertion that the Eucharist is a sacrifice in virtue of its relation to a sacrifice which Christ is now offering in heaven has not been unchallenged. It was in fact attacked in a massive volume which appeared practically simultaneously with Gore's own, *The Eucharistic Sacrifice*, by Dr. A. G. Mortimer, which was written to controvert Mr. F. E. Brightman's pamphlet with the same title and also the views expressed by Fr. Puller at the Oxford Conference of 1899. To discuss the controversy which followed would lead us too far from our subject; its course is outlined in Dr. F. L. Cross's *Darwell Stone*,[32] where it is pointed out that Dr. Stone was able to show that Brightman's teaching was less one-sided than Mortimer believed. It may, however, be suggested that, just as it is erroneous to place all the emphasis upon Calvary, it is also erroneous to place all the emphasis upon the heavenly session, and that the same deficiencies which characterised the Fulham Conference are to be found, though in a lesser degree, in Gore's own discussion.

There is only one section of Gore's book which seems to me to be thoroughly unsatisfactory, namely that in which he treats of the mode of the Eucharistic Presence. Gore was, as is well known, most definitely opposed to

[30] *The Body of Christ*, p. 208.   [31] Ibid., p. 213.
[32] Op. cit., pp. 69–70.

the extra-liturgical cultus of the Blessed Sacrament. In the preface which he wrote to the fourth edition of his book in 1907 and which makes explicit reference to the then recent report of the Royal Commission on Ecclesiastical Discipline he wrote as follows: 'I believe that some practices connected with the Tabernacle and the Monstrance involve an extension of the use of the sacrament which diverges so widely from Christ's intention as to be illegitimate. I would prohibit them in the Church of England for this reason; and every Bishop can legitimately prohibit any rite or service or prayer which is not in the Prayer Book.' (Gore had himself been a diocesan bishop since November 1901.) 'But', he added, 'not – precisely not – on the ground that they involve a doctrine which the Church of England excludes.'[33]

His own objection was that, as he believed, extra-liturgical devotion to the Sacrament was the product of a localised view of the Eucharistic Presence which, as a matter of history, had led to extremely infrequent communion on the part of the laity; the doctrine of transubstantiation had in fact caused the cultus of the reserved sacrament to take the place of communion.[34] Furthermore, it had led to communion itself being regarded as a merely temporary visit of the Saviour to the communicant.[35] For Gore, transubstantiation, infrequent communion, Benediction, and an individualistic and mechanical view of religion were all simply different manifestations of one and the same divagation from primitive Christianity – the loss of the great conception of the Church as the Body of Christ.

[33] *The Body of Christ*, p. viii.   [34] Ibid., pp. 136–7.
[35] Ibid., pp. 121–2.

And with this loss there had gone the development of a subjectivistic devotion to the manhood of our Lord, what Dr. F. J. A. Hort called by the name of 'Jesus-worship'.[36] Gore was quite clear that this divagation had affected Protestants no less than Catholics: 'If the early church', he wrote, 'had been in the constant habit of singing such hymns as "Jesus, lover of my soul", is it not very likely it would have also sung "Jesus, I adore thee on thy altar throne"?'[37] He seemed, however, to be far more fearful of its effects upon Catholics than upon Evangelicals. In the very preface in which he expressed his resolution to prohibit extra-liturgical devotions he wrote as follows about 'the serious divergence from our standards' that he found in certain members of the Evangelical school: 'But I believe that the practical devotional attitude of such teachers goes far to rectify the doctrinal defect: and I am most anxious not to scrutinise too closely the type of teaching in question.'[38] No such reserve as this characterised his judgment upon the more extreme Anglo-Catholics.

I have discussed elsewhere in this book[39] the legitimacy of extra-liturgical devotions and I shall therefore say little about the matter here. It must, I think, be admitted that Gore saw very much further than most of his contemporaries into the real nature of the degeneration that overtook popular Christianity in the Middle Ages. The subjectivism, psychologism, individualism and clericalism of mediaeval Christianity to which Dom Gregory Dix drew attention nearly fifty years later in *The Shape of the Liturgy* had not passed

[36] *The Body of Christ*, p. 106.
[37] Ibid., p. 109.
[38] Ibid., p. vi.
[39] Ch. xi *infra*.

unobserved by Charles Gore, though his strictures upon it seem to have been almost unnoticed at the time. I do not think, however, that Gore saw its real origin, as Dom Dix did, in the loss of the eschatological sense of Christianity which came over the Church after the establishment of Christianity as the official religion of the Roman Empire.[40] Nor do I think that Gore sufficiently recognised that not all the sacramental developments of the Middle Ages are necessarily undesirable. Had he been as generous in his attitude to extreme Anglo-Catholics as he was to extreme Evangelicals he would, I think, have been as ready to tolerate 'Jesus, I adore thee on thy altar throne' as 'Jesus, lover of my soul'. But it was a peculiar characteristic of Gore that, while he was himself by contemporary standards a very definite Anglo-Catholic, he could be very rigid towards those whose Catholicism went beyond his own.

There is more than a touch of irony in the way in which Gore was led to elaborate a theory of the Real Presence which would have the consequence that he required. In his discussion of transubstantiation he is quite ready to admit that modern Roman theologians interpret it in a way which avoids the condemnation of the doctrine expressed in the twenty-eighth Article of Religion. But he still condemns it as 'a verbal incumbrance due to an inopportune intrusion into church doctrine of a temporary phase of metaphysics'.[41] What is our surprise then, to find him appealing to the philosophy of his own time for the basis of his own

[40] See *The Shape of the Liturgy*, ch. xi, 'The Sanctification of Time'.

[41] *The Body of Christ*, p. 120.

doctrine! 'Modern philosophy of all schools', he
writes, 'recognises no distinction between substance
and accidents – knows no substance other than that
"something objectively real" which is constituted by
the qualities or relations under which alone any object
is known in experience.'[42] The 'modern philosophy'
to which he appeals is, of course, a quasi-Kantian
idealism. 'Metaphysical study', he writes, 'makes us
conscious how much the mind (the perceptive or intui-
tive faculties in us as distinct from the moral or
spiritual) has to do with actually constituting the objects of the outward world – the trees, the animals, the
persons. Mind, as it is in me and in all men, not only
perceives these things as ready-made, but also has to do
with making them to be.'[43] It is not however upon the
mind of the individual that the reality of physical
objects depends. 'The trees and flowers do not depend
on *my* mind for their existence, but on the action of that
common reason in which all men more or less effectively
share, but which, at the bottom, has its origin out of
the divine reason.'[44] Now Gore's assertion is that, in
the case of the Eucharistic Presence, faith plays the
same part that in the case of physical reality is played
by reason. 'The spiritual presence of Christ in his body
and his blood (and all that goes with it) rests not on the
precarious faith of any individual, but is so relative to
the faith of the church as a whole – that common
faculty which rests at bottom on the activity of the
Holy Ghost – as that apart from faith, or for one who
in no way shares it, it can no more in any intelligible
sense be said to exist than the beauty of nature can be

[42] *The Body of Christ*, p. 120.   [43] Ibid., p. 150.
[44] Ibid., p. 152.

said to exist for what is quite without reason.'[45] And the implication – which is, of course, fatal to any extra-liturgical cultus of the Sacrament – is that it is only when Christ is being received with faith in the act of communion that he can be said to be present in the Sacrament.

Gore's argument is, it can hardly be denied, extra-ordinarily ingenious, and it rests upon the established theological principle that, whereas physical objects are apprehended by our natural powers (of which reason is one of the chief), spiritual realities are apprehended by faith. But its conclusion stands or falls with the quasi-Kantian idealism which underlies it. If, for example, we denied that the mind plays any part in constituting the physical object but merely apprehends the existence of an object already constituted, then the parallel argument would assert that faith plays no part in constituting the reality of the Eucharistic Presence but only apprehends it as something already existing. And then, presumably, extra-liturgical devotion would be legitimate, if not indeed obligatory. If, at the other extreme, we held that physical objects are entirely constituted by the mind of the individual percipient (without any reference to Gore's mysterious 'common reason in which all men more or less effectively share'), the parallel argument would assert that the Eucharistic Presence exists entirely in the mind of the faithful communicant. And then we should be receptionists, if not indeed Zwinglians. It is little short of astounding that Gore, having rejected transubstantiation on the ground, among others, that it was the result of the introduction into Christian theology of a contemporary

[45] Ibid., p. 152.

17

metaphysical theory, should avowedly base his own doctrine of the presence upon the metaphysical theory which was characteristic of his own time. One can only suppose that he believed that theory to have an absolute and lasting character; time has, however, certainly falsified any such belief.

I would summarise this discussion by repeating that, in spite of certain defects which are obvious to us as we look back on his work half a century later, Gore's book *The Body of Christ* is worthy of much more attention to-day than is a good deal of the writing on the Eucharist that has appeared in the intervening period. For, with the exception of the question to which I have just devoted attention, his thought was remarkably free from what one might describe as conventional Anglican inhibitions. This does not mean that he was in any way lacking in his conviction of the fundamental Catholicity of the Church of England. He was, however, quite clear that that Catholicity can be vindicated only on a basis that is wider and deeper than Anglicanism itself. 'The main object of this book', he wrote in the preface to the fourth edition, 'is to set the specifically Anglican teaching of our formularies on a larger background, by going back behind the Reformation and the middle ages upon the ancient catholic teaching and upon the Bible. I seek to elaborate the eucharistic doctrine in what I think the truest and completest form. I have to admit that Anglican standards are in certain respects defective, and even misleading when taken by themselves.... But after all the Anglican Church does not claim to stand by itself. It refers back behind itself to the ancient and catholic church.'[46]

[46] *The Body of Christ*, p. vii.

This is a confession and an appeal which has been made more recently in the report published in 1947 under the title *Catholicity*. It was substantially repeated by the former Archbishop of Canterbury when he said: 'We have no doctrine of our own – we only possess the Catholic doctrine of the Catholic Church, enshrined in the Catholic Creeds, and those creeds we hold without addition or diminution. We stand firm on that rock.'[47]

[47] At a public meeting on 30 January 1951.

Chapter Ten

'PRIVATE MASSES'

UNTIL the recent revision of the rubrics of the Roman Missal the term *missa privata* was the normal term used to describe a mass celebrated without chant and the ceremonial assistance of deacon and subdeacon. It thus corresponded to our term 'low mass', though it was extended to include what is frequently called *missa cantata*, that is to say a mass which, although there is neither deacon nor subdeacon, is celebrated with more than one server, with the accompaniments of portable lights and possibly incense, and with the chant sung by a choir. It is clear from this that the word *privata* did not mean 'private', as indicating the absence of a congregation, but was simply the past participle of the verb *privare* and implies nothing more than that the mass is shorn of some of its full accompaniments. Nevertheless, in common use the term 'private mass' has come to mean a mass celebrated by a priest with a single server, who frequently does not communicate and in fact is often a young unconfirmed boy, without the presence of any other members of the laity.[1] It is this service, and not what is strictly denoted by the term *missa privata*, that I intend to discuss here.

It must be admitted that the early history of private

[1] The Constitution of the Second Vatican Council on the Sacred Liturgy uses the term *missa singularis* (para. 57).

masses, in this sense of the words, is not, from the theological point of view, entirely satisfactory. They arose at a period when the laity had very largely lost the understanding of their true function in the liturgical action, when the liturgy had come to be viewed not as something in which priest and people were involved together but as something which was done by the priest for the sake of the people, and when the sheer numerical multiplication of masses had come to be regarded as in itself of spiritual efficacy. In regard to this last point it is perhaps worth noting that the Roman Church itself has found it necessary to prohibit a priest, except on special occasions or for special reasons, from celebrating mass more than once in a day, though it seems difficult to deny that there is some sense, however difficult it may be to define it, in which two masses are twice as good as one, just as in *some* sense, other things being equal, to pray for twenty minutes is twice as good as to pray for ten. It is also probable that the rather undesirable custom of paying the clergy by means of mass stipends has at times been not without effect, though it can have very little to do with the revival of private masses in the Anglican Church, where the custom is almost entirely unknown. But in any case the origin of a practice has no necessary connection with its legitimacy or its desirability, and it should be possible to discuss a theological question simply as matter of theology.

It has sometimes been suggested that the modern movement for private masses in the Anglican Church arose in the male religious communities, when priests, whose duties as parochial clergymen had, as a matter of course, necessitated their celebrating the Holy

Mysteries several times a week or even daily, discovered that, as members of a community where there was only one mass a day, they would henceforth be subjected to the very considerable deprivation of celebrating only at very long intervals. I think it is true that some priests who had never felt the need, or even in some cases seen the legitimacy, of private masses may in fact have been led in this way to press for their introduction, but I believe that private masses had become a recognised practice in many Anglo-Catholic parishes long before most of the religious communities had been confronted with the question. (It is sometimes important to remember that professed religious are not by any means always 'advanced' in their churchmanship.) I imagine that, like a good many other practices, the daily mass of the priest was copied by post-tractarian Anglo-Catholics from contemporary Roman Catholicism as being simply 'part of the whole thing' and that it then maintained and extended itself because it was found to be a source of spiritual strength and a real assistance to holiness. And this would seem to be *pro tanto* a very strong argument for it.

It may help to clear the ground for the discussion if we recognise at the start that no branch of Catholic Christendom teaches that any priest has either a duty or a right to say mass every day, or even very frequently, except in so far as the needs of the people under his charge require it. Even in the Latin section of the Roman Communion, although the priest's daily mass is, in practice, almost universal, the only duty in the matter that the moral theologians assert to be binding on the priest simply in view of his ordination is that he should say mass 'from time to time'. Nevertheless, what is neither a duty nor a right may be both legitimate and highly desirable. And it is the legitimacy and the desirability of the daily mass, whether 'private' or 'public', that I wish to argue here.

I shall take as the starting-point of my argument the theological truth that, although in a secondary and descriptive sense we may rightly describe each celebration of the Holy Eucharist as 'a mass', in the primary and ultimate sense there is only one Mass, offered by the great High Priest, Jesus Christ, at the Last Supper, on Calvary and in Heaven. (There are various theories about the relation between these three 'moments' of Christ's sacrificial act, but they do not concern us here.[2]) Or, if to put the matter in this way seems to do too much violence to our habitual use of words, we might simply say that there are many masses, but only one sacrifice. In this ultimate sense we do not celebrate *masses* or attend *masses*; we celebrate *mass* and attend *mass*. For every earthly mass is simply the Church's participation in the one heavenly Mass. We human beings, composite creatures consisting not of pure spirit but of matter and spirit interwoven in unimaginable complexity, live by our very nature in the extendedness and scatteredness of space and time, and the Eucharist makes accessible to us, at our different points of space and moments of time, the one extra-spatial and supra-temporal redemptive activity of Christ, 'who ever liveth to make intercession for us'.

The question with which we are concerned, then, is this: how can a priest best associate himself with, and take part in, this activity, when there are more priests

[2] See ch. v *supra*.

available at a particular place and time than are needed as celebrants to meet the needs of the laity? There are three possible answers.

The first is that the superfluous priests should simply attend mass as members of the congregation, perhaps occupying special seats and wearing choir-dress, and should communicate in the same way as the laity. This seems to be the method envisaged, as regards cathedral and collegiate churches, by the fourth rubric at the end of the Anglican Communion office. No branch of Christendom, as far as I know, prohibits this practice; the Roman liturgical authorities so far recognise it as to prescribe that a priest so communicating shall put on a stole for the purpose. (It is, however, perhaps worth noting that in the Eastern Orthodox Church a non-celebrating communicant priest does not receive the Eucharistic gifts together by administration from the chalice with a spoon after the commixture, but takes the two kinds separately from the altar himself immediately after the celebrant; he is, therefore, not receiving as a layman, although he is receiving as a non-celebrant.) No one, I imagine, would wish to prohibit this practice, but it is difficult to maintain that it should be the normal way for a priest to communicate. For it seems to contravene directly the principle that in the Eucharist each order should perform its proper function, its own *leitourgia*. It is sometimes defended on the ground that every priest was a layman before he became a priest, and that the character of priesthood supplements, but does not abolish, the lay character; a man must be baptised and confirmed before he can be ordained. This argument is, I think, valid in so far as it proves that the practice under discussion is *legiti-*

mate; a priest who communicates as a layman is not usurping a function that is not his, as a layman would be who acted as celebrant. But, although a priest communicating as a layman is not acting as something which he is not, he is not acting as everything that he is; he is not exercising his full character, he is not fulfilling the status which he actually has in the Body of Christ. And therefore the practice, though legitimate, does not seem to be *desirable*; it introduces an element of confusion into the structure of the Church.

The second possible answer to our question is that all the priests present should act as joint celebrants; that we should revive the practice of concelebration, which was once general throughout the Church and which is still common in the East. (In the West it appears to have died out by the beginning of the thirteenth century; in the Latin Church it survived only at ordinations. Theoretically, there is a great deal to be said for it; Père Bouyer, in his fine work *The Paschal Mystery*, has pointed out its special suitability for Maundy Thursday, when the rule is still maintained that, at least ideally (for exceptions have now been made for the Mass at which the Bishop consecrates the holy oils and for extra masses which may be needed for the sake of the faithful), the rule is still maintained that there should be only one mass in the day in each church. In the first edition of this book I remarked that the Roman authorities had shown themselves so ready in recent years to countenance liturgical changes (as, for instance, in the permission for evening masses and in the drastic revision of the services of Holy Week) that it would be unwise to prophecy that concelebration would never be seen again in the West, marked as would be the break in established tradition that it would involve. Now, in the Constitution on the Sacred Liturgy which was enacted at the second session of the Second Vatican Council, the change has come about, and paragraph 57 reads as follows:

§ 1. Concelebration, whereby the unity of the priesthood is appropriately manifested, has remained in use to this day in the Church both eastern and western. For this reason it has seemed good to the Council to extend permission for concelebration to the following cases:

(i) (*a*) On Maundy Thursday, not only at the mass of the Holy Chrism, but also at the evening mass.

(*b*) At masses during Councils, Bishops' Conferences and Synods.

(*c*) At the Mass for the blessing of an abbot.

(ii) Also, with the permission of the Ordinary, to whom it belongs to decide whether concelebration is opportune, and to regulate the way in which it is done:

(*a*) At conventual mass, and at the principal mass in churches when the needs of the faithful do not require that all the priests available should celebrate individually;

(*b*) At masses celebrated at any kind of priests' meetings, whether the priests be secular clergy or religious.

However, the practice of individual masses ('private masses' in the popular sense) is explicitly safeguarded, for the paragraph continues:

§ 2. (i) It is for the bishop, however, to regulate the discipline of concelebration in the diocese.

(ii) But each priest shall always retain his right to celebrate mass individually (*missam singularem celebrandi*), though not at the same time in the

same church [as a concelebrated mass], nor on
Maundy Thursday.[3]

The actual method by which concelebration is to be
arranged, like most of the other details of liturgical
reform, is left for later arrangement, though it may well
differ from one region to another and will presumably
be settled in the first instance by the action of the local
hierarchy. Paragraph 58 of the Constitution simply
says that a new rite for concelebration is to be drawn
up and inserted into the Pontifical and the Roman
Missal, without indicating how much latitude this new
rite will allow. But already several more or less
'experimental' concelebrations have taken place,
notably those presided over by Pope Paul VI at the
opening and close of the third session of the Second
Vatican Council.

A word ought perhaps to be added about the common notion that the practice of concelebration has
somehow lined up the Eastern Orthodox Church with
moderate Anglicanism against the Roman Church
with its system of private masses. The precise opposite
appears to be the case. For both concelebration and
private masses rest on the principle that a priest, when
he is at mass, ought, at any rate normally and ideally,
to act as a priest and not as a layman, and are sharply
contrasted with the view that a priest ought to communicate as a layman whenever he can.

And this brings us to the third possible answer to
our question, which is that each priest should say what
is sometimes misleadingly described as 'his own mass',

[3] The words in [...] are not in the Latin text but are inserted in
Fr Clifford Howell's translation and no doubt give the intended
sense of the document.

whether this is necessary for the purpose of giving communion to the faithful or not. The practice is, of course, capable of misinterpretation. If, for example, it were believed, as apparently in some mediaeval circles it was believed, that every mass is a separate action, in which the celebrant, as principal agent, sacrifices Christ afresh for the particular intention which he has in mind, then the practice of private masses would encourage gross superstition. The fault would lie, however, not with private masses as such, but with the erroneous Eucharistic theology, and that erroneous theology would certainly not be corrected simply by prohibiting private masses. If, on the other hand, our Eucharistic theology is sound and it is realised that the different priests saying their different masses at their different altars are doing not *different* things but the *same* thing, that they are all taking part in the one eternal Liturgy whose celebrant is Christ and that their priesthood is only a participation in his, then the multiplication of masses emphasises the real unity of the mass and the true nature of the Church's corporate character as nothing else can. This may sound paradoxical, but I believe it to be true. For there is a very serious danger in certain circles which have been superficially affected by the liturgical movement, of a complete misunderstanding as to what the corporate nature of the Church and of the Eucharist is. Where all the emphasis is placed upon the desirability of the whole communicant body being present and communicating at the same mass, and when not only private masses but any masses in excess of the bare minimum required in order to give communion to the faithful are denounced as an individualistic abuse, the

impression is only too easily produced that what makes
the mass one and corporate is simply the fact that a lot
of people are together in the same place at the same
time. Logically this would involve having only one
mass each day in each diocese, celebrated by the
bishop. But the very purpose of the mass is that the
one redemptive act of Christ should be made accessible
to us who are scattered about in space and time, so
why should we be afraid of multiplicity, since multiplicity is simply the condition under which, by our
nature, we bodily creatures live? What makes the mass
one and *corporate* is not the fact that a lot of people are
together at the same service, but the fact that it is the
act of the *one* Christ in his Body (*corpus*) the Church.
And I can think of no better way of making anyone
understand wherein the unity and the corporateness of
the mass really consists than to take him into a church
in which a number of priests are simultaneously celebrating private masses and to say: 'Look at those men
at their various altars all round the church, each of
them apparently muttering away on his own and having nothing to do with the others. In fact they are all
of them doing *the same thing* – the same essentially the
same numerically – not just a lot of different things of
the same kind, but the very same identical thing; each
of them is taking his part as a priest in the one redemptive act which Christ, who died for our sins and rose
again for our justification, perpetuates in the Church
which is his Body through the sacrament of his body
and blood.'

I have spoken of the mass as making the redemptive
act of Christ accessible to us in different places and at
different times; and in saying this I have described it

as it appears to us. But what the mass really does, of course, is to gather those different places and times into the one redemptive act. It does not scatter Christ over the various altars; it draws the various altars into the one Christ. It does not divide Christ up among the individual communicants; it builds them into him. We do not really receive him; he receives us. The mass is the sacrament of unity, not of division or dispersion. But then we always see things upside down; that is what comes of being creatures. Thus the Incarnation, which is in its inner reality, as the Athanasian Creed tells us, 'the taking up of manhood into God', appears to us as 'God coming down from heaven to earth'. Neither the Incarnation nor the mass brings about any change in God, any more than something happens to the sun when, as we say, it 'sets'.

Of course, like anything else, private masses can be understood in an individualistic and divisive sense; so can acts of communion. Catholic priests sometimes talk about 'saying *my mass*'; Catholic and Protestant lay-folk alike often talk about 'making *my communion*'. Either term can manifest a thoroughly one-sided and uncatholic attitude to the sacrament, but neither of them need do so. It is quite undeniable that mediaeval and post-mediaeval piety have been deeply infected with the diseases of individualism and psychologism; they have tended to look upon religion as concerned simply with the sanctification of the individual soul and to measure that sanctification in terms of emotion. And nowhere have these tendencies been so prominent as in the realm of the liturgy. But I do not think that the remedy is to abolish private masses; it is to make it plain what the mass really is. And if that is done, private masses, quite apart from any other value that they have, emphasise, as perhaps nothing else can, the fact that the unity and the corporateness of the mass are made not by men but by God. For actually the term 'private mass' is a misnomer. No mass is really private. Mass said by a priest with one server in a heathen African village is as corporate as High Mass sung in St. Peter's by the Pope in the presence of five hundred bishops and twenty thousand of the laity For it is the act of Christ in the *Corpus Mysticum*, his Body, which is the Church.

My conclusion therefore is that the frequent, and even daily, celebration of mass by any priest is both legitimate and desirable, and that the renewed understanding of the true nature of the Church and the liturgy, which has been so marked a feature of both the thought and the life of the Church in recent years, does not in any way necessitate the disuse of 'private masses'. But I would repeat the assertion which I made at the beginning of this discussion, that, apart from special reasons such as are involved in the pastoral responsibility of a parish priest towards his people, such frequent celebration cannot be held to be either a right or a duty. And there are indeed cases in which to insist upon its exercise would clearly be wrong, for a priest may well be called by God to undertake work in which it is physically or morally impossible. In the Anglican Church especially such instances are obvious; in the Roman Church also there are cases like that of the priests in France who, in order to share the life and work of sailors and fishermen, have deliberately deprived themselves for long periods of the possibility of saying mass. And there will probably always be priests, particularly in our own Communion, who, while in no way lacking in devotion to the Blessed Sacrament, do not feel moved to celebrate the Holy Mysteries very frequently. In the Latin Church itself, there are priests to whom the idea of 'private masses' is unattractive or even repugnant.[4] This is surely a matter in which there should be the utmost tolerance and forbearance on all sides. For it is true of the heavenly, as of the earthly manna, that he that gathers much has nothing over, and that he that gathers little has no lack.

[4] Cf., e.g., Hans Küng, *The Living Church*, p. 213; T. Klauser, *The Western Liturgy Today*, pp. 15ff., 41.

Chapter Eleven

'ADORATION' AND 'BENEDICTION'

I INTEND in this concluding chapter to discuss briefly three questions: (1) whether it is legitimate and desirable that any extra-liturgical devotion should be paid to the sacramental presence of our Lord in the consecrated elements of the Eucharist, (2) whether, if such extra-liturgical devotion is legitimate and desirable, it is legitimate and desirable that it should take the form of a public service, and (3) whether, if some form of public service is legitimate and desirable, it is legitimate and desirable that it should take the form of the service commonly known as 'Benediction'.

(1) On the first question, as Dom Gregory Dix pointed out some years ago,[1] the crucial moment in the development of Eucharistic piety comes not with the emergence of extra-liturgical devotions in the late Middle Ages but with the emergence of intra-liturgical devotion to our Lord round about the end of the fifth century. This does not mean that the Church had previously been in any doubt about the reality of the Eucharistic Presence;[2] her belief in it was explicit and could on occasion manifest itself in startling and, as it would appear to many modern Christians, even irreverent ways. The Church was, however, in her earliest days so intent upon the performance of the Eucharistic

[1] *A Detection of Aumbries* (1942), pp. 55f.
[2] Cf. p. 72 *supra*.

259

action that she had no attention to spare for anything else. The Eucharist was, in its essence, the sacramental offering to the Father of the one true Sacrifice of Jesus Christ, and not a service of devotion to Christ himself. Nevertheless I do not think that many Anglicans would hold that the introduction into the Eucharist of prayer, either silent or audible, addressed to the Lord who is sacramentally present, is a superstitious or ungodly thing. It must, however, be admitted that such prayer can, if it is not carefully regulated, seriously disturb and unbalance the whole Eucharistic action, and this, moreover, not only or mainly in churches where the service is of an 'advanced' type. A striking example can be found in the kind of sung Eucharist which is common in those Anglican churches which would describe themselves as 'prayer-book catholic' and which include a number of our cathedrals. In these churches it is the normal custom for the choir, immediately after the recital of the narrative by the celebrant, to sing the 'Amen' and then, with little or no interval, the *Agnus Dei*, which in turn is immediately followed by the Communion. Now I do not, of course, deny that such a service is a perfectly valid Eucharist, but it must, I think, be admitted that a stranger to our rite would receive singularly little impression of the one thing which the Eucharist and it alone can perform, namely the offering to the Father of the sacrifice of Christ. What he would observe are two features which, in themselves, could be equally well performed with the reserved Sacrament, namely the adoration of the Lord Christ sacramentally present, expressed by the *Agnus Dei*, and the reception of Holy Communion. Whatever it may be and do in its inner reality, the consecration-prayer would *appear* to such a stranger to be nothing more than a means of bringing about the sacramental presence for these two purposes. And I do not think that it is only a stranger who would receive this impression. It would, I believe, be found, if one could carry out the necessary investigation, that such an attitude as I have described is common to many of our most devout communicants. They believe that Christ is present, and they come to worship and to receive him. This is indeed much, but it leaves out of consideration the primary fact that the Eucharist was instituted as the perpetual *anamnesis* of the sacrifice of Christ.

Now, to whatever dangers it may be exposed, I do not wish in any way to deny the legitimacy and the praiseworthiness of intra-liturgical devotion to our Blessed Lord. But I would urge that one ought not to deny the legitimacy of extra-liturgical devotion either. *Any* kind of devotion to Christ in the Eucharist is a development, it is a use of the Sacrament for a purpose other than that for which it was primarily instituted, and, as I have indicated, it can very easily come to overshadow that primary purpose. There are, I suggest, three ways in which this lack of proportion can be corrected without taking the extreme measure of prohibiting the offering of any Eucharistic devotion to our Lord at all. The first is by careful and sustained teaching about the true nature of the Eucharistic action. The second is by such a reform of the liturgical rite as will make explicit the nature of the Eucharist as the Church's sacramental offering of the Sacrifice of Christ to the Father. And the third is by providing means for the expression of devotion to the sacramental presence *outside* the immediate context of the Liturgy, so that within the Liturgy itself such devotion may not become disproportionate or exaggerated.

Such provision for extra-liturgical devotion would, of course, be wholly reprehensible if the sacramental presence of our Lord did not remain in the elements when they are reserved. It was apparently the view of the late Dr. Gore that the presence in the reserved elements is intermittent, being confined to the occasions when they are actually being received in communion.[3] I do not think that such a view has been commonly held, and it is difficult to see what grounds there could be for it other than an unconscious desire to find some theory of the presence which would allow the reserved Sacrament to be used for communion but for no other purpose. More recently it has been fairly widely urged that, although our Lord is present in the reserved Sacrament, he is present for the purpose of communion and therefore ought not to be recognised in any other way. I must confess that such a view of the Eucharistic Presence seems to me to be impossibly sophisticated and, no less than the view of Dr. Gore, to have been unconsciously elaborated for a predetermined purpose. That *theories* of the presence should be elaborate and involved seems to me to be natural and harmless, for they are the business of theologians who are presumably capable of understanding them. But the facts about the Eucharist which bear directly upon the life and worship of the ordinary Christian must surely be simple and direct, and I cannot imagine him

[3] Cf. *The Body of Christ*, 4th ed., pp. 131f. I have already remarked that Gore, having attacked transubstantiation as involving the importation of a particular metaphysic into theology, himself adopted an idealist metaphysic in arguing against extra-liturgical devotions (cf. p. 241 *supra*).

being anything but hopelessly confused if he is told that
his Lord and Saviour is present in the reserved Sacrament but that no notice must be taken of his presence
because he is there only for the purpose of communion.
After all, the primary purpose of the Incarnation itself
was not that Christ should be worshipped but that he
should redeem the world; nevertheless he accepted and
encouraged the homage of those who could see beneath
the outward appearance to the inner reality. The
'divine incognito', of which we have heard so much
recently, is not a scriptural term, and it can at most
express only one side of the truth; Scripture tells us
that, when the Word was made flesh and dwelt among
us, we beheld his glory. There is, of course, a truth expressed by our Lord's words to St. Mary Magdalene,
Noli me tangere, which has its bearings upon both the
Incarnation and the Eucharist; we must never allow
our desire of enjoying the presence of Christ to hinder
the performance of his redemptive work. But the danger
which is here involved is one which threatens Christian
discipleship at every point. It is no more connected
with Eucharistic devotion than with Christian devotion
in general, and it is no more connected with extra-
liturgical devotion than with intra-liturgical. Subjectivism, psychologism and individualism have infected Christian spirituality in all its forms; they can be
found in the low-church Anglican at a quiet 'said
celebration' quite as much as in the extreme Anglo-
Catholic at Benediction. They are certainly not to be
expunged simply by suppressing extra-liturgical devotion to the Sacrament. And if the incarnate Lord is
present in the reserved Sacrament in any but a purely
metaphorical sense, it is surely both lawful and desirable that his disciples should worship him there.

(2) There are a good many Anglicans who would go as far as this, but would maintain that this extra-liturgical devotion ought not to be embodied in any public form of service. While maintaining that the *purpose* for which the Sacrament is reserved is the communion of those who are unable to be present at the liturgy, they would not wish to prevent anyone who found his or her devotion assisted by praying before the reserved Sacrament from indulging in this practice. They would, however, object to any kind of organised service in connection with the reserved Sacrament and they would prefer that the Sacrament was kept in some quiet and secluded corner of the church where it would not be exposed to the attention of the casual visitor and where the devout worshipper would be free from disturbance. It seems to me that this attitude, however well-meant, is fundamentally mistaken and that whatever dangers there may be in the cultus of the reserved Sacrament are likely to be very much encouraged by it. For the fundamental facts about the Blessed Sacrament are its publicity and its centrality. It is not a secret treasure, hidden away in a corner to be the object of devotion of the abnormally pious; it is the gift of Christ to his body the Church. The method of reservation which is advocated by many – though fortunately a diminishing number – of our bishops, and which was explicitly prescribed in the 1928 Prayer-book, whereby the consecrated elements are placed in a safe in the church wall and removed from association with the altar, seems calculated to encourage almost every wrong view of the reserved Sacrament that is conceivable. Could anything be more likely to detach the reserved Sacrament from its organic connection

with the Church's Liturgy than the provision that the
place of reservation 'shall not be immediately behind
or above a Holy Table'? I should not wish to dis-
courage in any way the practice of private devotion
before the reserved Sacrament, but it is most important
that such devotion, like every other kind of private
prayer, should be kept in the context of the corporate
life of the Church and its Liturgy. Any attempt to limit
or confine the cultus of the reserved Sacrament,
whether by restricting it to the silent private prayer of
individuals, or to meetings of devout confraternities, or
to services held on week-day evenings, can only encourage the very distortions of belief and piety that it is
desired to avoid. It is therefore, I would suggest, most
desirable that the Blessed Sacrament should normally
be reserved in as central a place as possible, upon the
high altar of the church, and that regularly some form
of public devotion to the Eucharistic Presence should
be held, if possible when the main body of the congregation is assembled.

(3) And this brings me to my third question, whether
it is legitimate and desirable that such public services
should take the form that is commonly called 'Benediction'. In a large number of Anglican churches,
mainly confined, I believe, to the provinces of Canterbury and York, the common form of service held before the reserved Sacrament is that which is known
either as 'Devotions' or 'Adoration', which may be
roughly described as the service of Benediction with
the actual benediction left out. That is to say, at the
point in the service where normally the priest would
make the sign of the cross over the people with the
monstrance or ciborium containing the Sacred Host,

there is a pause, usually a bell is rung and incense is offered, and the priest and people bow low in adoration before the sacramental presence. This seems to me to be a perfectly legitimate form of devotion, but it lacks certain desirable features which the fuller service contains. For, as the name 'Adoration' suggests, the truncated form of service is almost wholly concerned with the human activity of worship directed to the incarnate Lord. Whatever the inner truth may be, *psychologically* the emphasis falls almost entirely upon what *we*, the congregation, are doing. In the full rite of Benediction, on the other hand, the blessing of the people with the Sacred Host as the climax of the service reminds them inescapably of the fact that, in our relation with God, it is he, and not we, who is the primary agent and who takes the initiative; and this is, I would suggest, of the highest significance. 'The glory of God', writes Père Charles, 'does not consist in receiving from us something that will make him richer. It consists rather in giving us the means of being no longer nothing.'[4] It is indeed our highest privilege and our most insistent duty that we should worship God, but it is salutary that when we come to worship him we should be reminded in the most forceful way that his response to our worship is to give his blessing to us. I have heard it argued against the service of Benediction that no one can say what precise benefit is supposed to be conferred when the priest makes the sign of the cross with the Host over the people, but I cannot see very much force in this objection. No one, so far as I know, can say what precise benefit is supposed to be conferred when a priest raises his hand towards

[4] *Prayer for all Times*, II, p. 60.

the people and pronounces a formula of blessing, but
this is not usually held to invalidate the practice. It
might well be possible to devise a form of service in
connection with the reserved Sacrament that was
better than the service of Benediction, but Benediction
seems to be at least a very satisfactory one, and it has
moreover very considerable practical advantages. It is
concise and flexible, it can be performed with sim-
plicity or elaboration as circumstances may dictate, it
is thoroughly congregational and does not need the
assistance of a trained choir. And I do not think that
anyone who is used to taking part in it will deny its real
power and value.

My conclusion is, therefore, that if we approach the
matter without prejudices or inhibitions, we shall
answer all our three questions in the affirmative. It is,
of course, undeniable that extra-liturgical devotions to
the Blessed Sacrament represent a very marked development from primitive practice. But they are, I
think, the manifestation of a far deeper development
that lies behind them, namely the concentration of
devotion, both in the Sacrament and outside it, upon
the Incarnate Son of God as being not only the
Saviour through whom we have access to the Father
but as being himself the direct object of our worship.
From the beginning, in their personal attitude to their
Redeemer, Christians have been ready and glad to fall
before him echoing the words of St. Thomas's confession, 'My Lord and my God'. At the end of the seventh
century the *Agnus Dei* found its way into the Western
rite, and in the East we can even find liturgies in which
the Eucharistic canon was addressed to the Son and not
to the Father. In the main, however, it has always

been the Father to whom the *liturgical* prayer of the
Church has been directed; what we might describe as
the 'official' pattern of the Church's prayer has been
ad Patrem per Filium in Spiritu. It was in the twelfth century in the West that there broke out that flood of devotion to the incarnate Lord that is associated with the
name of St. Bernard and of which Dr. Prestige has
written so movingly in the last chapter of his book
Fathers and Heretics. From that day to this it has never
ceased to bulk large in the religious life of Western
Christendom, and it has invaded, and indeed distorted, the understanding, by plain men and theologians alike, of the Eucharistic action itself. The cultus
of the Blessed Sacrament is only one, though perhaps
the most impressive of its manifestations. Misplaced as
it has sometimes been, in itself it is wholly good. And
now that we are beginning to recover a true sense of
the nature of the Liturgy as Christ's offering to his
Father of himself and his mystical Body, and so no
longer to think of the Eucharist as primarily our own
worship of Christ, it would seem to be more, rather
than less, desirable that our devotion to Christ *outside*
the liturgical action should be maintained and developed. Unless we are going to write off the whole
history of devotion to the sacred humanity as a sheer
mistake, we can hardly exclude that devotion from the
sphere of Christ's sacramental presence. Since, therefore, the liturgy itself is primarily concerned with something other than that, namely the offering to the Father
of the one true sacrifice, we can hardly be wrong if
we see the extra-liturgical cultus of the sacramental
presence as one of God's many good gifts to his household the Church.

THEOLOGY AND LITURGY

Some comments on the Liturgical Constitution of the Second Vatican Council

THE Constitution on the Sacred Liturgy, which is the chief tangible product of the first two sessions of the Second Vatican Council, is a document which, on account of the radical changes which it prescribes in the text and conduct of the services of the Church and not least for the widespread introduction of the vernacular, is sure to attract attention and stimulate experiment far beyond the boundaries of the Communion which it directly and immediately affects. It would, therefore, be a great pity if, in their concern with its practical proposals, those who study it were to skip over or to give no more than a casual glance at the admirable statements, concerning both the nature of the Church's Liturgy and the underlying facts of redemption on which the Liturgy is based, with which the successive chapters of the Constitution begin. There is hardly a word in them with which any reasonable Anglican could disagree; they make copious and accurate use of the words of Scripture and they would provide excellent material for both meditation and preaching. It is by the kind permission of Fr. Clifford Howell, S.J., that I am able to quote extensively from the fine translation which he has made and which is published by Whitegate Publications of 26a Castle Street, Cirencester, Gloucestershire.

The first chapter, on General Principles for the Restoration and Promotion of the Sacred Liturgy, begins with a

splendid announcement of the redemptive work of God in
Christ:

> God who 'wills that all men be saved and come to the
> knowledge of the truth' (I Tim. ii, 4), 'who in divers
> manners spoke in times past to the fathers by the prophets'
> (Heb. i, 1), when the fulness of time had come, sent his
> Son, the Word made flesh, anointed by the Holy Spirit,
> to preach the Gospel to the poor, to heal the contrite of
> heart, to be a 'bodily and spiritual medicine', the
> Mediator between God and man. For his humanity,
> united with the person of the Word, was the instrument of
> our salvation. Therefore in Christ 'the perfect achieve-
> ment of our reconciliation came forth, and the fulness of
> divine worship was given to us.'

Immediately the inclusive character of Christ's redemptive
work, as involving not only the Cross but also the Resurrection and Ascension, is stressed, with a skilful introduction of
the Easter Preface:

> The wonderful works of God among the people of the
> Old Testament were but a prelude to the work of Christ
> the Lord in redeeming mankind and giving perfect glory
> to God. He achieved his task principally by the paschal
> mystery of his blessed passion, resurrection from the dead
> and glorious ascension, whereby, 'dying, he destroyed our
> death and rising, he restored our life.'

And, in a patristic insight which Hoskyns endorsed in his
commentary on St. John's Gospel, we are told:

> For it was from the side of Christ as he slept the sleep of
> death upon the cross that there came forth 'the wondrous
> sacrament of the whole Church' (*Const. de Sacr. Lit.*,
> para. 5).

Immediately the Constitution passes on to declare how
the saving work of Christ is brought to the world by the

Apostolic commission of the Word and Sacraments, and here again the paschal note is struck:

Just as Christ was sent by the Father, so also he sent the apostles, filled with the Holy Spirit. This he did that, by preaching the gospel to every creature, they might proclaim that the Son of God, by his death and resurrection, had freed us from the power of Satan and from death, and brought us into the kingdom of his Father. His purpose also was that they might accomplish the work of salvation which they had proclaimed, by means of sacrifice and sacraments, around which the entire liturgical life revolves. Thus by baptism men are plunged into the paschal mystery of Christ; they die with him, are buried with him and rise with him; they receive the Spirit of adoption as sons 'in which we cry: Abba, Father' (Rom. viii, 15), and thus become true adorers whom the Father seeks. In like manner, as often as they eat the Supper of the Lord they proclaim the death of the Lord until he comes. For that reason, on the very day of Pentecost when the Church appeared before the world, 'those who received the word' of Peter 'were baptised'. And 'they continued steadfastly in the teaching of the apostles and in the communion of the breaking of bread and in prayers ... praising God and being in favour with all the people' (Acts ii, 41–47). From that time onwards the Church has never failed to come together to celebrate the paschal mystery: reading those things 'which were in all the scriptures concerning him' (Lk. xxiv, 27), celebrating the Eucharist in which 'the victory and triumph of his death are again made present' (*repraesentatur*) and at the same time 'giving thanks to God for his unspeakable gift' (II Cor. ix, 15) in Christ Jesus, 'in praise of his glory' (Eph. i, 12), through the power of the Holy Spirit (para. 6).

It is striking how the mediaeval and post-mediaeval

concentration upon the sheer immolation of Christ on the Cross and in the Mass has here given place to the patristic emphasis, embodied in the ancient liturgies themselves, on the Church as the community of those who have both died and risen with Christ and who now rejoice with him in his victory. And, while a welcome emphasis is placed upon the fact that it is Christ himself who is the principal minister of every sacrament and of the preaching of the Word, it is also made plain that he associates his Body the Church with him in this great work:

> To accomplish so great a work, Christ is always present in his Church, especially in her liturgical actions. He is present in the sacrifice of the Mass, not only in the person of his minister, 'the same now offering, through the ministry of priests, who formerly offered himself on the cross', but especially under the eucharistic species. By his power he is present in the sacraments, so that when a man baptises it is really Christ himself who baptises. He is present in his word, since it is he himself who speaks when the Holy Scriptures are read in church. He is present lastly, when the Church prays and sings, for he promised: 'Where two or three are gathered together in my name, there am I in the midst of them' (Mt. xviii, 20).

> Christ indeed always associates the Church with himself in this great work wherein God is perfectly glorified and men are sanctified. The Church is his beloved Bride who calls to her Lord, and through him offers worship to the Eternal Father.

The Constitution then drives home the threefold nature of the liturgy (and here we may notice that the word 'liturgy' throughout the document is used in the widest sense to include not only the Eucharist but all the public and official worship of the Church) as an act of Christ, a visible and tangible act, and an act of the Church:

> Rightly, then, the liturgy is considered as an exercise of

the priestly office of Jesus Christ. In the liturgy the sanctification of man is signified by signs perceptible to the senses, and is effected in a way which corresponds with each of these signs; in the liturgy the whole public worship is performed by the mystical body of Jesus Christ, that is, by the head and his members.

From this it follows that every liturgical celebration, because it is an action of Christ the priest and of his body which is the Church, is a sacred action surpassing all others; no other action of the Church can equal its efficacy by the same title and to the same degree (para. 7).

Another all too frequently forgotten note is now introduced, when we are reminded both of our condition as sojourners on earth in this life and of the never-ceasing and glorious worship of heaven, and furthermore of the great eschatological event to which all the Sacraments look forward and whose reality will persist when Sacraments have passed away:

In the earthly liturgy we take part in a foretaste of that heavenly liturgy which is celebrated in the holy city of Jerusalem towards which we journey as pilgrims, where Christ is sitting at the right hand of God, a minister of the holies and of the true tabernacle; we sing a hymn to the Lord's glory with all the warriors of the heavenly army; venerating the memory of the saints, we hope for some part and fellowship with them; we eagerly await our Saviour, the Lord Jesus Christ, until he, our life, shall appear and we too will appear with him in glory (para. 8).

Now, having reached this exalted note, we are given a salutary and somewhat abrupt reminder that 'the sacred liturgy does not exhaust the entire activity of the Church' and are presented with the missionary challenge of Romans x, 14–15. We are also reminded of our own sinful condition:

Therefore the Church announces the good tidings of

salvation to those who do not believe, so that all men may know the true God and Jesus Christ, whom he has sent, and may be converted from their ways, doing penance. To believers also the Church must ever preach faith and penance; she must prepare them for the sacraments, teach them to observe all that Christ has commanded, and invite them to all the works of charity, piety and the apostolate (para. 9).

Nevertheless the liturgy is the summit towards which the activity of the Church is directed; at the same time it is the fount from which all her power flows. For the aim and object of apostolic works is that all who are made sons of God by faith and baptism should come together to praise God in the midst of his Church, to take part in the sacrifice and to eat the Lord's supper (para. 10).

And so the connection between the liturgy and personal holiness is uncompromisingly expounded:

The liturgy in its turn moves the faithful, filled with 'the paschal sacraments', to be 'one in holiness'; it prays that 'they may hold fast in their lives to what they have grasped by their faith'; the renewal in the eucharist of the covenant between God and man draws the faithful into the compelling love of Christ and sets them on fire. From the liturgy, therefore, and especially from the eucharist as from a fount, grace is poured forth upon us; and the sanctification of men in Christ and the glorification of God, to which all other activities of the Church are directed as towards their end, is achieved in the most efficacious possible way (para. 10).

There is, however, no suggestion that the liturgy produces its effects in a purely automatic way; the succeeding paragraphs stress the need of devout and active participation on the part of the faithful and the correlative duty of the parish clergy to instruct them to this end. Furthermore explicit stress is laid upon the duties of private prayer and ascetic discipline and warm commendation is given to popular forms of devotion, so long as they 'accord with the sacred liturgy, are in some fashion derived from it and lead the people to it, since, in fact, the liturgy by its very nature far surpasses any of them' (para. 13). And the active participation of the laity in the liturgy is declared to be a theological consequence of their status as baptised Christians:

> Mother Church earnestly desires that all the faithful should be led to that full, conscious and active participation in liturgical celebrations (*ad plenam illam, consciam atque actuosam liturgicarum celebrationum participationem*) which is demanded by the very nature of liturgy. Such participation by the Christian people as 'a chosen race, a royal priesthood, a holy nation, a redeemed people' (I Pet. ii, 9; cf. ii, 4–5), is their right and duty by reason of their baptism.

Therefore:

> In the restoration and promotion of the sacred liturgy this full and active participation by all the people (*totius populi plena et actuosa participatio*) is the aim to be considered before all else (para. 14).

and all the subsequent provisions about the adequate training of the clergy in liturgical theology and praxis and about the radical revision of the liturgical rites themselves are governed by this overriding consideration of the whole Christian people as the redeemed and worshipping Body of Christ.

We come to an equally admirable and concise theological statement at the beginning of the chapter on the Mystery of the Holy Eucharist, and once again the intimate union between Christ and the Church is made plain:

> At the Last Supper, on the night when he was betrayed, our Saviour instituted the eucharistic sacrifice of his body

19

and blood. He did this in order to perpetuate the sacrifice of the Cross throughout the centuries until he should come again; and he wished to entrust to his beloved spouse, the Church, a memorial of his death and resurrection, a sacrament of love, a sign of unity, a bond of charity, a paschal banquet in which Christ is eaten, the mind is filled with grace and a pledge of future glory is given to us (para. 47).

We may note that, although use is made of the classical phrase 'the sacrifice of the Cross', this is almost immediately amplified in the phrase 'a memorial of his death *and resurrection*' and the eschatological reference to the future glory is skilfully introduced by the words quoted from the antiphon to the Magnificat at the second vespers of Corpus Christi. This paragraph is immediately followed by one in which the active participation of 'Christ's followers' (*Christifideles*) is developed; they should not be there as 'strangers or silent spectators' (*extranei vel muti spectatores*), but they should take part in the sacred action 'conscious of what they are doing, with devotion and full collaboration' (*conscie, pie et actuose*). The very significant term 'offerers' is applied to them: 'by offering the immaculate victim, not only through he hands of the priest *but also with him* (*non tantum per sacerdòtis manus, sed etiam una cum ipso offerentes*) they should learn to offer themselves; though Christ their mediator, they should be drawn day by day into ever more perfect union with God and with each other, so that finally God may be all in all' (para. 48).

The chapter on The Other Sacraments and the Sacramentals opens with an important reminder that the sacraments, in addition to their primary functions are means of instruction, and it is for this reason that the revision of their existing rites and ceremonies is to be undertaken:

> The purpose of the sacraments is to sanctify men, to build up the body of Christ and finally to give worship to

God; because they are signs they also instruct. They not only presuppose faith, but by words and objects they also nourish, strengthen and express it (*alunt, roborant, exprimunt*); that is why they are called 'sacraments of faith'. They have indeed the power to impart grace, but, in addition, the very act of celebrating them effectively disposes the faithful to receive this grace fruitfully, to worship God duly and to love each other mutually.

It is therefore of the highest importance that the faithful should easily understand the sacramental signs ... (para. 59).

It is, however, in the opening paragraphs of the chapter on the Divine Office that the Constitution reaches the height of its theological eloquence, when it asserts that, through his Body the Church, Christ associates the whole human race with the song of praise which, as the Word and Son of the Father, he utters in the eternal realm:

Christ Jesus, high priest of the new and eternal covenant, taking human nature, introduced into this earthly exile that hymn which is sung throughout all ages in the halls of heaven. He joins the entire community of mankind to himself (*universam hominum communitatem ipse sibi coagmentat*), associating it with his own singing of this canticle of divine praise (*eandemque in divino hoc concinendo laudis carmine secum consociat*).

For he continues his priestly work through the agency of his Church which is ceaselessly engaged in praising the Lord and interceding for the salvation of the whole world. She does this, not only by celebrating the eucharist, but also in other ways, especially by praying the divine office (para. 83).

Again:

When this wonderful song of praise is duly performed by priests and others who are deputed for this purpose by

the Church's ordinance, or when the faithful pray together with the priest in the approved form, then it is
truly the voice of the Bride addressed to her Bridegroom;
it is the very prayer which Christ himself, together with
his body, offers to the Father (para. 84; the word 'offers'
is not in the original).

So not only clerics and religious, but the laity too, are seen as
fulfilling a most exalted function when they take part in the
divine office:

Hence all who render this service are not only fulfilling
a duty of the Church, but also are sharing in the greatest
honour of Christ's spouse, for by duly offering (*per-
solventes*) these praises to God they are standing before
God's throne in the name of their Mother the Church
(para. 85).

It is therefore no matter for wonder that everything is to be
done both to make the offices intelligible to the laity and to
encourage the clergy and laity to recite the office together.

The chapter on The Liturgical Year recalls the essential
nature of Sunday as the day of the Lord's resurrection:

Holy Mother Church considers it her duty to celebrate
the saving work of her divine Spouse by devoutly recalling
it to mind on certain days throughout the course of the
year. Every week, on the day which she has called 'The
Lord's Day', she keeps the memory of her Lord's resurrection; once in the year, by the most solemn festival of the
Pasch, she celebrates his resurrection together with his
blessed passion.

In passing, one may note the slightly odd mention of the
Passion in this passage. One would expect both Sunday and
Easter to be seen as including the whole paschal mystery of
passion and resurrection, in line with what has been
previously said about the Eucharist, but I do not suppose

Appendix

that anything more is implied in this than the fact that in the Liturgical year, as it is now celebrated, Easter Day comes in close chronological relation to Good Friday. The following passage interestingly suggests that Advent should be thought of rather as the end than as the beginning of the liturgical year and is a further indication of the recovery of the sense of eschatology:

> As each year passes by, she [sc. the Church] unfolds the whole mystery of Christ, from the incarnation and birth until the ascension, the day of Pentecost and the expectation of blessed hope and of the coming of the Lord (para. 102).

The paragraph which comes next, dealing with the feasts of the Blessed Virgin, brings together, in a marvellously concise way, the various emphases which characterise the best and most balanced manifestations of contemporary Mariology, in contrast to those which not many years ago seemed to have acquired unrestrained ascendancy:

> In celebrating this annual cycle of Christ's mysteries, Holy Church honours with especial love the Blessed Mary, Mother of God (*Dei Genetricem*), who is inseparably involved in the saving work of her Son. In her the Church holds up and admires the most perfect fruit of the redemption, and joyfully contemplates, as in a faultless image, that which she herself desires and hopes fully to be (para. 103).

The insistence that Mary's part in redemption, as expressed in her reply to the divine message in Luke i, 38, cannot be treated as independent of the redemptive act of her divine Son (*indissolubili nexu cum Filii sui opere salutari conjungitur*), the emphasis on the fact that Mary, while involved in the work of redemption, is herself one of the redeemed (*praecellentem Redemptionis fructum*), and the notion, which is so congenial to the Eastern Orthodox, that Mary is in a very real sense an image of the Church, all these are most welcome. We may recall in this context the way in which the Fathers see both Mary and the Church as the Second Eve[1] and the symbolic identification of Mary with the Church, especially in relation to the figure of the woman in Revelation xii, made by both the Anglican scholar Sir Edwyn Hoskyns[2] and the Protestant Frère Max Thurian.[3]

A minor indication of the recovery of an eschatological outlook is provided by the mention in paragraph 106 that 'by a tradition handed down from the apostles and going back to the very day of Christ's resurrection, the Church celebrates the paschal mystery every eighth day', for the description of Sunday as the eighth, rather than as the first, day of the week expresses the Biblical and patristic insight that, by their entry into Christ's resurrection, his people have been taken out of the recurrent cyclic processes of this world and have been transferred into the new age of the Kingdom of God.

> With good reason [the Constitution continues] this, then, bears the name of 'the Lord's Day' or 'Sunday' (*dies Domini seu dies dominica*). For on this day Christ's faithful should come together into one place so that, by hearing the word of God and taking part in the eucharist, they may call to mind the passion, resurrection and glorification of the Lord Jesus, and may thank God who 'has begotten them again, through the resurrection of Jesus Christ from the dead, unto a living hope' (I Pet. i, 3).

Here again, we see brought together in the liturgical celebration of Sunday the truths of the one great redemptive act, in which passion, resurrection and ascension are combined, of the rebirth of Christians into the living Christ, of the hope of future glory, and of the indissoluble connection

---

[1] Cf., for examples, my *Christ, the Christian and the Church*, pp. 124f.
[2] *J.T.S.*, April 1920, pp. 210f.
[3] *Marie, Mère du Seigneur, Figure de l'Eglise, passim.*

of Word and Sacrament. It is, therefore, not surprising that we are told that only the very greatest feasts may be allowed to overshadow the Lord's own Day and that, in the liturgical calendar the cycle of the mysteries of salvation must be given precedence over the feasts of the saints (para. 108 cf. 111). And the unity of the great act of our redemption receives further stress from the instruction that the 'sacred paschal fast', which is to be celebrated everywhere on Good Friday, is where possible to be prolonged throughout Holy Saturday 'so that the joys of Easter Sunday may be attained with uplifted and clear minds' (para. 110).

In the above comments I have deliberately refrained from discussing the details of the prescribed liturgical reform but have confined myself to those passages which bear directly upon theological issues. It will, I think, have become clear that any notion that the Council has concerned itself purely with practical problems to the neglect of theological considerations is very far from the truth. It is rather the case that, by bringing their theological thinking to bear upon the central subject of the worship which it is the Church's supreme duty and privilege to offer to God, the Council fathers have been able to concentrate upon the basic theological theme of Redemption and in doing this to recover to a remarkable extent the balance which characterised the outlook of the patristic period and which has tended to be lost in many of the later developments. For this reason the Constitution on the Liturgy may prove to be of ecumenical importance from a theological no less than from a liturgical point of view.

A

Addai and Mari, SS., 60, 69
Allchin, A. M., 83
Ambrose, St., 186f., 208
Andrewes, L., 236
Anselm, St., 208
Aradi, Z., 126
Athanasius, St., 90
Athenagoras, 9
Attwater, D., 66
Augustine of Hippo, St., 31, 37, 43, 92, 100, 137, 156, 180, 186f., 215f., 237
Aulén, G., 82, 168f.

B

Baillie, D. M., 82, 156f., 167
Barlow, W. H., 229
Barth, K., 133
Becon, T., 208

Bellarmine, Robert, St., 124
Benoit, J. D., 82, 155f., 167
Benoit, P., 58
Benson, R. H., 116
Bernard of Clairvaux, St., 268
Bérulle, P. de, 87
Billot, L., 121, 143
Bouyer, L., 80, 116, 151, 181, 251
Brevint, D., 124f.
Bridges, R., 85
Brightman, F. E., 188, 238
Brilioth, Y., 108
Brooks, P., 185
Browning, E. B., 40
Bull, G., 110
Bute, J., Marquis of, 66

C

Cabasilas, N., 99, 164, 180

Cajetan, 147
Callahan, D. J., 197
Calvin, J., 67, 108, 165, 185, 204
Cano, M., 120
Casel, O., 150f.
Charles, P., 266
Cicero, 149, 216
Cirlot, F. L., 182
Clark, F., 101, 107, 110f.
Clark, N., 161
Comper, F., 116
Condren, C. de, 86f.
Congar, Y., 37
Couratin, A. H., 49
Cranmer, T., 42, 67f., 184, 186, 208
Creighton, M., 227
Cross, F. L., 209, 238
Cullmann, O., 82, 157

D

Dahl, N. A., 161
Davies, H., 67
Davis, H. F., 144
de Broglie, G., 154
de la Taille, M., 53, 82, 126f., 141, 146, 213, 217, 220, 227
de Lubac, H., 11, 37

de Lugo, J., 121, 136, 140
Denys the Carthusian, 101, 112
Descartes, R., 174
de Vaux, R., 94
Dimock, N., 229f.
Dix, G., 24, 50f., 63f., 108, 141, 213, 232, 240f., 259
Dowden, J., 209
Drucker, P., 44
Dugmore, C. W., 183f., 209
Du Moulin, C., 166

E

Einig, 235
Elizabeth I, Queen, 184
Evdokimov, P., 103
Every, G., 65, 83

F

Farrer, A. M., 143
Fisher, G. F., 245
Fisher, John, St., 114
Franzelin, J. B., 121

G

Galy, J., 86
Garrett, T. S., 64
Gore, C., 44, 227f., 262
Goudge, H. L., 200
Gratian, 99
Gregg, J. A. F., 15
Gregory of Nyssa, St., 186
Gregory Palamas, St., 7
Gregory the Great, St., 207

H

Hall, F. J., 9
Harnack, A., 186
Hebert, G., 144, 171
Hicks, F. C. N., 83, 88, 107, 113, 126f.
Higgins, A. J. B., 50
Hilary of Poitiers, St., 11
Hippolytus, St., 24, 55, 60, 68, 179
Holland, H. S., 44
Hooke, S. H., 96
Hooker, R., 37, 41
Hort, F. J. A., 240
Hoskyns, E. C., 85, 209f., 270, 280
Howell, C., 253, 269

I

Ignatius of Antioch, St., 70, 72
Innocent III, Pope, 65
Irenaeus, St., 72
Isaac of Stella, 116

J

Jeremias, J., 58, 161, 189
Jewel, J., 109, 184f., 209
John of the Cross, St., 7
Journet, C., 82, 141, 146f., 154, 158
Jungmann, J. A., 80, 151f.
Justin Martyr, St., 72, 190

K

Kelly, J. N. D., 186, 190
Kidd, B. J., 67, 107
Kirk, K. E., 16
Klauser, T., 258
Koenker, E. B., 125, 151
Küng, H., 258

L

Latomus, B., 116

Laud, W., 110
Leenhardt, J., 82, 157f., 167
Leo XIII, Pope, 114
Lepin, M., 126
Lessius, L., 121, 140, 143
Lewis, C. S., 27
Loofs, F., 186
Lossky, V., 8
Luther, M., 66f., 108

M

Macdonald, A., 130
MacGregor, G., 82, 159f.
Mackenzie, K. D., 141
Manners-Sutton, C., 28
Marson, C., 44
Masure, E., 33, 82, 86f., 112, 121, 136f., 146, 156, 173, 213f., 218, 232, 235
Melanchthon, P., 120
Mersch, E., 37, 86, 183
Michell, G. A., 55, 68, 182
Monsabré, J. M. L., 125, 129
Mortimer, A. G., 238
Moule, C. F. D., 83
Moule, H. C. G., 229

N

Neunhauser, B., 151
Newman, J. H., 139

O

Olier, J. J., 87

P

Parker, T. H. L., 133
Parker, T. M., 113, 186
Paschasius Radbertus, 99
Paul VI, Pope, 253
Penido, M. T.-L., 223
Peter Damian, St., 27
Peter Lombard, 209
Pighius, P., 116
Pius V, Pope St., 66
Pocknee, C. E., 80
Prenter, R., 83
Prestige, G. L., 268
Puller, F. W., 227f.

Q

Quick, O. C., 23, 200

R

Rahner, H., 154
Rahner, K., 19
Ramsey, A. M., 171
Ratcliff, E. C., 55, 99
Ratzinger, J., 19
Reid, J. K. S., 133
Richelieu, A. J. du P.,
Duke of, 28
Ridley, N., 204
Robinson, J. A. T., 201
Roguet, A.-M., 126

S

Sage, P., 145
Salmeron, A., 121
Sanday, W., 227
Sarapion, 68
Schatzgeyer, C., 115
Scheeben, M. J., 138,
194f.
Schillebeeckx, E. H., 196f.
Shakespeare, W., 59
Simon, U. E., 163
Smyth, F. H., 83, 190f.
Söhngen, G., 153f.
Spens, W., 127f., 137,
220, 227
Srawley, J. H., 50

Stephenson, A. A., 111,
116f., 132, 218
Stone, D., 110, 121, 238
Suarez, F., 124
Synge, F. C., 190

T

Talbot, E. S., 200
Tavard, G. H., 106, 109
Taylor, J., 114
Temple, W., 175
Tertullian, 75, 209
Thalhofer, V., 126
Thomas Aquinas, St., 2,
36, 48, 100, 110, 112,
117f., 137, 140, 149,
167, 208, 212f.
Thorndike, H., 209
Thorold, A., 136
Thurian, M., 82, 160f.,
173, 189, 280
Trethowan, I., 87, 136,
144

V

Vasquez, G., 121, 140
Vonier, A., 82, 131f., 143,
146, 147, 154, 217,
219f., 230

W

Wace, H., 227, 230
Waggett, P. N., 101
Waterland, D., 229
Wilberforce, R. I., 37, 133
Williams, C., 42
Wolsey, T., 28

Y

Yerkes, R. K., 87f.

Z

Zwingli, U., 67, 108

Printed in Great Britain
by Amazon